Wannsee House and the Holocaust

Wannsee House and the Holocaust

by
STEVEN LEHRER

McFarland & Company, Inc., Publishers
Jefferson, North Carolina, and London

ISBN 0-7864-0792-1 (illustrated case binding : 50# alkaline paper)

Library of Congress cataloguing data are available

British Library cataloguing data are available

On the cover: The Wannsee House in 1992

Manufactured in the United States of America

*McFarland & Company, Inc., Publishers
Box 611, Jefferson, North Carolina 28640
www.mcfarlandpub.com*

Ein Hospital für arme, kranke Juden.
Für Menschenkinder, welche dreifach elend
Behaftet mit den bösen drei Gebresten,
Mit Armut, Körperschmerz und Judentume!

Das schlimmste von den dreien ist das letzte,
Das tausendjährige Familienübel,
Die aus dem Niltal mitgeschleppte Plage,
Der altegyptisch ungesunde Glauben.

Unheilbar tiefes Leid! Dagegen helfen
Nicht Dampfbad, Dusche, nicht die Apparate
Der Chirurgie, noch all die Arzeneien,
Die dieses Haus den siechen Gästen bietet.

A hospital for poor, sick Jews.
For human-children, who are miserably
burdened with the three evil afflictions,
poverty, body-pain and Jewry!

The worst of the three is the last,
The millennial familial evil,
That nuisance dragged from the Nile valley,
The old Egyptian unhealthy beliefs.

Incurably deep sorrow! No help against it,
Not steam-bath, not shower, not the surgical instruments,
Not even all the medical arts
That this house offers its sick guests.

Heinrich Heine
Verse written in Paris after the dedication of
the new Jewish Hospital in Hamburg (1842)

Contents

Acknowledgments   ix
List of Illustrations   xi
Introduction   1

I.   The Wannsee Villa and Fritz Haber   3
II.   Friedrich Minoux Buys the Wannsee Villa
      and Enters Politics   17
III.   Aryanization, Friedrich Minoux, and the
      Plundering of the German Jews   36
IV.   Friedrich Minoux Defrauds the Berlin Gas Company   48
V.   Reinhard Heydrich and the Nordhav Foundation   53
VI.   Planning to Murder the Jews of Europe   64
VII.   Ordinary Germans, the Catholic Church, and
      the Holocaust   109
VIII. The Wannsee Villa After the Wannsee Conference   131

Appendix A: A Jew Defined   137
Appendix B: Letters   140
Appendix C: The Wannsee Protocol   146
Appendix D: Biographies of Wannsee Conference Participants   154
Appendix E: Eichmann's Testimony in Jerusalem About the Conference   174
Appendix F: Notes on the Film "The Wannsee Conference"   180
Chapter Notes   181
Bibliography   187
Index   191

Acknowledgments

The help of the following persons is gratefully acknowledged:

Gaby Müller Oelrichs
Haus der Wannsee Konferenz
Berlin

Dr. Johannes Tuchel
Gedenkstätte Deutscher Widerstand
Berlin

Karl Wilhelm Klahn
Stadtarchiv
Burg auf Fehmarn

Annette Samaras
Ullstein Bilderdienst
Berlin

Dr. Claudia Steur
Dr. Klaus Hesse
Stiftung Topographie des Terrors
Berlin

List of Illustrations

1. The Wannsee House, 1992   4
2. Paul O. A. Baumgarten, architect of the Wannsee House   5
3. Friedrich Minoux   18
4. Reinhard Heydrich in the uniform of
   an SS Obergruppenführer (General)   54
5. Wedding photo of Reinhard and Lina Heydrich   55
6. Reinhard Heydrich's house on Fehmarn   56
7. Heydrich's house in Berlin: Augustrastra(e 14   61
8. Dining room, Wannsee House, 1922   70
9. Robert M. W. Kempner   78
10. Reinhard Heydrich's funeral   87
11. Reinhard Heydrich's grave   87
12. Adolf Eichmann on trial in Jerusalem   95
13. Joseph Wulf   133
14. Martin Luther   155
15. Josef Bühler conferring with Hans Frank and
    Dienstleiter Schalk of the Reich Labor Office   156
16. Dr. Roland Freisler   157
17. Otto Hofmann   160
18. Gerhard Klopfer   161
19. Rudolf Erwin Lange   163
20. Alfred Meyer   165
21. Dr. Georg Leibbrandt   165
22. Heinrich Müller   167
23. Erich Neumann   168
24. Dr. Wilheml Stuckart   171

Introduction

On a wintry Tuesday, January 20, 1942, in the Berlin Villa Am Großen Wannsee 56–58, the Chief of the Security Police (SS) and the Security Service (SD), Reinhard Heydrich, notified the Nazi government bosses of the planned deportation and destruction of the Jews of Europe. At this meeting, the notorious Wannsee Conference, all of the participants offered Heydrich their full support and cooperation.

The foundations of the Wannsee Villa and the Holocaust were both laid during the same year, 1914. The First World War, which began in August 1914, was the foundation for the Holocaust. The war and the Versailles Treaty, which the victorious Allies imposed on Germany in 1919, made possible the rise of Adolf Hitler. Had there been no war, Hitler probably would have spent his life as an obscure Munich painter of architectural scenes.

A prosperous Berlin merchant, Ernst Marlier, began building his new Wannsee Villa in 1914. In 1921, the postwar economic problems in Germany forced Marlier to sell the Wannsee Villa to an industrialist, Friedrich Minoux.

Minoux, a tailor's son, took a lively interest in politics and developed plans in 1923 to form a right-wing dictatorship. Shortly before the Munich ("Beerhall") Putsch in November 1923, the failed attempt to overthrow the Bavarian government, Minoux had established close contact with the principal plotters, one of whom was Hitler.

Minoux did not remain a wealthy business figure. In 1938 he was indicted for massively defrauding the Berlin Gas Company, the biggest swindle of the Nazi era. He died of starvation shortly after the victorious Allies released him from Brandenburg Prison in 1945.

In 1940, from his jail cell in Berlin, Minoux sold the Wannsee Villa to a foundation controlled by the SS, called the Stiftung Nordhav. Reinhard Heydrich set up the Nordhav Foundation in 1939, nominally to build "vacation spas" for members of the Nazi security police. In fact, by creating this foundation, Heydrich had formed a highly personal instrument of power.

The Stiftung Nordhav became part of one of history's cruel ironies. Heydrich and his henchmen plundered the cash to fund the Stiftung Nordhav from German Jews being deported to the east. The money the Nazis stole from these Jews paid for the Wannsee Villa, where the Endlösung (final solution), the mass murder of the Jews of Europe, was announced.

"God will give him blood to drink!" was the curse, of a man hanged for witchcraft, that fell upon the inhabitants of Nathaniel Hawthorne's *House of the Seven Gables*. The Wannsee Villa bears a certain eerie resemblance to Hawthorne's fictional creation, its inhabitants cursed by the evil period of German history to which the house stood witness. In this book, the story of the graceful old mansion and its owners will be told, alongside the annals of the times, to present aspects of the Holocaust that may be unfamiliar to many English-speaking readers.

Research for this book involved many German-language sources, including Third Reich documents. All translations are by the author unless otherwise noted. A number of the documents quoted in the text may be found reproduced in full in the appendices.

The Wannsee Villa
and Fritz Haber

Wannsee signifies two things to Berliners. The first is the residential district of Wannsee, one of the best addresses in Berlin, with its elegant villas set in large gardens. The second is the lake of Wannsee, or rather the two lakes, the Großer and the Kleiner (Great and Little) Wannsee.

Wannsee is a favorite recreation area. It has the largest beach in Berlin, and along its shores are other beaches, with sailing and rowing clubs, cafés, restaurants, terraces overlooking the Großer Wannsee, and a variety of attractive foot paths and walks.

The Großer Wannsee, which has an area of two hundred sixty hectares (six hundred forty acres), is part of a basin gouged out during the Ice Age. The northern end runs into the River Havel with its international shipping traffic. At the southern end is the Wannsee bridge, which carries a major highway, the Königstrasse, from Berlin to Potsdam. A string of small lakes connected with one another runs southwestward in a long trough, also dating from the Ice Age.

The district of Wannsee is one of the oldest areas of settlement within Berlin. It consists of three parts which were amalgamated in 1899: the settlement colony around the train station; the villa colony of Alsen on the west side of the Wannsee, established in 1863; and the village of Stolpe on the Stolpchensee, one of the small lakes. Stolpe, which first appears in the records in 1299, has a lovely old church, built by Karl Friedrich Schinkel, the Prussian court architect who also designed the Iron Cross. In Bismarckstrasse, on the Kleiner Wannsee, is the tomb of the dramatist Heinrich von Kleist, who together with Henriette Vogel committed suicide here in 1811.

The road known as Am Großen Wannsee runs along the western bank of the larger lake. The elegant house at Nos. 56–58, now called the Wannsee House or Wannsee Villa, was the scene of the Wannsee Conference.

The land under the Wannsee Villa had been incorporated into the north-

The Wannsee Villa.

ern border of the colony of Alsen only ten years before the house was built. Alsen is a residential area lying directly on the lake of Wannsee. Wilhelm Conrad, a prominent banker and industrialist, and Gustav Meyer, the first director of gardens for the city of Berlin, had established Alsen's borders in 1869. In the following years, industrialists and artists moved to the area for the summer months — among them the publisher Ferdinand Springer and the artist Max Liebermann, whose works the Nazis exhibited as degenerate art. The court painter of the Kaisers, Anton von Werner, built a summer home in Alsen in 1887. Alsen is near the town of Potsdam, country home of the rulers of Prussia, but is also close to Berlin.

A prosperous Berlin merchant and factory owner, Ernst Marlier, bought the land for the Wannsee Villa on April 30, 1914, from the Prussian government. Marlier was a solidly built man with a thick mustache, a large nose, and a full head of neatly parted, black hair. He dressed meticulously, occasionally wearing a vest and a jaunty straw boater.

Marlier's land was one of the most beautiful plots in the area. For the 26,415 square meters of land, Marlier paid 449,055 marks, or 17 marks per square meter. Shortly before, he had bought 4,163 square meters of adjacent land for 58,282 marks.

As architect for his new 1,500-square-meter Wannsee house, Marlier chose Paul O. A. Baumgarten, a student of the architect Alfred Messel. A proponent of neoclassical and Greek revival styles, Messel had designed Wertheim's Department Store and the offices of AEG (Allgemeine Elektricitäts-Gesellschaft), both in Berlin. Baumgarten had built houses in Alsen, among them the house of Max Liebermann. Marlier's finished house was quite stunning, as a contemporary observer noted: "The home blends well with the park landscape and stylized garden. The building has a broad terrace, but is so situated as to give a modest appearance without an overwhelming monumentality of form."

On the ground floor, the main rooms opened from a central doorway to the rear garden front. A central axis was bounded by a bay window in the library at one end and a conservatory at the other. In the center of the axis, a one-and-a-half-story hallway was connected to salons and a large dining room. Baumgarten filled these rooms with elegant furniture, knickknacks, and copies of well-known works of art. Especially noteworthy were the library door, the columns in the dining room, the marble fountain in the conservatory, and the two ground-floor fireplaces.

Baumgarten lavished special care on the landscaping of the park-like garden. As one observer remarked, the garden was "a cultural monument ... that should be preserved for posterity."

Paul O. A Baumgarten, architect of the Wannsee Villa. Baumgarten had been a student of the architect Alfred Messel, a proponent of neo-classical and Greek revival styles. Messel had designed Wertheim's Department Store and the offices of AEG (Allgemeine Elektricitäts-Gesellschaft), both in Berlin. Baumgarten had built houses in Alsen, among them the house of the painter Max Liebermann. (Ullstein Bilderdienst)

Ernst Marlier and his wife Margarete were conspicuously proud of their exquisite home. But the inflation in Germany that followed World War I caused Marlier considerable difficulties. On September 6, 1921, he sold the Wannsee Villa and land to a foundation, the Norddeutsche Grundstücks-Aktiengesellschaft-AG. The industrialist Friedrich Minoux controlled this foundation, and he paid 2.3 million marks for the property: three hundred thousand marks in cash, and two million marks in the form of a mortgage. The yearly interest rate was 5 percent, with a prohibition against paying off the two-million-mark balance before October 1926. Along with the house, Friedrich Minoux bought many of Marlier's furnishings, including a rare Gobelin tapestry that adorned one of the dining room walls.

Ernst Marlier was only one of many Germans who suffered because of the four-year-long war. Almost everyone thought that the fighting would last no more than a month or two and that the soldiers would be home before the leaves fell.

In fact, World War I might have been very short but for a single scientific discovery. In August 1914, when war broke out, Britain clamped a naval blockade on Germany. Nitrates from Chile were one vital import immediately cut off. These compounds were essential for the production of both fertilizer and explosives. When they invaded Belgium, the Germans were able to seize twenty thousand tons of Chilean saltpeter in the port of Anvers. However, once this material had been used up, the Kaiser's government would have had to sue for a quick peace.

The scientific discovery that rescued the German war effort was the Haber Process, a method for the industrial synthesis of ammonia from nitrogen and hydrogen, two plentifully available elements. The ammonia could easily be substituted for the unavailable imported nitrates.

A German Jew, Fritz Haber, developed this process in 1909. Haber was fervently patriotic, like the majority of German Jews, but his story is more ironic than most. Besides prolonging the bloody, ruinous war that made possible the rise of Hitler, Haber introduced the horrific gas warfare that killed one hundred thousand soldiers and injured a million more. And in a final brutal twist, this genius of a chemist invented Zyklon B, the cyanide insecticide the Nazis used to murder millions of other Jews. Without Fritz Haber, there would have been no Wannsee Conference.

The Story of Fritz Haber

Fritz Haber was born in Breslau (now Wroclaw, Poland), on December 9, 1868. His mother died when he was born. From his earliest childhood, his family and teachers saw that young Fritz was endowed with superior intelligence. Haber père, a successful businessman who dealt in pharmaceuticals and dyes, instilled in his son the Prussian virtues: hard work and a sense of order, duty, and discipline.

Chemistry had fascinated Fritz Haber as a student. He studied at three universities: Berlin, Heidelberg, and the Charlottenburg Technische Hochschule, which awarded him a Ph.D. He did postdoctoral work at the Eidgenossiche Technische Hochschule in Zurich, then joined his father's business, but soon decided on a different career path, university chemist. Because university careers were generally open only to Christians, he converted to the Lutheran faith.

Haber first took up organic chemical research at the University of Jena, but its orthodox methods gave him little satisfaction. In later years he delighted in telling how chance brought him at the age of twenty-five to a junior post at the Technische Hochschule of Karlsruhe, where he immediately threw himself with tremendous zest into the teaching of physical chemistry (a subject in which he was essentially self-taught) and into research. His intensive early researches in electrochemistry and thermodynamics gained him the position of associate professor of physical chemistry (1898); his reputation was much enhanced by his book *Grundriss der technischen Elektrochemie auf theoretischer Grundlage* (1898; "The Theoretical Basis of Technical Electrochemistry") and especially by *Thermodynamik technischer Gasreaktionen Vorlesungen* (1905; *The Thermodynamics of Technical Gas Reactions,* 1908), a pioneering work that had considerable influence on teaching and research. A colleague described Fritz Haber as impulsive, capricious, lively, and an excellent teacher who could speak knowledgeably about almost any subject

In turn-of-the-century Germany, university positions paid very little. A professorial assistant (Privatdozent) or associate (Ausserordentlicher Professor) was paid nothing at all; what income he received came from tutoring students. Only a professor received a regular salary.

To earn some money, Haber consulted for industry and filed patents, but his work ethic unsettled some of his peers. Haber was initially refused a chair in physical chemistry; another chemist, Wilhelm Ostwald, remarked, "When one works with above average intensity, one provokes instinctive opposition from colleagues." In 1906 Haber was finally appointed to the position of full professor.

In 1901 Fritz Haber married thirty-year-old Clara Immerwahr, daughter of another respected Jewish family in Breslau, whom he had known since his adolescence. Clara's ambition rivaled that of her fiancé and propelled her to become the first woman awarded a doctorate in science (chemistry) from the University of Breslau.

Fritz Haber was not as attentive to his wife as he might have been. In a letter, Clara wrote:

> What Fritz has gained during the past eight years, I have lost, and I am filled with a profound bitterness. I have always thought that life is not worth living unless a person can develop all her talents and experience everything the world has to offer. This is what convinced me to marry, even if a part of me resisted. If my happiness was ephemeral ... the cause is Fritz's dominating behavior at home and in marriage, besides which anyone perishes who doesn't assert herself more ruthlessly than he ... I ask myself whether superior intelligence makes one person more precious than another, and if much of me, that has gone to the devil because it has gone to the wrong man, is not more valuable than the most important electronic theory.

Contemporary photographs show the dominating presence Clara described. Haber looks remote and formal, towering over everyone in the picture, with a bald pate, a starched collar, a pince-nez, and a supercilious air. "I was German to a degree which no one today would believe," said Haber in 1933. To Chaim Weizmann, another celebrated chemist and future first president of

Israel, he remarked, "I was more a great military leader, more a captain of industry. I was the founder of huge enterprises. My work opened the way to a vast expansion of the German army and German industry. All doors were open to me."

In his laboratory, Fritz Haber was able to solve a problem that had defied his predecessors for more than a century: how to synthesize ammonia from hydrogen and nitrogen, a reaction called nitrogen fixation. A master of both theoretical and experimental chemistry, Haber attacked the synthesis problem without regard for the practical applications that a solution might yield. With a young English collaborator, Robert Le Rossignol, he studied minutely the temperatures and pressures necessary to combine hydrogen and nitrogen to produce significant quantities of ammonia.

Haber discovered that the synthesis of ammonia required extreme conditions never before achieved in a laboratory: a temperature of 600°C and pressure of more than 200 atmospheres. Even then, very little ammonia formed. To accelerate the reaction, Haber realized he would need a catalyst, a metal surface on which the hydrogen and nitrogen atoms could combine. Haber and Le Rossignol tried every available metallic element until they found that osmium, a rare, dense metal, caused a remarkable acceleration of the reaction. On July 2, 1909, they demonstrated their process to the directors of the Badische Anilin und Soda Fabriken (BASF), one of the largest German chemical companies. Their reactor produced seventy drops of ammonia per minute. To convert the ammonia to fertilizer would be simple.

In 1909 the saltpeter mines of Chile were the principal source of nitrate fertilizer. The capacity of these mines was limited, and by 1940, German experts predicted, they would be exhausted. A second source of nitrates was gassified coal, but this source was totally inadequate to satisfy the enormous demand.

Nitrogen, on the other hand, exists in unlimited quantities in the air around us, and hydrogen is easy to produce from gassified coal. The ammonia Haber and Le Rossignol made by combining these two elements could be used as fertilizer, or, treated with sulfuric acid, it would form nitrates.

Convinced of the profitable possibilities of the Haber Process, the BASF directors assigned two of their best chemists, Carl Bosch and Alwin Mittasch, to ratchet up the process to an industrial scale. BASF instructed the two chemists to devote as much time as necessary and spare no expense. In the meantime, the company took an option on one hundred kilograms of osmium, virtually the entire world stock.

There was never a need for BASF to exercise its option. Mittasch tested four thousand possible catalysts in ten thousand trials of ammonia synthesis. He finally selected iron, a cheaper and much more abundant metal than osmium, mixed with small amounts of aluminum, calcium, and potassium oxides. On September 9, 1913, the first industrial installation began generating between three and five tons of ammonia daily, a thousand times what Haber and Rossignol had made. Today, world production of ammonia for agriculture is a hundred thousand times as great, yet Mittasch's catalyst is still at the heart of the method. No one has ever found anything better, though ammonia synthesis is less hazardous now than in Haber's time. On September 21, 1921, an explosion in a plant at Oppau, on the Rhine, killed 561 people and left another 7,000 homeless.

Haber received large royalty payments and the 1918 Nobel Prize in Chemistry for his process. Carl Bosch was awarded a Nobel prize in 1931 for developing a new technique for high pressure ammonia production. Alwin Mittasch has been almost forgotten.

Because of the hugely profitable nature of his discovery, Haber immediately became embroiled in controversy. An Austrian company which had financed his initial experiments contested his patents. Other companies also wanted a part of this gold mine of a process and fought to break the patents.

In 1910 Kaiser Wilhelm II founded the Kaiser Wilhelm Society for the Advancement of Science, a semipublic research organization to promote German science. Leopold Koppel, a Jewish banker, provided financing, and proposed organizing an institute for physical chemistry under Fritz Haber's direction. Haber made strong demands, all of which were met: a chair at the University of Berlin, membership in the Prussian Academy of Sciences, and an annual salary of 15,000 marks (about $75,000 today).

With Walther Nernst, who received a 1920 Nobel prize for formulating the third law of thermodynamics, Haber persuaded Albert Einstein to leave Zurich and come to Berlin. In addition, Haber attracted many outstanding young scientists who wanted to work with him. The chemist Emil Fischer, who won the Nobel Prize in 1902 for determining the structures and synthesis of sugars, was another eminent scientist at the Kaiser Wilhelm Institute.

When war broke out in August 1914, Haber volunteered for military duty — he had already served as a young man — but was rejected because of his age. Instead of making him a soldier, the war ministry appointed him chief of its chemical section, with responsibility for war matériel. In December 1914 he tested an artillery shell filled with tear gas, but the gas dispersed too rapidly in the open air to have any military value. Then a physical chemist working with him, Otto Sackur, was killed in a laboratory explosion while synthesizing other chemicals to be tested as armaments.

Haber quickly hit on the idea of using chlorine in canisters as a chemical weapon. Chlorine is a highly corrosive yellow-green gas, two-and-a-half times heavier than air. It violently attacks mucous membranes in the eyes, nose, mouth, and throat. Inhaled into the lungs, it causes asphyxia and death.

Haber proposed to use the wind to carry chlorine over enemy lines. The chlorine would flow into the trenches, forcing soldiers to flee into the open air, where they would make easy targets.

The chief of staff, Erich von Falkenhayn, loved the idea, but it seemed to violate one of the Hague Conventions, which the Germans had signed and ratified in 1899 and 1907. The first convention declared that "the signatory powers agree to abstain from using any projectile, the sole function of which is to diffuse asphyxiating or harmful gas."

Falkenhayn saw a subtle distinction between firing a projectile filled with toxic gas, versus releasing the gas from a canister and allowing the wind to disperse it. The Hague diplomats had not foreseen wind dispersal. Promoted to the rank of captain in the reserves, Haber was immediately charged with preparing the gas canisters. In his book, *The Toxic Cloud*, Ludwig Haber, Fritz Haber's son, wrote, "[The high command] found Haber to be a determined, brilliant spirit, an extremely energetic organizer, and a man devoid of scruples."

Haber threw himself into his assigned task, organizing the production of hundreds of tons of chlorine and thousands of gas canisters. Oblivious to personal danger, he trained special troops to test the canisters and supervise their installation in trenches at the front. He recruited his own collaborators as well as numerous other chemists. Otto Hahn who won a 1944 Nobel prize for nuclear fission, protested that gas warfare was contrary to international law. Haber retorted that the French had broken the law first by shooting tear gas projectiles at the Germans in August 1914. According to Dietrich Stolzenberg and Ludwig Haber, Fritz Haber's assertion was false. Stolzenberg adds: "Haber's activities and behavior at the time give the impression that he was obsessed with his self-imposed task."

Indeed, Fritz Haber's unbounded ambition may have led him to believe that he alone could win the war. To accomplish his aim, he planned to diffuse chlorine gas toward the Allied lines along a front of twenty-five kilometers, killing and routing enemy soldiers. The German infantry would then pierce the Allied defenses. Haber warned the German high command not to use gas until the most propitious moment and to equip German troops with gas masks.

The German commanders at the front were not anxious to participate in a gas attack. As the commander of the XV Army Corps, General Berthold von Deimling wrote in his memoirs, "I must admit that the task of poisoning the enemy like rats was repugnant to me, as it would be to any respectable soldier."

Duke Albrecht of Wurtemberg was more willing to try gas. The Duke's troops were engaged in one of the fiercest battles of the Western Front, at the town of Ypres, thirty kilometers from the Belgian coast. Ypres was under attack as the key point that blocked a German approach to the English Channel.

Haber's gas troops installed 5,730 gas canisters, containing 150 tons of chlorine gas, along a front of five kilometers. The east wind, which was to carry the gas to the enemy, could be expected only one day in three and was quite variable because the sea was so close. Ludwig Haber wrote: "Here was Haber himself, an academic in uniform, paunchy, rarely without a cigar, pockets bulging, surrounded by young acolytes who managed to look respectful, busy, and unconventional in dress and bearing." Surviving German documents from the war refer to Fritz Haber, in highly deferential terms, as Geheimrat (privy counselor) Haber. Such was his prestige that he was able to persuade the reluctant Otto Hahn, who commanded a company of machine gunners, to serve as an "active observer." James Franck and Gustave Hertz, who shared a 1925 Nobel prize, lent a hand. But the physicist Max Born, another future Nobel laureate and member of Haber's institute, refused. Hugo Stolzenberg, father of Haber's biographer, supervised the filling of gas canisters at the front. Troops placed the unwieldy containers, each weighing one hundred kilograms, in the German trenches around Ypres on the nights of April 10 and 11, 1915. The gas masks Haber recommended never arrived. Ludwig Haber described the battle:

> The first order to prepare the gas for attack was given on April 14th at 10:30 PM and canceled at 1:45 AM April 15th. The second order came on April 19th at 4 PM but was also canceled ... The third alert was given on April 21st at 5 PM, repeated at 4 AM on April 22, and again at 9 AM.
>
> The troops, the "Pioneer commandos," had little chance to rest. They were certain that the Allies knew what the Germans were planning, and they were right. Three weeks before, German prisoners had told the French about the installation of the gas canisters, and the French had seen the test explosions in March. But the French did not pay heed to the warnings ... The simultaneous opening of 6,000 canisters, dispersing 150 tons of chlorine over 7,000 meters in ten minutes was spectacular ... Franco-Algerian soldiers in the front lines were submerged and choking. Those who did not suffocate after terrible spasms took flight, but the gas pursued them. The front broke.

The British soldier-poet Wilfred Owen has left us an even more vivid description of a German gas attack:

> Bent double, like old beggars under sacks,
> Knock-kneed, coughing like hags, we cursed through sludge,
> Till on the haunting flares we turned our backs
> And towards our distant rest began to trudge.

Men marched asleep. Many had lost their boots
But limped on, blood-shod. All went lame; all blind;
Drunk with fatigue; deaf even to the hoots
Of tired, outstripped Five-Nines that dropped behind.

Gas! Gas! Quick, boys!— An ecstasy of fumbling,
Fitting the clumsy helmets just in time;
But someone still was yelling out and stumbling,
And flound'ring like a man in fire or lime...
Dim, through the misty panes and thick green light,
As under a green sea, I saw him drowning.

In all my dreams, before my helpless sight,
He plunges at me, guttering, choking, drowning.

If in some smothering dreams you too could pace
Behind the wagon that we flung him in,
And watch the white eyes writhing in his face,
His hanging face, like a devil's sick of sin;
If you could hear, at every jolt, the blood
Come gargling from the froth-corrupted lungs,
Obscene as cancer, bitter as the cud
Of vile, incurable sores on innocent tongues,—
My friend, you would not tell with such high zest
To children ardent for some desperate glory,
The old Lie: Dulce et decorum est
Pro patria mori.[1]

The German gas attack at Ypres caused fifteen thousand casualties, of which five thousand were deaths. Yet the great victory Fritz Haber envisioned did not materialize. As Ludwig Haber wrote: "The Germans advanced carefully. Following the clouds, they were as surprised as their adversaries. The German advance was retarded, not by enemy resistance, but by pockets of gas in trenches and ruins ... The hesitance of the Germans and nightfall saved the French by giving them time to regroup ... The initial satisfaction of the Germans rapidly changed to disappointment when, on April 23, they received the order to advance but met an increasingly tough resistance." The German generals had thrown away the unique tactical and psychological advantage of attacking an unprotected, unprepared enemy. Haber returned to Berlin a few days later, frustrated and fatigued.

---

[1]*The ironic Latin line is from Horace, Odes, III. ii. 13, "It is sweet and fitting to die for the fatherland."*

On May 1, the Habers received dinner guests. During the night, while Fritz Haber slept, Clara, depressed over her husband's role in gas warfare, killed herself with Fritz's service pistol. The shot awakened her fourteen-year-old son Hermann, who discovered her body lying in a pool of blood in the garden. Next morning, Fritz Haber returned to the front. From his post, he wrote to a friend: "For a month, I doubted I would hold out, but now the war with its gruesome pictures and its continuous demands on all my strength has calmed me."

Haber continued to devote himself to chemical warfare and was entirely satisfied with his work. But after the first German gas offensive, the Allies began using chlorine gas and the more dominant west wind to pummel their enemy. Undaunted, Haber continued to research new, more terrible weapons.

When the Germans decided to annex Belgium and northern France, and considered invading England, Haber got his patron Koppel to urge the minister of war to finance a Kaiser Wilhelm Foundation for military technology. Haber also asked his friend Carl Duisberg, director of the Bayer dye corporation, to propose the creation of a Kaiser Wilhelm Institute for chemical warfare, which Haber would direct. Yet when he made these demands in 1916, Haber was convinced that Germany would lose the war.

On December 17, 1916, Wilhelm II approved the creation of the military foundation, with Fritz Haber, Emil Fischer, Walter Nernst, and three other eminent chemists as directors. But members of the Kaiser Wilhelm Institute were initially reluctant to collaborate with the new foundation, since "killing people" was not part of their charter. They eventually saw the light, and in September 1918 the institute director accepted six million marks from the war ministry.

Immediately after the armistice, November 11, 1918, the Allies declared Haber and Nernst war criminals and demanded their extradition. Haber fled to Switzerland and became a Swiss citizen, a privilege accorded to very few people. The Allies soon abandoned their extradition demands, and Haber returned to Germany to help rebuild the country. In total disregard of the Versailles Treaty, he also conducted secret poison gas research.

Chemical warfare had become a profitable business. The Spanish government wanted gas to put down the Abd el-Krim revolt in Morocco. The Soviet government concluded a covert agreement with Germany to buy chemical weapons. To satisfy the demand, the Prussian War Ministry built a secret chemical warfare laboratory near Wittenberg, where Martin Luther had preached four centuries earlier. Fritz Haber ran the laboratory through an intermediary, Dr. Hugo Stolzenberg, who had been his subordinate during the war. Ludwig Haber described Stolzenberg as "a plausible rogue, who, in other circumstances, could have convinced anyone that it would be possible to grow mushrooms in the desert."

Haber seemed to be a man with no regrets. He insisted that his chemical weapons were more humane than powerful explosives because many soldiers survived a gas attack. But he never mentioned that survivors were often horribly burned and suffered terribly the rest of their lives. One survivor was the young Adolf Hitler, who was temporarily blinded in a gas attack on October 14, 1918. "That night," said Hitler, "I resolved that if I recovered my eyesight, I would enter politics."

Until Hitler came to power, Haber continued to advise the German government regarding its secret production of chemical weapons. He also devoted himself to rebuilding his institute, reviving German science, and renewing contacts with foreign scientists. Although he may have been a domestic tyrant, in his laboratory he gave his young collaborators considerable freedom to pursue their interests. Just after the war, Haber's own interest was in helping Germany compensate its former enemies.

Haber had decided to save his country by finding a way to repay the gargantuan war damages assessed by the Versailles treaty. He knew that a ton of sea water might contain five to ten milligrams of gold. He would therefore develop a method to extract this gold. In total secrecy, Haber obtained funds to hire fourteen young collaborators, and, disguised as ship's crew, they sailed with him to Rio de Janeiro. His preliminary shipboard analyses of sea water samples en route confirmed his estimate of gold content. But because of the great variability in gold concentration from sample to sample, he took the samples back to his Berlin laboratory. After careful analyses of sea water from many parts of the world, Johannes Jaenicke, one of Haber's assistants, reported that the average gold concentration was only 0.1 percent of original estimates. In 1926 Haber gave up gold prospecting.

Haber's second marriage failed not long afterward. In 1917 he had married Charlotte Nathan, a seductive, independent-minded woman, a passionate traveler twenty-one years his junior. Charlotte was definitely not the teutonic ideal, a Kinder, Kirche, Küche (children, church, kitchen) wife, nor was she subservient like the late Clara. Being married to a man who was hardly ever home, and exhausted when he was, did not appeal to Charlotte. They had a son, Ludwig, and a daughter, Eva, before she divorced Fritz in 1927.

By early 1933, Fritz Haber was worn out. As he wrote to a friend: "I fight with ebbing strength against my four enemies: insomnia, the economic claims of my divorced wife, my lack of confidence in the future, and awareness of the grave mistakes I have committed..."

In April 1933 the Nazis decreed that all Jewish civil servants, including those at the Kaiser Wilhelm Institute, were to be relieved of their duties. Max Planck, president of the Institute, called on Reichschancellor Hitler to plead that Jewish scientists be allowed to keep their jobs. Hitler replied that he had nothing against Jews except that they were all communists. When Planck protested that expelling these excellent scientists could only hurt German science, Hitler slapped his knees, spoke more and more rapidly, and worked himself into such a towering rage that Planck fled the room.

Although he had been allowed to keep his job because of his military service record, Fritz Haber resigned from the Kaiser Wilhelm Institute on April 30, 1933. In his resignation letter, he wrote: "For more than forty years I have selected my collaborators on the basis of their intelligence and their character and not on the basis of their grandmothers, and I am not willing for the rest of my life to change this method which I have found so good."

Haber devoted his efforts to finding posts abroad for his Jewish colleagues. Einstein, who had already emigrated, announced that he would not return to Germany because it no longer recognized "civil liberties, tolerance, or equality of its citizens before the law." The Nazi press responded with a flood of invective and demanded that the Prussian Academy of Sciences impose disciplinary sanctions.

Planck thought that Einstein was still a German, even though living abroad, and should have sided with Germany, irrespective of the faults of the new regime. He therefore decided that Einstein could no longer be a member of the Academy. When Planck presented his decision to the other Academy members, Haber concurred. Only the Nobel laureate Max von Laue had the courage to condemn Planck's disgraceful judgment.

In late 1933 Haber left Germany for a job in England. At Cambridge, William Pope, the professor of chemistry, warmly welcomed his old chemical warfare adversary. But the laboratory technicians, who had fought in the trenches, took pains to avoid Haber. He stayed in Cambridge only four months.

The Daniel Sieff Research Institute in Rehovot, Palestine (now the Weizmann Institute of Science), offered Haber the directorship of its physical chemistry section. He accepted with the proviso that he would find the climate and living conditions agreeable. On a trip to the opening ceremonies for the Sieff Institute, Haber had a heart attack and died at Basel, Switzerland, on January 29, 1934, at age sixty-five. Had he lived another decade, he would have been forced to confront the most awful aspect of all his work.

When, in 1919, the Allies had forbidden German chemical warfare research, Haber decided to devote himself, publicly at least, to agriculture. He was named National Commissioner for Pest Control and founded a company, the German Society for Pest Control, to produce insecticides. One of his products was a highly toxic insecticide, hydrocyanic acid, forced under pressure into porous particles and stored in airtight cans. Ordinary sodium or potassium cyanide crystals, although corrosive, are relatively stable and do not vaporize when exposed to air. But Haber's porous particles, spread over a field, immediately released poison gas, hydrocyanic acid, which killed any insects nearby. The particles also released a nontoxic odorant, which warned humans in the vicinity to get out of the way. The German patent office awarded the new insecticide patent number 438,818.

A Frankfurt company, Degesch, and a Hamburg company, Tesch and Stabonow, manufactured Haber's new insecticide for use in fields and buildings infested with insects.[2] The material was called Zyklon B (Cyclone B). The first test of Zyklon B was in a ship of the Hamburg-America Line. Astounded German entomologists raved over the "elegance of the process." Zyklon B proved to be a huge commercial success.

One day during World War II, a Dr. Peters, director of the Society for the Fight Against Insects, received a secret order from the SS. The Society was to deliver Zyklon B to the Auschwitz concentration camp, but the crystals were to contain no odorant. An SS officer explained that the poison was to be used to kill criminals, the incurably ill, and the mentally retarded. Dr. Peters was not to say anything about the order, on pain of death.

Another group of victims was announced at the Wannsee Conference: the Jews. Among the millions of Jews the Germans murdered with Zyklon B were Fritz Haber's relatives and many of his friends.

---

[2]In 1946, the British executed Dr. Bruno Tesch and his general manager, Karl Weinbacher, on the testimony of a bookkeeper, though Tesch maintained he had no idea the Zyklon B his company produced was being used to murder people. Since 1947 a German firm, Testa, has continued to manufacture and sell Zyklon B, which is now called Cyanosil.

2

Friedrich Minoux Buys the Wannsee Villa and Enters Politics

Friedrich Minoux, the second owner of the Wannsee Villa, was born March 21, 1877, in the city of Mutterstadt in the Pfalz region of Germany. He was of humble Christian origins. In a *Reichshandbook of German Society,* Minoux described himself as the "son of a simple tailor." His father, the tailor Michael Minoux, was born August 27, 1834, in Mundenheim (today Ludwigshafen), the son of a gardener. On December 31, 1861, Michael Minoux married the seamstress Katherina Reffert, a shoemaker's daughter, who had been born May 7, 1824, in the town of Eppstein.

Michael Minoux and Katherina Reffert Minoux had three children, a daughter Anna Maria, born August 23, 1862, a son Michael, born September 8, 1863, and a daughter Barbara, born September 20, 1866. Barbara died at age three on March 8, 1869, and Katherina Reffert Minoux died a short time later.

After the death of his wife, Michael Minoux married her sister, Magaretha Reffert, in 1872. With Margaretha he had three more children: another Barbara, born March 5, 1875, a son Friedrich, who died in Mutterstadt on December 13, 1875, and another son Friedrich, the future owner of the Wannsee Villa. In June 1890 Margaretha Minoux died, followed by Michael Minoux in March 1892. In later school records, Friedrich Minoux's older sister Barbara is listed as his guardian.

Friedrich Minoux was educated in the Gymnasien (high schools) of Speyer and Mannheim and was a middling student. His best grade was an "A" in behavior, which may be contrasted with the "D" he received in diligence. His best grade in the 1892 school year was a "B" in religion during the second trimester; in the third trimester he received a "B-" in religion, general mathematics, physics, and gym. He received a "C" in French and geom-

Friedrich Minoux. A tailor's son, Minoux took a lively interest in politics, and developed plans in 1923 to form a right wing dictatorship. Shortly before the Munich (Beerhall) Putsch in November 1923, the failed attempt to overthrow the Bavarian Government, Minoux had established close contact with the principal plotters, one of whom was Hitler. But Minoux did not remain a wealthy business figure. In 1938 he was indicted and imprisoned for massively defrauding the Berlin Gas Company, the biggest swindle of the Nazi era. He died of starvation shortly after the victorious Allies released him from Brandenburg Prison in 1945.

etry, a "C+" in Greek grammar, a "C-" in German, Latin, and history, and a "D" in Latin style and Greek reading. In spite of one recorded episode of "unacceptable behavior," he graduated in 1893.

Minoux fulfilled his compulsory military obligation in Field Artillery Regiment number 5 of Landau, where he worked on the military railroads as a cook. Later he served as a gunner and a railroad station assistant. He began his service at age seventeen and served two years longer than the one year required of a volunteer.

After leaving the military, Minoux went to work as an office boy for the Essen Gas and Water Works. Here he had an exemplary career. In three years he rose to cashier's assistant; within another year he was a bookkeeper; six months later he was a cashier, and then he became financial vice president. On November 1, 1906, he became a state secretary and supervisor of the state finance bureau, on March 1, 1908, first officer for sales of the Gas and Water Works, and on April 1, 1910, director of sales. Now successful enough to take a wife, Friedrich Minoux married the twenty-five-year-old Maria Karoline Hente, nicknamed "Lilly." Two daughters, Johanna and Monika, followed.

On April 30, 1912, Minoux entered into the service of Hugo Stinnes, whom he had met in 1908. Stinnes (1870–1924), an industrialist who emerged after World War I as Germany's "business Kaiser," controlled coal mines, steel mills, hotels, electrical factories, newspapers, shipping lines, airlines, and banks.

Hugo Stinnes had been trying to dismantle the Rhein-Westfall Electrical Works, but he was meeting very tough resistance because of Minoux. Stinnes felt he could best overcome these difficulties by hiring his adversary. In doing so, he did more than defuse a slightly unpleasant situation. In a short time, Minoux had become a powerful figure in the mighty Stinnes organization. Along with a fiery temperament, Minoux had a real head for business and was constantly cooking up schemes. Contemporary photographs show a small man with close-cropped hair, a mustache, and a pair of eyes that would unnerve any adversary over a dueling pistol at twenty paces.

In the beginning, Minoux was interested in the graphics and paper industries, especially paper manufacturing. Later his interests broadened to include automobile manufacturing, coal mining, and steel production. In the inflationary expansion following World War I, Minoux profited immensely. By 1919 he had become a general director of the Stinnes Organization and a director of the United Berlin Coal Dealers AG, another large industrial combine.

The German press soon took note of Minoux's activities. As the *Deutsche Allgemeine Zeitung* reported: "The newspaper owner Hugo Stinnes naturally has no interest in lower paper prices, but a double interest in higher prices: he is a paper manufacturer, and also profits from the vertical integration of his newspaper trust, since every price rise gives him an advantage over his competitors. But Stinnes and his former general director Minoux have not advertised their pricing policies...How much has Stinnes benefited from the government price supports for paper? Certainly a part of his costs have been returned to him."

Minoux had his own business interests, apart from those he shared with Stinnes, and he made huge profits from takeovers and other speculative maneuvers during the postwar German inflation. His income was around three hundred fifty thousand gold marks yearly, this money forming the basis of the later fortune he amassed. During the same period, he made two hundred million gold marks for the Stinnes companies. In one of these years of high income, 1921, Minoux acquired the Wannsee Villa. He proceeded to develop an active political and social life. His living expenses were large. Besides a housekeeper, he employed a cook, a head gardener, a chauffeur, and other household help.

The Wannsee Villa was the site of evening receptions and political gatherings with prominent speakers. Central to these events were the dining room and lakeside terrace. Minoux had moved into the Wannsee Villa with his wife; but after a few years, ostensibly for reasons of health, she took up residence in another house belonging to her husband in Garmisch-Partenkirchen, a Bavarian Alpine town six hundred kilometers south of Berlin.

Friedrich Minoux and the German Hyperinflation

The German hyperinflation of 1923 was caused, to a great extent, by World War I and the terms of the Versailles peace treaty. To pay for the war, the Kaiser's ministers borrowed gold from Germany's citizens, giving paper notes in return. Repayment, the Germans assumed, would come from the defeated French and English. After all, Otto von Bismarck, the Iron Chancellor, had imposed an indemnity of five billion francs on the beaten French in 1871. This money paid for Bismarck's wars and later financed the rapid postwar growth of Berlin. To meet the vastly greater costs of World War I, Imperial Finance Minister Karl Helfferich was ready to demand one hundred fifty billion marks when the fighting ended. But the Germans lost.

"The hour has struck for the weighty settlement of our accounts," said Georges Clemenceau, the French Premier, to German Foreign Minister Count Ulrich von Brockdorff-Rantzau. The year was 1919. World War I had ended with an armistice seven months before. The scene was the Hall of Mirrors in France's Versailles Palace, where Louis XIV, the Sun King, had once reigned. The victorious Allies declared to the representatives of a defeated Germany that there were to be no negotiations. The Germans were simply to receive the terms that the Allies had agreed on.

The reception the vengeful French gave to Brockdorff-Rantzau, a thin, pale professional diplomat with a monocle, must have alerted him to expect the worst. They forced his special train, filled with one hundred eighty diplomats and experts preparing to argue the German case, to skulk along at ten miles an hour. The Germans were thus compelled to see the devastation their armies had inflicted on the countryside of northern France. In Versailles, the French housed the German delegation in an isolated hotel surrounded by barbed wire and made them carry their own bags upstairs.

The French terms were harsh. Clemenceau demanded total payment for all of France's war damages, its five million dead and wounded, its four thousand ruined towns, and twenty thousand destroyed businesses. He declared that the Germans must pay up to a hundred years if necessary, with interest. British experts calculated that the Germans owed a total of eight hundred billion marks, which was more than all the German national wealth.

The Allies summarily rejected a German counteroffer of one hundred billion marks, without interest. Instead, they demanded an immediate initial payment of $5 billion in gold, along with considerable quantities of coal, chemicals, and shipping, to be delivered by May 1921. The final amount to be paid was left to future negotiations. Winston Churchill called the reparations "a sad story of complicated idiocy." They led to an unending dispute between Germany and the Allies and were a partial cause for the ruinous fall of the German mark.

At first, the decline in value of the mark was not precipitous. Between 1918 and the summer of 1921, the mark slid in value from 4.20 to the dollar to 75, a significant descent. But people were more preoccupied with hunger and the shortage of food.

By the summer of 1922, the value of the mark had fallen to 400 to the dollar. On June 24, 1922, right-wing radicals assassinated Walther Rathenau, the millionaire Jewish minister of reconstruction, and shook what little faith anyone had left for prospects of a German recovery. From 400 per dollar, the mark sank to 7,000 by the beginning of 1923, and every week it slumped further.

January 1923 was a disaster. The government of Chancellor Josef Wirth collapsed. President Friedrich Ebert, a former saddle maker, tried to build a more conservative coalition that could win the support of big business and deal with the inflation. He selected as chancellor William Cuno, the director of the Hamburg-America shipping line. Cuno's elegant manners and appearance temporarily disguised his total inability to help govern a disintegrating Germany. ("Cuno is a fat cigar," Walther Rathenau had once said, "which will have to be smoked some day because of its lovely band.")

The bickering over reparations went on. The Germans asked for a moratorium and delayed their deliveries of raw material, while they tried to negotiate better terms. France's vindictive premier, Raymond Poincaré, refused to tolerate such tactics. In fact, he was anxious for any pretext that would allow the French to claim a violation of the Versailles Treaty and justify an invasion of Germany. "Whatever happens," he had told British Prime Minister Bonar Law, "I shall advance into the Ruhr on January 15."

When the Germans continued to stall, the French complained formally that the Germans had not delivered half the two hundred thousand telephone poles due for shipment to France during 1922. The Germans blamed their state governments for the delay, since the governments owned the forests with the trees to be cut down for telephone poles. The British did not take the French complaint seriously. History had recorded no such political use of wood as the French were making since the Greeks had built a horse outside Troy, said Sir John Bradbury, the British envoy.

Then the French made a new complaint regarding dilatory coal deliveries from the Ruhr. Disregarding British protests, they sent a Franco-Belgian "technical commission" to the Ruhr on January 11, 1923, to investigate the matter. The French discovered that the German Coal Syndicate had just moved from the Ruhr to Hamburg. The French, who had already sent a few troops to "protect" their commission, followed up with more troops. The German government immediately suspended all reparations deliveries and called on German citizens in the Ruhr to passively resist the French invasion. The French response was to dismiss any Ruhr official who disobeyed them and to arrest anyone who attempted to use force against them. On March 31, French troops fired on a crowd of workers at the Krupp Works in Essen, killing thirteen. By then, the French had put the entire Ruhr under their military rule, depriving Germany of its industrial center, the source of 80 percent of its coal, iron, and steel, the means for its economic recovery.

The German mark collapsed. From a rate of 7,000 to the dollar in January, when the French occupied the Ruhr, it slumped to 160,000 by July. The German government, to subsidize the idled Ruhr workers, churned out banknotes. At the Ullstein publishing headquarters on the Kochstraße in Berlin (where Ullstein is still located), government officials requisitioned the printing presses to produce increasingly worthless paper. One of the owners, Hermann Ullstein, recalled: "All doors were locked and officials of the Reichsbank were placed on guard. Round the machinery sat elderly women, staring fascinated at those parts of the presses from which the finished products came pouring out. It was the duty of these women to see that the billion mark notes were placed in the right baskets and handed to the officials. They had to keep an eye on every single billion. Officials are so funny sometimes."

Friedrich Minoux's engagement in German politics began at this time and was two pronged. First, Minoux appeared before the public with his own plan for stabilizing the mark and overcoming the inflation that had by then wiped out the savings of the middle class and wrought havoc. Second and more ominously, Minoux began to ally himself with conspiratorial right-wing radicals who were active in the army. He was probably a member of a group that was agitating to form a dictatorship; this group included an obscure former corporal, Adolf Hitler.

Minoux's efforts to stabilize the mark caused some conflict with Hugo Stinnes, who was making a fortune from the inflation. Still, the two continued to profit from the downward spiraling currency. The Reichstag (parliament) made a special inquiry into their activities, and on June 22, 1923, Minoux was called to testify. He defended his mentor Stinnes aggressively and excoriated the *Frankfurter Zeitung*, the newspaper that discovered his role in Stinnes's machinations: "Where did Stinnes get the money? He has a cadre of collaborators, who gladly worked with him. No Hugo Stinnes and no *Frankfurter Zeitung* has so much money that they could force this cadre to undermine German interests! Stinnes and I would also never contemplate such a thing. I regret having to appear before this committee. Our workday has sixteen hours; if everyone worked as we did, sixteen hours a day, Germany would be in better shape! Then...this committee would have never convened." Quite a tumult followed Minoux's testimony. A few weeks later, the regime of Reich Chancellor Gustav Stresemann attacked Minoux for his arrogance before the Reichstag, accusing him of working for the inflation rather than against it.

Karl Helfferich, now the government food minister, had suggested stabilizing the mark by tying it to rye. There was considerable official discussion of this suggestion, and Minoux offered his advice. On August 23, 1923, in the newspaper *Deutsche Allgemeine Zeitung*, Minoux wrote an article, under the pseudonym Friedrich Pilot, suggesting the use of gold to stabilize the mark. Under the title "Elimination of inflation and financial reform with a gold-based currency," Minoux described his program. Paper money would be eliminated; every individual and corporation would pay a uniform 5 percent income tax; the government would issue high-interest bonds and thereby bring order to the capital markets; the newly issued gold mark would be fixed at a rate of 4.2 to the dollar. Within one year, Minoux wrote, there would be financial stabilization, and the crazy system of taxation would be replaced by a rational one. The economically valuable classes would ascend to the fore; the lazy and wasteful members of the economic body would be banished, and the working people would benefit. Minoux saw no disadvantages to his proposals, but he recommended that, if there were any, the state should deal with them. Furthermore, he did not advocate a change in the length of the workday.

In the turbulent Germany of 1923, Minoux's proposed economic reforms had radical political implications. As Hermann Bücher, President of the Association of German Industries, noted: "Herr Minoux's reforms could be instituted very quickly. But I believe they would only be possible with an absolute dictatorship. If we create this dictatorship, I am willing to participate. Then the reforms will be a cure." Bücher's position is not surprising, because the Association of German Industries had previously endorsed a gold standard.

Minoux's pseudonym, Friedrich Pilot, did not conceal his identity for very long. On September 1, 1923, the newspaper *Berliner Tageblatt* reported: "We are perhaps not revealing a secret when we report that the article was not written by Hugo Stinnes, but that it was written by one of the leaders of the Stinnes Organization, very close to Stinnes himself."

On the evening of August 27 or 28, Reich Chancellor Gustav Stresemann met with Hugo Stinnes, Friedrich Minoux, and other leading business figures. On August 30, 1923, Stresemann mentioned this encounter at a meeting of his cabinet. The finance minister, Hans Luther, agreed to consider a gold standard.

The government's finance and currency committee convened on September 6. Both Minoux and the banker Hjalmar Schacht addressed the committee. Minoux reiterated his taxation plan and his recommendation of a gold standard, and he again rejected using rye to stabilize the currency: "The urban population will be inclined to suspect agrarian manipulations; these, to me, are indissolubly bound to the word *rye*." Also, Minoux rejected a separation of currency reform and governmental finance reform; the one must accompany the other, and both must be accomplished soon. Hjalmar Schacht concurred: "...for that, which Herr Minoux has said, is, in my opinion, completely right. If we are not successful in once again winning trust in state finances, then no other measures will help us. Without the people's trust, we cannot accomplish the large national tasks which we have come here to discuss..." It is not surprising that, after the committee expressed further support for Minoux, they recommended the tax assessment he advocated, while declining Karl Helfferich's rye standard "because a rye currency would cause large fluctuations of German rye prices and would have no value in international trade." On the same day the finance minister reported to the cabinet Minoux's recommendations for a gold standard. Critics of Minoux's suggestions for currency reform held that they would take too long to implement and that Minoux had overvalued the national wealth. In the end, the government did not implement the Minoux plan.

Instead, the mark was stabilized by issuing a so-called Rentenmark secured by land. Only in 1924 did the government introduce a gold mark, under the aegis of Hjalmar Schacht, the Reichsbank President.

Minoux's involvement in the currency reform led to a break with Hugo Stinnes. On September 9, 1923, an anonymous article appeared under the title "Truth" in the Stinnes newspaper *Deutsche Allgemeine Zeitung*. Attributed to a "leading industrialist," the extensive article indicated that lengthening the workday from eight hours to ten hours would provide a needed basis for overcoming the inflation. The anonymous author, none other than Hugo Stinnes himself, postulated that "only then is it conceivable that the mark can be stabilized by means of the suggestions of Friedrich Pilot, previously published in this newspaper."

According to Stinnes's biographer Peter Wulf, the difference of opinion about the length of the workday was not the only cause of tension between Stinnes and Minoux. A second cause was the political-economic program that Minoux had developed for General Hans von Seeckt. Chief of the Imperial General Staff during World War I, Seeckt was head of the Reichswehr (army) from 1920 to 1926.

Seeckt was a strange general, a frail man with a long neck, slender hands, and a Father Christmas face. He was a connoisseur of art and wine, a wanderer through Europe, Africa, and India. A soldier since the age of nineteen, he had been a brilliant World War I staff officer, the mastermind of the Gorlice breakthrough in the east and the Soissons breakthrough on the Western Front. When the war ended in defeat, Seeckt wept. Military combat was to him a quasi-mystical experience; as he once remarked, "War is the highest summit of human achievement. It is the natural, the final stage in the historical development of humanity." Germany was to him a spiritual entity: "The Reich! There is something supernatural in this word. It embraces far more and connotes something other than the conception of a state."

Seeckt was the military member of the German delegation to Versailles, so he knew first hand how fiercely the French planned to enforce German disarmament. Though he had reluctantly signed the peace treaty, he now felt that his duty as army commander was to thwart the treaty in any way he could.

He also believed that the Versailles limit of one hundred thousand troops prevented him from defending his eastern frontier, so he organized a secret eastern army of twenty thousand so-called "work commandos," which soon became known as the "Black Reichswehr." His long-range goal was to build a new army that could defeat the French when the next war came.

Minoux's program for Seeckt had subordinated Stinnes's single interest, the lengthening of the workday, to multiple other economic reforms. On October 7, 1923, Minoux and Stinnes had a contentious confrontation. As Stinnes later wrote to Minoux, "Your remarks at our meeting deepened my impression that, in the last few months, you have found your association with me to be a disturbing impediment to your political work and final life's mission. You are a person with unique abilities to master the present difficulties. I certainly would never have stood in your way if you had come to me in the quiet, amicable manner commensurate with our twelve year friendship. But you did not, and you hurt me deeply, even though I am well acquainted with your fiery temper. Nevertheless, I wish you all the best and thank you for your incomparable services. Without you, our firm would never be what it is today."

To his son, Hugo, Jr., Stinnes was more candid in his appraisal of Minoux's political talents: "It is my impression that Minoux could easily play the role he wants if he knew how to lead. But his messianic faith has led him often to uninhibited expression of wrongheaded ideas. In the dangerous and slick world of politics, one must be able to shut one's trap, and never run off at the mouth, or at least seldom, and only in good company." Although Minoux and Stinnes had split as business partners, they remained political confederates during the following weeks.

Friedrich Minoux and Plans for a Dictatorship

In 1923, Friedrich Minoux was in close contact with right-wing German politicians and extremist military groups. His goal was the building of a politically strong, authoritarian regime which would be able to nullify the intervention efforts of the victorious Allied powers. On February 21, 1923, Minoux moderated a discussion in his Wannsee Villa between General Seeckt and the former army general quartermaster, Erich Ludendorff, the German general who was mainly responsible for Germany's military policy and strategy in the latter years of World War I.

Ludendorff, a man with a granite character and a gluttony for work, had won the right to wear the coveted red stripes of the general staff at age thirty in 1895. He had a thick body, a blond mustache over a harsh down-curving mouth, a round double chin, and that bulge at the back of the neck which Ralph Waldo Emerson called the mark of the beast.

When World War I ended, Ludendorff had hidden in a Berlin boarding house, then disguised himself with false whiskers and fled briefly to Sweden. But he had an iron nerve under fire. During the November 1923 "Beerhall" Putsch, Ludendorff, Hitler, and their confederates attempted to overthrow the Bavarian government. As Ludendorff, accompanied by Hitler and two thousand other men, marched toward Munich's Odeonsplatz, the state police opened fire. Eighteen men were killed. A comrade yanked Hitler to the ground, dislocating his left shoulder. Ludendorff, oblivious to the bullets whizzing past his head, marched straight through the police cordon and into the arms of a lieutenant who arrested him.

According to Ludendorff's memoirs, Hugo Stinnes had arranged the meeting with Minoux and Seeckt, which Reichschancellor Wilhelm Cuno was also supposed to have attended. The occasion for the meeting was the French occupation of the Ruhr and what could be done about it. Ludendorff recalled later: "I had no favorable impressions. I sensed no clarity about the situation or the desire to act. But I told General von Seeckt I would try to work with the groups to defend against France. Only through unity of the groups and the army could anything meaningful be accomplished. I was skeptical of General von Seeckt's idea of using force to expel the French, but I was equally doubtful that passive resistance would be of any value." Seeckt wanted nothing to do with the right wing paramilitary organizations, of which Ludendorff considered himself a representative. Seeckt feared that any cooperation with these groups might allow them to assume a leading role. The Reich Defense Minister, Otto Geßler, reported later that Seeckt had told him, with unconcealed satisfaction, that Ludendorff was deeply irritated at the end of the meeting. Thereafter, relations between Ludendorff and Seeckt did not improve, but in the following months there were many more meetings between Seeckt and Minoux.

A Lieutenant General Lieber witnessed one meeting between Minoux and Seeckt. He later reported: "Minoux explained his program to Seeckt. It was gigantic in all areas and would change Germany's whole internal structure. It would mean a life and death fight, but if successful would lead to the recovery of Germany. Minoux's powerful personality completely overawed Seeckt." Minoux had gained an opposite impression and later described Seeckt as an "empty safe." Yet Seeckt's written "Government Program" contained in its section "Economy and social laws" the handwriting of Friedrich Minoux, as well as references to Minoux's August 1923 suggestions for currency reform and other changes: "Decisive renunciation of all Marxist theories and measures, in particular those dealing with socialization... Right of the government to oversee vital industries.... Unemployment benefits.... Legal regulation of the length of the workday.... Retention of the eight hour workday..." Seeckt made an intensive effort to effect these and other goals. But too many events were roiling German domestic politics.

On August 13, 1923, Chancellor Gustav Stresemann's first cabinet entered office. On September 26, passive resistance to the French occupation of the Ruhr was discontinued. On September 27, Reich president Friedrich Ebert took over from defense minister Geßler the task of putting down the leftist radical governments of Thuringia and Saxony. On October 3, Stresemann's first cabinet dissolved, and a second cabinet was created three days later. On October 21, separatists in Aachen declared a "Rhine Republic." On October 22, the army marched into Saxony. On October 23 and 24, a communist uprising in Hamburg failed. On November 2, because of the loss of the Social Democratic Party (SPD) minister, Stresemann's cabinet was no longer able to function. On November 5, the army completely occupied Thuringia and Saxony. On November 9, 1923, Hitler's National Socialist "Beerhall" Putsch in Munich failed.

During these eventful months, Friedrich Minoux worked ceaselessly behind the scenes. A day after the dissolution of Stresemann's first cabinet, General Kurt von Schleicher, in the Reichschancellery, suggested the naming of five ministers, among them Geßler, Seeckt, and Minoux. But Minoux declined.

Yet his political involvement did not end. In the following weeks, rightist circles continued to advocate the formation of a "Directorate" with dictatorial powers, which would be organized after the Stresemann government had been toppled. The members of the Directorate were to be: Seeckt; the Bavarian General State Commissioner, Alfred Ritter von Kahr; the German ambassador in Washington, Otto Wiedtfeldt; and Friedrich Minoux. Seeckt apparently had plans for an all-party directorate, in order to reduce the importance of Reichspresident Friedrich Ebert.

In the meantime, Minoux was still in touch with the Bavarian separatists, among them Ritter von Kahr and Otto von Lossow, the commanding army general in Bavaria. Minoux anticipated the possibility of first forming a dictatorship in Bavaria, which would then spread throughout all of Germany. Seeckt, however, was not enthusiastic about this plan, preferring instead that the dictatorship originate in Berlin.

But Seeckt's proposed plans came to naught. Reichspresident Ebert rejected all calls for a dictatorship and remained steadfastly committed to a democratic government. Under no circumstance would he countenance attempts to overthrow the Weimar Republic. On November 9, 1923, Seeckt took power over the government for four months but made no attempt to institute a dictatorship. In the meantime, Minoux had distanced himself from Seeckt and was now working with the plotters in Bavaria.

Friedrich Minoux and the Hitler "Beerhall" Putsch

Minoux traveled to Munich on October 25, 1923, to meet with Ludendorff, Kahr, Lossow, and Hans Ritter von Seißer, chief of the Bavarian police.

Ludendorff later described the meeting: "Herr Minoux came to my house, accompanied by Lossow and Seißer.... According to my recollection, he had received a request to travel to Berlin to take over a ministry in conjunction with the forming of a dictatorship; Seeckt was to be Reichschancellor. But Minoux first wanted my opinion. He told me he was inclined to become a minister, but not in a Seeckt government. He had developed his political ideas considerably, but they were much too one-sided, economically speaking, and had no appeal for me. No doubt Minoux will remember more details of our talk than I do..." Kahr's colleague, Hans von Seißer, had other recollections of the meeting: "We were with Ludendorff for an hour. All three of us tried to get him to convince Hitler not to do anything rash. Ludendorff gave me his word with a handshake that he would do nothing without informing me first. This promise was freely given; I did not demand it. In the following days Ludendorff neither reneged nor hedged on what he had said. Just before we were to leave, Hitler appeared, but there was too little time for any further meaningful discussion." In 1924, Hitler was tried and convicted for his role in the Putsch to overthrow the government, and he received a prison sentence. Ludendorff was acquitted and turned even more decisively against Minoux's economic program. It was "too populist, not sufficiently anti-Semitic, and too materialistic."

Minoux maintained that the help of the Jews could not be renounced in any currency stabilization plan. He also advised that two eminent Jewish bankers, Carl Joseph Melchior and Max M. Warburg, be recruited as financial advisors. Warburg had met Ludendorff in 1918, shortly before the armistice. An agitated Ludendorff was demanding that Germany declare bankruptcy, and Warburg thought the general had lost his nerve. A few months later, Warburg and Melchior accompanied Count Ulrich von Brockdorff-Rantzau to the Versailles Peace Conference as part of the German delegation.

Konrad Heiden, Hitler's biographer, described Ludendorff's reaction to Minoux's advocacy of Melchior and Warburg: "Minoux's talents impressed Ludendorff, but Minoux's political views were another matter entirely. That Minoux ever had anything to do with Seeckt vexed Ludendorff, but far worse was Minoux's belief that Germany could not be governed without Jews. How could Minoux even suggest involvement with people like Melchior or Warburg? 'My dear Herr Minoux, what you say is truly wonderful, but to me it's all a bit too commercial,' to which Minoux replied in such a harsh manner that Ludendorff recoiled."

Hitler decisively rejected Minoux's philo-Semitic stance. In its verdict on the "Beerhall" Putsch, April 1, 1924, the Munich court accepted and repeated Hitler's angst regarding a Minoux-Seeckt directorate. As Hitler himself said, "A government with a Jewish finance minister would be a catastrophe for Germany."

After his failed talks in Munich, Minoux returned to Berlin and met with Seeckt on October 26. Seeckt now considered Minoux "to have taken a Bavarian turn," though in fact Minoux was still wary of the Munich plotters. Hans Ritter von Seißer recorded the next meeting of Seeckt and Minoux in the Wannsee Villa on November 2, 1923:

> A new cabinet will form in fourteen days, at most. There are doubts whether Seeckt will have the support he needs to create a directorate. Minoux does not want a putsch. Awaiting events in Bavaria. Hunger and cold becoming worse. Soon the unrest will bring calls for change. Minoux had a conference with Ebert, who would not think of trying to rule without parliament; even threats will not shake Ebert's resolve. Situation in Munich similar: economic reforms must not be separated from political ones. My impression is that Minoux is holding back until his moment arrives. He says that people who take part in a putsch will not be able to join the government. His attitude toward Hitler and Ludendorff is unchanged, as is his desire for involvement of the Jews. There are worries about what Hitler will do in Bavaria. A communication from Stinnes: Minoux should try to use his influence in Bavaria in order to prevent an uprising.

Minoux was certain a debacle was coming. He felt that the new Stresemann government would last only a short time. The economic situation would get worse, and political unrest would follow. In light of these events, Minoux believed, Reichspresident Friedrich Ebert could no longer reject calls for an authoritarian regime, in which Minoux would play a leading role. Minoux would then effect a financial healing of Germany by virtue of his "economic expertise" and his "Friedrich Pilot" plans. But under no circumstances would Minoux endanger his chances by involving himself in a Seeckt or Hitler-Ludendorff putsch.

It is interesting that the men around Seeckt and Ludendorff each thought Minoux was in the other's camp. As was mentioned, Seeckt thought that the Bavarians had won Minoux over, while Hitler and Ludendorff were convinced that Minoux was Seeckt's man. Hitler, in fact, thought Seeckt and Minoux were quite close and a danger to his own political plans. On October 25, 1923, Minoux had his only meeting with Hitler. Minoux offered Hitler as little support for his Bavarian plans as he would offer Seeckt in the following days.

In the short run, Minoux seems to have assessed the situation correctly. On November 2, 1923, the Social Democrats withdrew from the government; thereafter, Stresemann did not have a parliamentary majority. On November 23, 1923, after a vote of no confidence, he stepped down. A political centrist, Wilhelm Marx, replaced him as Reichschancellor, although most of Stresemann's ministers remained in office. Marx proceeded to pursue a business-friendly policy, meant to restore a rigorous economic stability. Seeckt remained the most powerful figure in the government, but he had given up his plans for a dictatorship.

Minoux's political plans were ruined. The German nationalists were still ready in mid-November 1923 to invite him to take part in a dictatorship with wide-ranging powers. But Stresemann had a strong aversion to this plan. Stresemann's attitude, along with the new, moderately right-wing Marx government and the estrangement between Minoux and Seeckt, all prevented the establishment of Minoux's directorate. In the following years, Minoux left politics and concentrated on his own economic endeavors.

Two questions arise about the political activities of Friedrich Minoux. First, did Minoux provide financial support to Hitler and the Nazi party, and second, exactly what relationship did Minoux have to the other far-right-wing nationalist groups?

George W. Hallgarten, the American ambassador, wrote in his memoirs that Minoux was in touch with the "paramilitary groups around Ludendorff, which he helped to finance." To support this assertion, Hallgarten cited the book *I Paid Hitler* by Fritz Thyssen, the heir to a German steel fortune. But in Thyssen's book, there is only one reference to Minoux as a supporter of Ludendorff: "Ludendorff... had already asked for and received the help of various industrialists, in particular Minoux and the Stinnes firm." There was not a word about Minoux financing the Nazis or other paramilitary organizations.

Some new studies have refuted the notion that Minoux or Stinnes financed the paramilitary groups. Henry A. Turner, in his book *German Big Business and the Rise of Hitler*, noted no involvement of these two men with the Nazi party. Moreover, Hitler made derogatory mention of Stinnes in speeches, and in *Mein Kampf* he disparaged Stinnes's lack of "eternal idea values" and assertion that only economic effort could revive Germany: "These words pronounced by a Stinnes created the most incredible confusion; they were picked up at once, and with amazing rapidity became the *leitmotif* of all the quacks and big-mouths that since the revolution Fate has let loose on Germany in the capacity of 'statesmen'."

Nonetheless, Minoux tried later to make use of his 1923 contacts with the Nazi party. In 1941 the Reich Justice Ministry prosecuted him for defrauding the Berlin Gas Company. In the records of the proceedings, the following appears: "Minoux claims that in 1923 the Führer had chosen him as his finance minister, that he had financed the activities of the Party, and had made possible the first speech of the Führer in the Ruhr after its occupation."

In fact, Hitler had not picked Minoux as his finance minister and kept his distance from the hot-tempered little entrepreneur. From the beginning of the French occupation of the Ruhr in January 1923, to the "Beerhall" Putsch in November, Hitler had never given a speech in the Ruhr region. Nor, as was noted above, had Minoux ever given money to the Nazis. In 1941 the jailed Minoux was simply saying what he thought might secure his release.

Friedrich Minoux's Business Activities
After His Split with Hugo Stinnes

After Minoux and Stinnes parted ways in 1923, the company Gute Hoffnungshütte, a machine works, offered Minoux the post of general director. Minoux rejected this offer because he did not want to move from Berlin to the town of Oberhausen. He also rejected a job offer from the German Potash Syndicate because the annual salary, one hundred fifty thousand reichsmarks, was too low. Instead, he founded a series of firms and involved himself with many others.

The nucleus of Minoux's interlocked business empire was his company, Friedrich Minoux, Inc. for Trade and Industry. To secure liquidity for his far-flung empire, Minoux invested one million marks to buy a share of a Berlin bank, Jacquier & Securius. This sum comprised a quarter of the bank's capital. Jacquier & Securius was a prominent Jewish private bank, founded in 1817 and located in the middle of Berlin in a building nicknamed the "Red Castle." During his time with the bank, Minoux took part in a 150 million goldmark project to build canals in Constantinople. In 1930 Minoux sold his interest in the bank in order to concentrate on his wholesale coal business.

While still working with Stinnes, Minoux had become involved with the Rota Boiler and Engineering Company, and here he demonstrated the sharp business practices that proved to be his downfall. The state railways had offered Stinnes a contract for the improvement of freight cars, which he refused. Minoux took the contract and with Rota was soon refurbishing locomotives as well. The business was quite profitable, and it quickly expanded from twenty to fifteen hundred employees. Minoux acquired buildings and machinery to do the work, then became a part owner of Rota.

But problems soon cropped up. The state railways were paying Minoux so much money that they decided they could do the work more cheaply in their own shops, and they tried to break their contract. In the course of this dispute, some employees of Rota and some state railway officials were indicted for fraud; one Rota official named März went to prison. März had been a foreman for the state railways when Minoux hired him as a manager of Rota.

During the trial Minoux appeared as a witness, but not under oath. The prosecutors suspected that he had suborned März to commit fraud. In the end, Minoux had to pay a fine of eight hundred thousand reichsmarks.

Despite this setback, Minoux continued to prosper. He was the founder and a board member of Prinator Machines, Inc., a maker of printing presses. He was a major shareholder of the German-Rumanian Petroleum Corporation

(Derupag). He had acquired half the shares of Derupag, later called Mawag (Mineral and Asphalt Works), for one million gold marks. Derupag closed down unused navy tank installations in the Kaiser Wilhelm Canal and built large distillation and refinery facilities, where Mexican crude was transformed into oil, gasoline, fuel oil, and synthetic resin. But Mawag made one large misstep by building an oil refinery in Marseilles. Minoux invested his profits in shares of the new refinery, which he was able to sell later only at a substantial loss.

The automobile business also attracted Minoux. After acquiring a share of the Berlin-Burger Ironworks, Minoux arranged a preliminary concession to sell Ford automobiles in Germany. But this deal came to naught.

Minoux devoted himself to some public service. In 1924 he joined the board of the Berlin State Electrical Works, Inc. (called Bewag) as economic advisor. Other board members were Berlin mayor Gustav Böß, three state representatives, eight city councilmen, two corporate officers, and an engineer. Minoux remained on the board until 1928, even though he was never able to acquire shares of Bewag, which were not for sale.

At the same time, Minoux was on the board of the Berlin State Waterworks and the Berlin Gas Company. His involvement with the gas company eventually led to charges of fraud, his imprisonment, and death.

After 1925, Minoux began taking bigger risks but seemed to have misplaced his golden touch. He became involved with a series of small German firms and squandered money. Also, with his Jewish banking partners, he had imported and sold English coal; a miners' strike subsequently caused more losses. Between 1926 and 1932 he lost at least three million reichsmarks.

Minoux's shady side soon got him in more trouble with the law. In 1924 Jacquier & Securius, as leader of a bank consortium, had acquired a majority of stock in the cigarette maker August Batschari. Minoux took over August Batschari in June 1926. On July 29, 1933, the government accused Minoux and an associate, Joseph Ludwig, of falsifying the records of the company to avoid paying taxes. However, to the chagrin of the state prosecutor, Minoux was able to refute the accusations.

The Great Depression and Friedrich Minoux

Within a few months of the Wall Street crash of 1929, a world-wide depression began. No country was so vulnerable to the contraction of credit and trade as Germany. Foreign investors called in their loans and capital flowed out of the country, causing companies to lay off workers or close entirely. During January 1930, German unemployment soared from 1.5 million to 2.5 million, and every month the number kept increasing. The unemployed received a dole of $17 a month, while those still employed had to take pay cuts. For example, a miner's salary sank from $47 a month in 1930 to $39 the following year.

The newspaper stories were grim. Berlin's *Deutsche Allgemeine Zeitung* reported that the number of customers at the city's pawnshops had doubled. In one week alone, five bankrupt bankers committed suicide. "The banker Max Cunow of Berlin was found dead in his bedroom Monday morning, shot through the head. The police announced that it was a suicide. A letter was found, citing financial difficulties..."

The Berlin unemployed huddled for warmth in public shelters. At one shelter in the Ackerstrasse, the crowd overflowed and a fight started. The police had to use their clubs.

Otto Friedrich, a *Newsweek* editor, interviewed Dr. Hans-Joachim Kausch, who had witnessed the depression as a Berlin newspaper correspondent: "What was it really like for the unemployed? They played cards. They demonstrated. Some became criminals. It was a sad time. You go to work, and hundreds of young men and young girls are standing around on the streets, just standing. In Berlin alone, a city of four million, there were 750,000 unemployed. They were drinking a little beer. They were walking in the forests. They were hungry." In the woods surrounding Berlin, the unemployed built tent colonies, where they lived from spring until frost. In nearby fields, peasants stood guard with rifles to prevent foragers from digging up their potatoes.

The economic crisis quickly brought the coalition cabinet of Social Democratic Chancellor Herman Müller to the point of collapse. Even the most optimistic reckoning predicted that unemployment payments would produce a deficit of $100 million. The conservatives demanded reduction in payments, the left demanded an increase in taxes on workers. The Catholic Center, now headed by Dr. Heinrich Brüning, worked out a compromise that provided for some sacrifices on both sides, but the Social Democrats felt they could not bargain about so fundamental an issue.

In November 1930, Friedrich Minoux met with Brüning and offered him a list of suggestions for overcoming unemployment. Among them were the following:

• The workday should be shortened from eight hours to six, but workers should be paid for a seven-hour day.
• The government should undertake public works projects that eventually would be self-supporting, for example, dams, canals, and highways.
• The government should carefully monitor work conditions without impairing the freedoms of the individual worker.
• All married men should be hired, while the employment of women should be curtailed, above all by the prohibition of paying female factory

workers less than their male counterparts. These measures should be combined with a youth tax of 5 percent on the income of thirty-year-olds and 25 percent on persons are forty and older.

  • Former country dwellers should be resettled in the country for agricultural work.

  • A 5 percent tax increase should be imposed on everyone whose work day could not be shortened. The government should increase tobacco and alcohol taxes and provide national health insurance.

Minoux's agenda, taxing, spending, and creating public works programs, resembled Franklin D. Roosevelt's New Deal, begun three years later.

But unlike Roosevelt, Friedrich Minoux was quite enthusiastic about the rise of fascism. Minoux was an executive committee member of the "Society for the Study of Fascism," founded in 1931. Among the other members was Major Waldemar Pabst, who in 1919 had been one of the plotters in the murders of the Jewish revolutionary socialists Karl Liebknecht and Rosa Luxemburg. By 1933 the society had ninety-six full members and one hundred ten corresponding members. Among these were thirty right-wing paramilitants and twenty Nazis. Seventy-five members were businessmen, including the banker and former finance minister Hjalmar Schacht and the industrialist Fritz Thyssen. Thirty other members were large land holders, including the former crown prince Friedrich Wilhelm. The Society saw its main task as disseminating Italian fascist ideas in Germany and unifying ideologically all right-wing extremist groups. Another aim was reforming German unions along fascist lines. The Society held once monthly evening meetings, at which Friedrich Minoux occasionally spoke.

Minoux gave one notable speech on December 15, 1932, at the Hotel Kaiserhof in Berlin. The title was "An Economic Turn Through Individual Social Economy." In his extensive "leading measures to combat unemployment," Minoux laid out a comprehensive program. He emphasized the "primacy of politics," demanded that the state set basic conditions for the economy, and extensively disputed other economic concepts. He rejected the notion of "Christian socialism," because of its presumably false premises, as well as the planned economy of Marxist socialism. He disparaged the economic reform measures the Soviet Union had instituted, saying that Germany should be defended against the introduction of these measures: "The fact that we have recently embraced new dances from Negro colonies, and that we in Europe have been repeatedly infected with Asiatic cholera, does not justify drawing our economic recipes from Asia." Minoux condemned economic organization from above and declared a planned economy, state capitalism, and state socialism to be unworkable. Instead of these measures, he advocated an "individual social economy":

"At the heart of our laws are families and property, a feeling of responsibility and a healthy sense of accomplishment, as well as a natural force driving the desire to work and save. While collectivism demeans all earthly values, individual industry advances human progress and material well-being. For me the matter is clear: the more collectivism, the worse the effect on total productivity." Minoux spoke at great length about trusts, monopolies, and syndicates. Interestingly, he mentioned that in 1918 he advised Hugo Stinnes to form a coal syndicate but that Stinnes only followed this recommendation temporarily. Minoux now demanded the elimination and prohibition of all syndicates and trusts, including "wage syndicates and tariff treaties." In their place, he advocated a state-determined minimum wage for many occupations. The nucleus of his planned reforms was (a) suppression of mammoth anonymous companies by revision of the regulations governing corporations, and (b) the "dethroning of anonymous capital" by comprehensive redistribution. Minoux wanted the huge companies, as well as banks, to be broken up into smaller organizations, within a specified period, and overseen by regional authorities. Monopolies valued at more than five million reichsmarks would not be allowed to exist without governmental permission.

This speech was Friedrich Minoux's last public attempt to exercise political influence. The Society for the Study of Fascism rapidly lost meaning after Hitler became chancellor in January 1933, and it was disbanded the following December. Thereafter, Minoux never joined the Nazi party or any Nazi political organization.

3

Aryanization, Friedrich Minoux, and the Plundering of the German Jews

When the Nazis came to power, one of their fundamental aims was to eliminate the Jewish presence in Germany. They began this endeavor by systematic theft of Jewish property, which they called "Aryanization." Though a philo-Semite, even Friedrich Minoux made money from disenfranchised Jews. Aryanization involved mostly small and mid-sized companies unknown outside of Germany. But at least one tragic Aryanization involved a world-renowned company, the music publisher C.F. Peters.

As Gordon A. Craig has written, antipathy toward the Jews was quite ancient. Even in Roman times, Jews were viewed with suspicion because their strict monotheism made no concessions to the deification of the emperors and the rites that celebrated this. In some parts of the Empire their stubbornness on this score led to anti-Jewish riots and pogroms.

With the rise of Christianity, such violent expression of hostility toward the Jews became a regular feature of Western life. To Christians, the Jews were a stubborn people who had refused to recognize Jesus as the Messiah and who were guilty of deicide, which, according to the Gospel of St. Matthew, they had themselves acknowledged by crying, at the time of Jesus's condemnation, "His blood be on us and on our children!" Jesus himself, according to the Gospel of St. John (8: 42–45), had declared them to be sinful and unregenerate ("Ye are of your father the devil, and the lusts of your father ye will do"), and his followers found it easy to believe that there was no crime of which the Jews were not capable. In the fourth century, St. John Chrysostom declared:

> I know that a great number of the faithful have a certain respect for the Jews and hold their ceremonies in reverence. This provokes me to eradicate com-

pletely such a disastrous opinion.... Since they have disowned the Father, crucified the Son, and rejected the Spirit's help, who would not dare to assert that the synagogue is not a home of demons? God is not worshipped there; it is simply a home of idolatry.... The Jews live for their bellies, they crave for the goods of this world. In shamelessness and greed, they surpass even pigs and goats... The Jews are possessed by demons, they are handed over to impure spirits.... Instead of greeting them and addressing them by so much as a word, you should turn away from them as from the pest and a plague of the human race.

The very exclusivity of the Jews, their preference during the Middle Ages for living in closed communities, made them the object of superstitious fear. No crime was committed, no child disappeared, without their being blamed. Obscene practices and ritual murder were said to be a normal feature of their religious observances. They were believed to be poisoners of wells and seducers of the young, with demonic powers which enabled them to call down earthquakes, pestilence, and tempests upon their Christian neighbors. During times of calamity, they became the victims of mob violence.

In Germany, sporadic outbursts of popular anti-Semitism were common throughout the Middle Ages and the early modern period. They were often encouraged by the Church, which sometimes made it easier for rioters to identify their victims by forcing Jews to wear distinctive items of dress (yellow patches or horned caps, which was the custom in Bamberg in the fifteenth century), or by Christian merchants who were jealous of the competition of Jewish peddlers, or by people who wished to free themselves from debt to Jewish moneylenders.

People with any sense of reality realized that the Jews generally stimulated economic life and brought prosperity to the localities in which they settled, and in many parts of Germany Jewish traders were placed under the protection of the emperor or local rulers. But the rights granted them varied from state to state and were limited in duration and always at the mercy of local conditions and the whims of town councilors.

In the sixteenth century, the Reformation led to an increase of intolerance. Martin Luther at first believed that the Jews would respond positively to the new dispensation and would renounce their past errors and embrace Christianity. As he wrote: "For our fools, the popes, bishops, sophists, and monks — the coarse blockheads! — dealt with the Jews as if they were dogs and not human beings. They have done nothing for them but curse them and seize their wealth. I would advise and beg everybody to deal kindly with the Jews and to instruct them in the Scriptures; in such case we could expect them to come over to us." When the Jews were unresponsive, Luther raged against them with a coarseness of language unequaled before the Nazi period. In a long treatise called "Concerning the Jews and Their Lies" (1543), he asked:

"What then shall we Christians do with this damned, rejected race of Jews?...Since they live among us and we know about their lying and blasphemy and cursing, we cannot tolerate them.... In this way we cannot quench the inextinguishable fire of divine rage...or convert the Jews. We must prayerfully and reverentially practice a merciful severity."

"This," he continued, would include "setting fire to their synagogues and schools and covering over what will not burn with earth so that no man will ever see a stone or cinder of them again...breaking and destroying their houses...so that they have to live in stalls like gypsies and learn that they are not the lords in our land as they boast and must live in misery and captivity," depriving them of their holy books, silencing their teachers, forbidding them the right to travel or to trade, and seizing their wealth on the grounds that "everything that they possess they have robbed and stolen from us by their usury."

The Germans did not put these harsh measures into general practice until four centuries had passed. But, because of Luther's personal animus and the heightened emphasis placed upon the text of the New Testament in Lutheran observance, the Lutheran church acquired a prejudice against the Jews that was never completely eradicated.

Before 1914 German anti-Semitism was a stubborn social undercurrent. Among the many German intellectuals who embraced it were the composer Richard Wagner and the historian Heinrich von Treitschke. The slogan, "The Jews are our misfortune (Die Juden sind unser Unglück)" is Treitschke's.[1]

Another historian, Theodor Mommsen, who in the late 1870s had been the first to take up arms against the anti-Jewish writings of his colleagues, sadly noted: "You are mistaken if you believe that anything could be achieved by reason. In years past, I thought so myself and kept protesting against the monstrous infamy that is anti-Semitism. But it is useless, completely useless.... It is a horrible epidemic like cholera — one can neither explain or cure it. One must patiently wait until the poison has consumed itself and lost its virulence."

Despite the pervasive anti-Semitism, Jews volunteered in droves to fight for the fatherland when war broke out in August 1914. Indeed, Jews were not new to the German army. They had fought against Napoleon in the wars of liberation, and seventy-one had won the Iron Cross, first awarded in 1813. Only their numbers in the military had increased. During World War I, of five hundred fifty thousand German Jews, one hundred thousand were in uniform and twelve thousand were killed in action. One of the most successful

---

[1]Der Stürmer *(The Stormer), the anti-Semitic, pornographic Nazi newspaper, carried Treitschke's slogan on the front page of every issue after 1927. The same slogan was on all* Stürmer *display cases in German cities and towns.*

fighter pilots, a Jew, Wilhelm Franke, received Prussia's highest military decoration, Pour le Mérite, and was killed in action.

But after 1918, in a radically different emotional atmosphere tinged by national humiliation and economic chaos, anti–Semitism flourished as never before. Every argument that Hitler used against the Jews had been made prior to 1914. The only difference was that the Nazis had the strength of their convictions and turned those arguments into a program of action.

They began their program by forcing the sale of Jewish businesses to non-Jews, a process called Aryanization. The tactics employed were harassment, boycott and credit restriction. Aryanization was a gradual process. In five years, all Jewish assets, estimated at ten to twelve billion reichsmarks in 1933, had been reduced by half.

In 1938 the pace of Aryanization increased. On April 26 all Jews were ordered to register their property. On June 14, in a third supplementary decree to the Reich Citizenship Law, a business was considered Jewish if the proprietor was a Jew, if a partner was a Jew, or if, as of January 1, 1938, a member of the board of directors was a Jew. Also considered Jewish was a business in which Jews owned more than one-quarter of the shares or more than one-half of the votes, or a business under predominantly Jewish influence. On July 6 a law established an extensive list of commercial services henceforth forbidden to Jews.

On the night of November 9, 1938, Kristallnacht, there were terror attacks on synagogues and stores. The attacks, long planned, had awaited only a pretext. Two days earlier, a Polish Jew, Herschel Grynszpan, had assassinated Ernst von Rath, Third Secretary of the German Embassy in Paris. The pretext now established, Security Police Chief Reinhard Heydrich ordered destruction of all Jewish places of worship in Germany and Austria. In fifteen hours the Nazis had burned one hundred one synagogues and demolished another seventy-six. Roving bands wrecked seven thousand five hundred Jewish-owned stores. The pillage went on through the night, and next day the streets were covered with broken glass, hence the name Kristallnacht. The final blow that destroyed Jewish economic life in Germany came on November 12, when Reichsmarschall Hermann Göring issued a ban on all Jewish business activity.

Aryanizations rose exponentially. For example, from 1938 until 1945 the citizens of Hamburg enriched themselves with the property of seventeen thousand of their Jewish fellow citizens. They bought Jewish businesses and real estate at fire-sale prices, as well as tons of household furnishings confiscated from Dutch, French, and Belgian Jews. "Simple housewives suddenly were wearing fur coats, and filling their homes with expensive furniture and carpets," said Gertrud Seydelmann, an eighty-four-year-old librarian who saw everything. The Nazis sold this booty at public auction, while sending many of its former owners to be gassed at Auschwitz or Treblinka.

The Hamburgers were not great fans of Hitler. Before 1933, few voted for him or cared for his strident anti-Semitism. A favorite song of the SA brownshirts, "When Jewish Blood Spurts from the Knife," left the Hamburgers cold, and a Party-organized boycott against Jewish stores, April 1, 1933, was a failure.[2] As late as January 1938, SS officials complained that their anti-Semitic propaganda "had no effect on a large part of the Hamburg population," according to historian Frank Bajohr's study.

The Jews of Hamburg had initially been spared persecution because the city was a center of international trade. The Hitler regime did not want its anti-Semitism to cause a boycott of the harbor or endanger commerce. But because of massive German rearmament, by 1938 the worldwide depression was no longer felt in Hamburg. Plundering of the Jews proceeded apace.

Everyone wanted a piece of the action. An Aryanization infrastructure flourished, complete with lawyers, notaries, and auctioneers. For every Jewish business, there were eighteen prospective buyers. The day after Kristallnacht, an "enrichment competition" erupted, in the words of historian Bajohr. In a few months, twelve hundred Jewish businesses had changed hands. Former employees were some of the biggest profiteers, yet only 20 percent of the new owners bothered to give their erstwhile bosses a fair price.

The government was the catalyst. Threatened with a concentration camp, the Brothers Gotthold sold their metal works. The local prosecutor tried to coerce another entrepreneur, Salomon Rothschild, by charging him with "racial desecration," intercourse between a Jew and an Aryan. Rothschild escaped punishment only because the putative victim, his employee, was able to demonstrate her virginity at a local hospital.

The average citizen began to benefit after the war started. In September 1939, four thousand freight cars, filled with the property of Jews who had fled, stood on the wharves. This property could not be shipped abroad, and the Gestapo decided to auction it off. Hamburg's auction houses did a booming business, collecting 5 percent of the 7.2 million marks the goods brought in. Thereafter, auctioneers received postcards asking when more "things were coming from Holland." Government officials wanted to keep for themselves the paintings and art objects taken from Belgian, French, and Dutch Jews. But Hitler ordered expanded distribution, with the intent of providing for Germans in the newly occupied eastern territories.

After eight thousand Hamburg Jews were deported in October 1941, their possessions came under the hammer. At first, sales were held in auction houses. When gasoline became scarce in 1942, the auctions took place in victims' homes. "Some of my library patrons told me to go to the harbor and

---

[2] The SA (Sturmabteilung — Storm Division or Storm Troop) was the early private army of the Nazi party.

load up on carpets, furniture, jewelry, and furs," said Gertrud Seydelmann, who refused to do so.

She was an exception. Historian Bajohr estimates that one hundred thousand Hamburgers enriched themselves with Jewish booty. By the time Allied bombers had reduced Hamburg to rubble and ended the pillage, thirty thousand tons of chairs, cabinets, bed linen, and clothing had arrived by train and ship. At war's end, half of the rooms in the city held Jewish property. Everyone knew where it came from.

Ironically, after the war, Jews who had fled Hamburg presented the town with a certificate of praise. They had left before the "enrichment competition" became a mass phenomenon. The Jews who had stayed behind and witnessed the Aryanization free-for-all said nothing. They had already been deported and murdered.

Friedrich Minoux, like the citizens of Hamburg, was not one to let a profitable opportunity pass him by, even if it involved an Aryanized business. Such an opportunity for him soon arose.

The Aryanization of the Okriftel Paper Company

Even after Minoux sold his interest in the Jacquier & Securius Bank in January 1931, he maintained his offices in the bank's headquarters, Stechbahn 3–4, until 1935. He dedicated himself principally to his wholesale coal business, but in 1938 he was involved in the Aryanization of the Okriftel cellulose and paper factory.

A Frankfurt businessman, Philipp Offenheimer, had founded Okriftel in 1896 with twenty-seven workers and two managers. Okriftel became a pioneer in the German cellulose industry. Offenheimer had recognized the value of bleached cellulose and had organized his company to produce this material. By the turn of the century, Okriftel dominated the German market for raw paper, carbon paper, and other cellulose products. Before Aryanization began, Okriftel had a yearly income of 8.5 million reichsmarks, while producing eighteen thousand tons of bleached cellulose and six thousand five hundred tons of high-quality paper.

Soon after the Nazi takeover, the chicaneries against the non-Aryan Okriftel began. First, the Berlin headquarters for wood distribution restricted the company's raw material allotment for spruce by 25 percent, thus reducing Okriftel's output. Nevertheless the balance sheet of July 1937 still showed a yearly income of 993,785.35 reichsmarks.

The Frankfurt chamber of commerce increased the pressure further. Professor Dr. Carl Lüer, president of the chamber of commerce, demanded that the owners of Okriftel sell the company to Aryans. The Fatherland

Truehand Company, Ltd. made an appraisal, considerably undervaluing Okriftel, in order to force a swift sale. Fatherland Truehand estimated the value of the business, on March 25, 1938, at 9.4 million reichsmarks. Okriftel's owners believed that the actual value of their company was 12 million reichsmarks, if they themselves had been able to liquidate all plants and equipment. Okriftel would have had a far higher value if it were sold in its entirety as a going business. In the following weeks, the pressure increased on Lucie Offenheimer, the widow of the founder; her son, Ernst; and her daughter, Marie Therese.

Friedrich Minoux probably learned from his right wing friends or his old associates in the paper business that the Offenheimers were being coerced to sell Okriftel. He bought the company on July 21, 1938, for 3.65 million reichsmarks. Of this sum, one million reichsmarks immediately went to the Finance Ministry as a "Reich flight tax." The remaining 2.65 million reichsmarks went to an escrow account in a Frankfurt bank.

During the November 1938 Kristallnacht pogrom, the Offenheimers managed to hide and emigrated shortly thereafter. They never received a penny from the sale of Okriftel.

Minoux had financed his purchase with only a small amount of his own money. Part of the price came from the Dresdner Bank, while another part came from a three million Reichsmark mortgage on Okriftel's land, which Minoux then mortgaged more heavily. Thus Minoux had obtained a business worth over twelve million reichsmarks with an investment that finally came to less than a million reichsmarks.

Despite the wartime shortages of raw materials and workers, Okriftel generated a healthy profit of two hundred twenty thousand reichsmarks in 1941. The company was Friedrich Minoux's last large asset and remained in his name at the end of the war. The cash that the Aryanized Okriftel threw off enabled Minoux to pay down a part of the substantial debts and fine he incurred when he was tried and convicted of swindling the Berlin Gas Company.

Most of the Aryanizations involved small to medium-sized businesses, such as Okriftel. But some large companies were also Aryanized. In 1934 the Nazis Aryanized the giant Ullstein Verlag, publisher of books, as well as five daily and eight weekly newspapers. In 1938 M. M. Warburg, the big Hamburg private bank, was Aryanized.

Sometimes complex negotiations were involved, for example, with the Rothschilds for control of the Witkowitz Steel Works in Czechoslovakia. During these negotiations, the Viennese Baron Louis Rothschild was held hostage. Other thorny cases involved the Weinmann and Petschek families, who controlled steelworks and coal mines in Germany. The Nazis were caught in a maze of foreign holdings and property transfers initiated by their prospective victims.

Like Okriftel, the majority of Aryanized companies were not known outside of Germany. But there was at least one prominent exception, the music publisher C. F. Peters.

The Story of C. F. Peters

Musicians and music lovers the world over know the Peters Editions of the musical classics. The scores are accurately reproduced from the original sources and clearly printed on high-grade paper. The pages lie flat when open on a music stand, unlike cheaper American editions which must be held with clips or weighted down.

The history of C. F. Peters began in 1800, when Franz Anton Hoffmeister (1754–1812) and Ambrosius Kühnel (1770–1813) founded the Bureau de Musique in Leipzig. The company's first publications were a collection of Josef Haydn's string quartets and a volume of Mozart's compositions for piano. By 1803 the Bureau de Musique had issued fourteen volumes of Johann Sebastian Bach's keyboard works. Ludwig van Beethoven wrote to Hoffmeister on January 15, 1801, after the first volumes had appeared: "My heart rejoices at your publication of the works of Sebastian Bach, since he was the greatest progenitor of our system of harmony. I hope to see the entire set soon." Beethoven submitted his own compositions to the Bureau de Musique for publication. By 1802 Kühnel and Hoffmeister had issued the second piano concerto in B flat op. 19, the E flat septet op. 20, the symphony number one in C major op. 21, and the piano sonata in B flat op. 22. But the publisher then asked for more than Beethoven wanted to give, as the composer wrote on April 8, 1802, in his messy, almost illegible hand: "Have you gentlemen both gone to the devil, suggesting that I write such a sonata? At the time of the revolutionary fever, certainly. But now that things are returning to normal, and Bonaparte has concluded a concordat with the pope, do you really want the sonata? If it were a mass for Saint Mary in three voices or a vesper, then maybe I would do it, even write a credo with big pound notes, but dear God, such a sonata. In these new Christian times — ho, ho, ho — I can skip it; nothing will come of it. I give my answer now in the fastest tempo...."

On January 2, 1805, Hoffmeister withdrew from the business and sold his interest to Ambrosius Kühnel. Renaming the company Neuer Verlag des Bureau de Musique, Kühnel proceeded to build a thriving enterprise by publishing the compositions of, among others, Giacomo Meyerbeer and Louis Spohr.

Ambrosius Kühnel died on August 18, 1813, and on April 1, 1814, his heirs sold his firm to a Leipzig book dealer, Carl Friedrich Peters (1779–1827), who renamed the company Bureau de Musique C. F. Peters, Leipzig. Spohr wrote to Peters on September 13, 1815: "Out of gratitude, I gave my manuscripts to

Herr Kühnel more readily than to other publishers. He has been my friend since he published my first compositions. He never demanded that I pay cash for a hundred copies of my own work, as Herr Härtel[3] did when he published my first concerto. And at the time Herr Härtel was very rich, while Herr Kühnel was still very poor." Spohr did not much care for Beethoven, as he wrote to the publisher on November 24, 1810: "I still haven't heard Beethoven's newest quartet. As for his last three quartets [op. 59], the newest [sixth] symphony and the Leonora overture, the symphony may have a few good points, but I really do not enjoy any of these works. They seem to me like rhapsodies composed by a crazy person...."

Peters had taken over the company at a difficult time and had many business problems. Nonetheless he managed to preserve his relationship with Spohr and to publish other promising composers, among them Carl Maria von Weber, Johann Nepomuk Hummel, and John Field. He also contracted with Beethoven for his Missa Solemnis but was unable to persuade the master to submit any further works. Yet the Peters musical instrument store managed to sell a grand piano to Johann Wolfgang von Goethe.

C. F. Peters became severely depressed and died in an insane asylum at Sonnenstein on November 20, 1827. Spohr wrote of Peters: "With deep sorrow I learned of the death of Herr Peters. The world has lost an active, reliable man." Peters's daughter Anna sold her father's company to a Leipzig tobacco manufacturer, Carl Gotthelf Siegmund Böhme (1785–1855).

Böhme snared an early Chopin composition, Bolero (op. 19), as well as Robert Schumann's Genoveva. But other publishers' pirating of C. F. Peters publications was a problem. On May 23, 1829, Böhme signed the so-called Conventional-Acte with four music publishing houses: Johann André, Breitkopf & Härtel, B. Schott's Sons, and Nikolaus Simrock. This agreement forbade pirating of musical compositions, and it was later approved by foreign publishers as well. Through the agreement, A. Farrenc in Paris received the French rights to Friedrich Kuhlau's works, while Thomas Boosey & Co. in London acquired the English rights to publish the Forkel edition of Bach's *Well-Tempered Clavier.*

At the same time, Böhme commissioned Beethoven's student Carl Czerny (1791–1857) to prepare a complete edition of Bach's instrumental works and *Kunst der Fuge.* Piano students today still use Czerny's *School of Velocity,* which looks like a collection of rejected Beethoven compositions that Czerny fished out of the master's wastebasket and recycled as finger exercises.

Böhme died on July 20, 1855, and left his company to a charitable foundation, under the direction of C. F. Peters's manager, A. Th. Whistling.

---

[3]*Gottfried Christian Härtel (1763–1857) was an owner of the music publisher Breitkopf &
Härtel and founder of the* Allgemeine Musikalische Zeitung.

Whistling continued to work with the same composers, mainly Spohr. On April 21, 1860, the foundation transferred control of C. F. Peters to Julius Friedländer, a Berlin music dealer. Friedländer introduced a faster music printing press, engraved plates, and glued pages that reduced production costs.

On April 1, 1863, Dr. Max Abraham bought C. F. Peters from Friedländer. Under Abraham, a Jewish lawyer, the company experienced its most phenomenal period of growth. From the beginning, Abraham had the far-sighted idea of making C. F. Peters and its publications a universal reference library of music.

Abraham's first move was to publish works of a new group of musicians and composers, among them Clara Schumann, Johannes Brahms, Hans von Bülow, and Franz Liszt. But Abraham's greatest coup was his recognition and publication of the young, little-known Edvard Grieg. Their relationship, at first a simple business one between composer and publisher, developed into a deep, enduring friendship. An 1889 contract with Grieg allowed C. F. Peters to publish almost all first editions of the Norwegian master's works. As a 1933 corporate history of Peters noted: "Whenever Grieg was in Leipzig, Abraham provided him with a 'room to work with Cerberus.'[4] The composer had built in his garden at Trolhaugen a solitary little house, where he could devote himself, undisturbed, to his art. But when Grieg was in Leipzig, he had the quietest and most isolated room in the Talstraße 10 [C. F. Peters] House, high up on the fourth floor, directly under the roof." Alas, East Germany allowed the Talstraße building to fall into disrepair after 1945, and the fourth floor partly collapsed. But in front of the window a chestnut tree, which Grieg liked to gaze out at for inspiration, still thrives. The tree is now under landmark protection.

Recognizing that Friedländer's improvements of the printing process were only a first step, Max Abraham became interested in a new rotational music press developed by Theodor Litolff. A Leipzig printer, C. G. Röder, was also interested in Litolff's machine. Röder wanted to apply a recently developed method for book printing, lithography, to the printing of music. A few publishers in Leipzig had already rejected Röder's prototype for a new press as impractical. But Max Abraham quickly grasped that this device could lead to more rapid production, higher output, and lower costs. "Abraham's confidence in Röder's discovery, and Röder's trust in Abraham's merchant genius" were to revolutionize the music publishing business.

In 1878, to produce the most accurate possible scores, Max Abraham hired Alfred Dörffel (1821–1905) as corrector and arranger. A one-time student

---

[4]*In Greek mythology, Cerberus was a three-headed dog that guarded the entrance to the underworld.*

of Felix Mendelssohn, Dörffel was called the "musical conscience" of Peters. The University of Leipzig awarded Dörffel an honorary doctorate in 1885 for his history of the Gewandhaus concerts. But Dörffel could not abide some modern composers, among them Max Reger. For years, Dörffel discouraged Max Abraham from publishing Reger, consigning the composer to a long, sad period of anonymous penury. Only in 1901, a year after Abraham's death, did C. F. Peters finally begin to issue Reger's works.

Still, music publishing was more than simply a business venture to Max Abraham. As he wrote, "I regard it as my holy task to see that the works of the great masters are conveyed in pristine form." Thus was born the Edition Peters Universal Library of Music. Abraham subsequently built a large public music library near the Leipzig town hall. The company also issued the works of Bach, Beethoven, Händel, Mozart, and Schubert in superbly printed new volumes at popular prices. Clara Schumann wrote of the new Peters editions: "They are excellent in every respect, clear and playable, and I would choose them above all others." The works no longer protected by copyright had green covers, while those protected by copyright were covered with pink. The pink or green covers, with the Peters insignia, became familiar to musicians and music lovers throughout the world.

At the pinnacle of his success, the sixty-nine-year-old Max Abraham became mortally ill. On December 8, 1900, just after the Peters centennial celebration, he committed suicide. Abraham's nephew, Henri Hinrichsen, took over the company. On December 9, after learning of Max Abraham's death, Edvard Grieg wrote to Hinrichsen: "He was to me, in the best sense, a fatherly friend, and he influenced and affected the course of my life as few others have. When we met forty years ago, our relationship was purely a business one. But under the businessman I soon discovered the philanthropist and well-wisher. These traits evoked in me a fondness for him, which has never diminished; on the contrary, it has continually grown." Under Hinrichsen, C. F. Peters published the works of new composers, including five symphonies of Gustav Mahler. Peters wanted to publish Richard Strauss's *Sinfonia Domestica*, but Strauss refused. When he finally offered another work, his *Alpensinfonie*, Peters refused it. But Strauss did revise and expand *Berlioz's Instrumental Teachings*, which Alfred Dörffel had originally translated. Other new Peters editions were Tchaikovsky's violin concerto, Max Reger's piano and organ works, and Reger's four-hand arrangement of Bach's Brandenburg Concertos. So close did Reger's relationship with Peters become that the composer died a few hours after a visit to Hinrichsen's home. And after Hugo Wolf died of syphilis, Peters published his *Mörike Lieder* and *Italienisches Liederbuch*.

Henri Hinrichsen was by this time a cultural lion of Leipzig. He received an honorary doctorate from the University of Leipzig in 1929, and his three sons, Max, Walter, and Hans Joachim, entered the firm. But when Hitler came to power in 1933, C. F. Peters was immediately affected.

A Leipzig city counselor named Hauptmann warned Wilhelm Weismann, Henri Hinrichsen's assistant, that C. F. Peters was no place for "a German man." Herr Hauptmann offered Weismann a position as head music programmer for Leipzig Radio. Weismann refused. A year later, the Nazis declared that Peters Editions were "undesirable" and that public institutions should not use them.

Henri Hinrichsen could not believe that the Nazis would harm him. But Walter and Max Hinrichsen had seen enough. Max left Germany in 1936 and went to work for a company in Chicago that represented C. F. Peters in America. On September 1, 1948, he founded the C. F. Peters Corporation in New York. In 1937, to the dismay of his father, Walter left for London, where he founded Hinrichsen Editions, Ltd. Only Hans Joachim stayed behind.

Despite all warnings, Henri Hinrichsen would not leave Leipzig. He said it was his duty to watch over the firm that his uncle, Max Abraham, had entrusted to his care. But after Kristallnacht, November 9, 1938, Hinrichsen's stewardship ended. The Nazis forced him to turn over C. F. Peters to SS Standartenführer (Colonel) Noatzke, giving the old publisher only a few minutes to clear out of the building.

Hans Joachim Hinrichsen fled through Belgium to France, where in 1940 the Nazis murdered him in the Perpignan concentration camp; the Nazis also killed his mother. Henri Hinrichsen was deported to the Theresienstadt camp and murdered there.

Meanwhile, C. F. Peters was Aryanized. A city counselor, Dr. Herrmann, who was a hunting companion of Hermann Göring, took control of the company. Dr. Johannes Petschull, a music publisher in Leipzig, became director.

Henri Hinrichsen had urged his friend Wilhelm Weismann to stay at Peters, and Weismann ended up running the company throughout the war. Because of the heavy air attacks, the most important documents and parts of the music library were moved to the small town of Eisenhammer in the Dübener Meadow, forty kilometers from Leipzig. C. F. Peters's two printers, C. G. Röder and Poeschel & Trepte, and its bookbinder, E. A. Enders, were completely destroyed. Miraculously, Peters's Leipzig offices at Talstraße 10 survived unscathed. Henri Hinrichsen's grand piano is still in the waiting room.

After the war, C. F. Peters was split in two. The East Germans took over the Leipzig offices, while the Hinrichsens established a new headquarters in Frankfurt. With the collapse of communism in 1989, the Hinrichsens finally regained their Leipzig property.

4

Friedrich Minoux Defrauds the Berlin Gas Company

Friedrich Minoux, one of the largest Berlin coal dealers, became a director of the newly created Berlin Gas Company in 1924. This directorship allowed him to massively defraud the company.

Eighty-one gas companies founded The Economic Union of German Gas Companies' Coke Syndicate, Inc. in Cologne in 1904. By 1919 the syndicate had grown to six hundred companies. The main purpose of the syndicate was to fix the price of coke used for gas production. The fixed price was possible because almost all the gas companies produced coke. A secondary purpose was the sale of the byproducts of gas production — tar, ammonia, toluol, benzene, and various oils.

To improve distribution and maintain uniform pricing, the syndicate had established the Gas-Coal-Production Association in 1912. In Berlin, the Coke Syndicate induced nine Berlin coal wholesalers to join the association. Their function was to sell all gas-coke produced by the syndicate in the Berlin area. After World War I and the postwar inflation, there was a large redistribution of the Coke Syndicate shares. Friedrich Minoux acquired more than a quarter of these shares, although his gas coal sales were relatively low, three to five thousand tons per year.

On March 13, 1924, Minoux and two partners, Max Kessler and Johannes Tiemessen, were able to make themselves sole purveyors of all gas-coke to the Berlin Gas Company. They arranged this profitable deal through their syndicate, now reorganized as the Gas Coal Sales Association. The Berlin Gas Company accepted this arrangement reluctantly, with good reason. Soon, the three partners had appointed friends to key positions at the gas company.

In the following years, Minoux, Kessler, and Tiemessen proceeded to enrich themselves at the expense of the Berlin Gas Company. Tiemessen and Kessler paid for personal expenses with a disguised gas company account. Minoux abetted the illegal activity of his two associates and was later named an accomplice in their theft. But his own method of illicitly enriching himself, price-fixing, was more subtle and lucrative.

The fixed price agreements Minoux arranged were supposed to assure the gas company a constant source of gas-coke. Instead, the agreements forced the company to buy coke at above-market prices. Even the so-called "summer-reduction price" was no reduction at all.

To maintain the fixed price agreements, Minoux and his partners bribed the gas company director, Adolf Schmidt, with tens of thousands of reichsmarks and perquisites. When Schmidt's son wrecked a car that the Coke Sales Association had provided, the association promptly bought the elder Schmidt a new one.

In May 1927, Jacquier & Securius, the bank in which Minoux was a partner, contracted with the Gas Coal Sales Association to accept full liability for any losses the association incurred for the fixed-price agreements. In return for this risk-free deal, the bank would get three quarters of the association's profits. Minoux then arranged to reinsure Jacquier & Securius. A Paris bank, Commerce, Industrie, Finances (CIF), acting as reinsurer, collected 95 percent of the money that went to Jacquier & Securius. CIF then sent the money back to Germany, to the accounts of Friedrich Minoux, Inc. But because CIF was a foreign company, no one in Germany could perform an audit. Minoux had thus created for himself, at least temporarily, a perfect money-laundering scheme.

When Minoux withdrew from the Jacquier & Securius Bank in 1930, his firm, Friedrich Minoux, Inc., replaced the bank as insurer. Minoux tried to have the English coal exporter, Mathwin & Son, in Newcastle-on-Tyne, act as reinsurer. But Mathwin & Son balked at the malodorous arrangement. The Minoux-controlled firm Proba Metal, Inc. subsequently became reinsurer.

In the end, Minoux and his partners swindled the Berlin Gas Company out of at least 7.4 million Reichsmarks. Besides the millions that went to Minoux, his partners, and to gas company director Adolf Schmidt in bribes, sixty to seventy thousand reichsmarks went to St. Michael's Catholic Church in Wannsee. In return, the church was to be named after Minoux's father.

For years the swindle continued. In 1930, a new gas company board member, the mayor, Dr. Fritz Elsas, became suspicious. He asked the director of the Frankfurt Gas Company, a Dr. Winkler, to investigate. Winkler noted the huge profits the Coke Sales Association was making. But Minoux and Schmidt attacked Winkler. They called him incompetent to evaluate the situation, and the Berlin Gas Company supported them.

In 1935, Minoux's scheme finally began to unravel. Four years before, an audit of all German communal service businesses had begun. When the auditors went over the books of the Gas Coal Sales Association and Minoux's other corporate entities, they spotted irregularities. At first, Minoux, Kessler, and Tiemessen succeeded in covering up their swindle. But on April 8, 1937, a witness wrote to the Frankfurt prosecutor, accusing Tiemessen of lying, fraud, and destruction of documents. The prosecutor fined Tiemessen fifty thousand reichsmarks.

Only a brief respite followed this slap on the wrist. In 1938 the state prosecutor again began investigating Minoux's activities. At the end of December, the police searched Minoux's house and his corporate offices. Hans Tiemessen was arrested in February 1939, Max Kessler in March. Minoux remained free while the prosecutor called in experts to examine the impounded material. On May 4, 1940, Minoux was finally arrested.

In December 1940, the state prosecutor produced a 443-page indictment. There were ninety-six witnesses. Kessler, Tiemessen, and Minoux were accused of defrauding the Berlin Gas Company and the Potsdam Gas Company from 1927 to 1938.

Minoux tried, through his old political contacts, to avoid a criminal trial, but to no avail. After a forty-three-day proceeding, the court sentenced Minoux, Tiemessen, and Kessler to five years imprisonment and five years probation. In addition, Kessler was fined three hundred thousand reichsmarks, Tiemessen one hundred twenty thousand, and Minoux six hundred thousand.

The Berlin Gas Company instituted a civil suit to recover damages and won from Kessler a 1.5 million reichsmark judgment. Kessler, now in Luckau Prison, had to surrender his collection of eighteenth- and nineteenth-century paintings, porcelain, and ceramics, valued at six hundred forty-four thousand reichsmarks, as well as his property in Sakrow, worth another eight hundred thousand reichsmarks.

Kessler's art collection did more than simply satisfy a damage judgment. In early 1940, Hitler's personal photographer, Heinrich Hoffmann, had seen the paintings in the Berlin Schlossmuseum, the former city palace of the Kaisers. Hitler was in the process of assembling an art collection for his new hometown museum in Linz, and Hoffmann wanted to offer Kessler's collection for the museum.

But Berlin city officials, particularly Mayor Ludwig Steeg, refused to give up Kessler's art collection. In a memorandum, Berlin City Treasurer Lindig remarked, "The mayor will do everything to keep the collection in the Reich Capital City, Berlin, at least the porcelain collection. The porcelain belongs to Berlin because of its history (porcelain manufacture, Frederick the Great, etc.), and has no relationship to the museum in Linz. Whether or not the paintings should go to Linz is debatable, especially if we are paid for them...."

The conflict over Kessler's art collection took place in the closing months of the war. After the Finance Office had released the art, the City of Berlin obtained it for 3.5 million reichsmarks, paid to the Berlin Gas Company. With the judgment it had already collected from Kessler, the Gas Company made more than three million reichsmarks on the art. By 1950 the collection had disappeared, and Max Kessler demanded that the Gas Company either return his art or pay him 3.5 million reichsmarks.

Hans Tiemessen did not survive as long as Kessler had. The court rejected his appeal, and he began his sentence in Luckau Prison. The Berlin Gas Company won a seven hundred fifty thousand reichsmark civil damage judgment against him and forced him to forfeit almost all his property. His wife Eugenie became ill as a result, and she died on September 20, 1943. Tiemessen died near Darmstadt, as he was being transported to another prison, on April 5, 1944, a year before the demise of Friedrich Minoux.

When his serious legal problems began, Minoux recognized that he, like Kessler and Tiemessen, could be liable for considerable civil damages. After he was arrested and jailed in May 1940, he arranged for a mortgage credit of one million reichsmarks in case of a fine. But he realized that he could no longer keep the Wannsee Villa. He therefore arranged for his attorney, Hans Helmut Kuhnke, to sell it.

Friedrich Minoux received a good price for the house, but he ultimately got very little money, and the Berlin Gas Company none at all. After the government had seized its share in taxes and other debts, only ten thousand reichsmarks were left over for the unhappy Minoux. On May 1, 1941, his family vacated the house.

Still, the Berlin Gas Company suspected that Minoux might be holding back even more money. In early 1942, the company hired a Berlin private detective named Arthur Müller to see if Minoux had any concealed assets. Müller wrote:

> My report in the matter of Friedrich Minoux is as follows: The household of Friedrich Minoux in Berlin Wannsee, *Am Großen Wannsee 56–58,* was dissolved on May 1, 1941. The SS bought the furnishings of the exquisite dining room, which contains a rare Gobelin tapestry, in March 1941. A moving firm was engaged and by the end of April or beginning of May 1941, the last objects were removed from the house and sent to a warehouse in Lichtenberg. The valuable oil paintings, however, are now in the house in Garmisch-Partenkirchen, where Frau Minoux has lived for years. Also, since May 13, 1941, Frau Lilly Minoux has registered her local address as Berlin-Dahlem, Max Eythstraße 12; the owner of this impressive house is the architect Prof. J. A. Breuhaus, who rented it furnished to Frau Minoux for one year. But Frau Minoux has lived in her house in Garmisch-Partenkirchen for many years, because she claims the climate of Berlin Wannsee is detrimental to her health.

On February 20, 1942, Private Detective Müller completed his surveillance:

As noted in my reports, Herr Friedrich Minoux has paid a year's rent in advance for Herr Prof. Breubaus' villa in Dahlem, Max Eythstraße 12. Herr Minoux paid the rent to Prof Breubaus' attorney, since the Professor lives in Kissingen. The possessions of Fräulein Behrens and the cook Fräulein Schröder were taken to the Breubaus villa from Wannsee, Königstraße 58, by Herr Schulze, the coal merchant. A small amount of furniture from the Wannsee Villa was taken to the home of Herr Minoux's daughter Monika in Grunewald, Hagenstraße 40. The furniture that had been stored in the warehouse in Lichtenberg was removed when the building was damaged in an air attack. I cannot determine where this furniture was taken, and where the rest of Herr Minoux's furniture might be, because those persons in the know are not talking. Minoux's chauffeur, Herr Gantner, has been in Berlin for the past few days and is again living with the coal merchant Schulze in Wannsee, Königstraße 58. Herr Gantner is once more employed in Minoux's office on Kurfürstendamm, and every morning he brings breakfast to his boss, Herr Friedrich Minoux, in his jail cell.... The villa rented in Max Eythstraße was emptied out on March 31. After April 1, 1942, an empty villa in Dahlem is supposed to be taken and the furniture now in the warehouse will be sent there. This imposing villa is said to have been rented on April 1 for five years. The location of this villa is still unknown.

When he began his sentence in Brandenburg Prison in June 1942, Minoux was sixty-five years old. He worked in the kitchen and the prison library, while engaging in an extensive correspondence with his attorneys, treasury officials, and the Berlin Gas Company. He also monitored the receipts from Okriftel and matters pertaining to his taxes. But, by the last months of the war, there was very little food. Minoux was starving to death when the victorious Allies released him in April 1945. He never recovered his health and died in Berlin-Lichterfelde on October 16, 1945. He was buried in the Alter Friedhof, the graveyard of a Protestant church in Wannsee's Lindenstraße.[1] His grave is now unmarked.

Friedrich Minoux had sold the Wannsee Villa to the Nordhav Foundation, a Nazi organization controlled by the infamous Reinhard Heydrich. To organize the destruction of the Jews of Europe, Heydrich convened the Wannsee Conference.

---

[5]*Minoux lies alongside distinguished neighbors: physiologist and physicist Hermann von Helmholtz (1821–1894); Nobel laureate chemist Emil Fischer (1852–1919), who committed suicide; Ferdinand Sauerbruch (1875–1951), one of the most famous surgeons in central Europe; and many members of the Siemens family.*

5

Reinhard Heydrich and
the Nordhav Foundation

Reinhard Tristan Eugen Heydrich was born March 7, 1904, in Halle, Germany. During the Third Reich, Heydrich was Heinrich Himmler's chief lieutenant in the SS; he instituted mass executions in occupied territories during the opening years of World War II. Arguably the darkest personality in the Nazi firmament, Heydrich was a talented man, whose ambition it was, without any doubt, one day to follow in the steps of or to supplant his boss Himmler.

Reinhard Heydrich was the son of Bruno Heydrich, a composer and conservatory director in Halle. At the age of fourteen, young Reinhard joined a Free Corps gang, in which he became schooled in street-fighting, terrorism, and looting. In 1922 he joined the Navy, rising to the rank of first lieutenant, but he was expelled in 1931 for a morals infraction, breach of promise, the lady in question being the daughter of a Kiel shipyard manager.

Heydrich joined the Nazi party and, soon after Hitler became chancellor, was appointed chief of the political department of the Munich police force, with control over the notorious Dachau concentration camp. In 1934 he was appointed SS chief for Berlin and was later made deputy chief of the SS under Heinrich Himmler. Blond, handsome, vain, and fiercely ambitious, Heydrich was also a fine violinist, a champion skier and fencer, a fearless pilot, and an outstanding organizer. A virtually friendless loner, he was pitiless in dealing with "enemies of the state"; he was so hated and feared by anti-Nazi elements throughout Europe that he was called "the Hangman."

Those who met Heydrich were impressed by his ambition, ruthlessness, and duplicity. Eugen Dollman, his interpreter on a trip to Italy in 1938, recalled: "Of all the great men with whom I came into contact, he was the only one I instinctively feared." Even within the Nazi security police, Heydrich was dreaded rather than loved. His own protégé, Walter Schellenberg, who later rose to head the German intelligence service, found his boss's very

Reinhard Heydrich in the uniform of an SS Obergruppenführer (general). Among his medals is an Iron Cross, First Class, which he was awarded for his Luftwaffe service at the beginning of the Russian campaign in 1941. Around the time this photo was taken, Heydrich called the Wannsee Conference to announce the decision to destroy the Jews of Europe. (Ullstein Bilderdienst)

appearance sinister: "He was a tall, impressive figure with a broad, unusually high forehead, small restless eyes as crafty as an animal's and of uncanny power, and a wide full-lipped mouth. His hands were slender and rather too long; they made one think of the legs of a spider. His splendid figure was marred by the breadth of his hips, a disturbingly feminine effect which made him appear even more sinister. His voice was much too high for so large a man and his speech was nervous and staccato."

Schellenberg described his chief as a born intriguer with "an incredibly acute perception of the moral, human, professional and political weaknesses of others.... His unusual intellect was matched by the ever watchful instincts of a predatory animal.... He was inordinately ambitious. It seemed as if, in a pack of ferocious wolves, he must always prove himself the strongest and assume the leadership." Wilhelm Hoettl, another member of the Nazi security service, remembered Heydrich as a man without a moral code: "Truth and goodness had no intrinsic meaning for him; they were instruments to be used for the gaining of more and more power.... Politics too were...merely stepping stones for the seizing and holding of power. To debate whether any action was of itself right appeared so stupid to him that it was certainly a question he never asked himself." His was "a cruel, brave and cold intelligence" and his life "an unbroken chain of murders." According to Pierre Huss, an American journalist who knew him well, Heydrich "had a mind and mentality something like an adding machine, never forgetting or lapsing into the sentimental...Nobody ever got a break or considerations of mercy." Heydrich disliked criticism and reacted badly to the inquiries of foreign pressmen: "A single evening of him on his best behavior was enough to convince every one of us that he was a bad one to deal with if you were on the wrong side of the fence."

Though by all accounts he was devoted to his three children (a fourth was born after his death), his relationship with his wife was strained. A compulsive womanizer, Heydrich was a familiar figure in the red-light district of

Berlin. He would often compel his subordinates to accompany him on epic binges in the bars and brothels of the capital, occasions dreaded by his staff since he was dangerously unstable when drunk and displayed a strong sadistic streak. They came to fear the afternoon phone call from their chief, the leering voice and the request that they join him for dinner and then "go places." Lina Heydrich resented her husband's infidelity, while he in turn suspected her of affairs, including one with Walter Schellenberg, and he had the security police watch her.

On July 30, 1939, Heydrich organized the Nordhav Foundation (Stiftung Nordhav) in Berlin. Soon to be chief of the Reich Security Main Office, Heydrich indicated that the express purpose of this foundation was the "creation and maintenance of refreshment and recreation houses for members of the security service of the SS and their dependents."

Nordhav was the name of a little farm on the Vitzdorfer Meadow, part of the Island of Fehmarn. A Lieutenant Witte had built this farm on part of a large tract of land called the Katharinenhof in 1760.

How did a little farm on an island in the Baltic come to lend its name to a foundation controlled by the Chief of the Security Police? The answer lies in the biography of Reinhard Heydrich. Lina Heydrich (née von Osten) had been born in the village of Avendorf on Fehmarn. Her parents, impoverished by the economic upheaval following World War I, had moved to the region. Her father was a schoolmaster, and she had relatives living on the island. On

Wedding photo of Reinhard and Lina Heydrich, Hamburg. On December 26, 1931, they were married in nearby Großenbrode, in a church ceremony heavy with Nazi trappings. (Bildarchiv Preußischer Kulturbesitz)

December 26, 1931, Reinhard Heydrich and Lina von Osten were married in nearby Großenbrode, in a church ceremony heavy with Nazi trappings.

In 1934 Lina Heydrich's parents were still living on Fehmarn. After returning from a visit, she reported, "I encouraged my husband to buy a house on Fehmarn as soon as possible. He could pursue his love of sailing there. He adored the idea...." However, the high price annoyed him, as he wrote to the mayor of Fehmarn on October 25, 1934:

> I thank you for your letter of October 18, 1934.
>
> You indicate that the price should be 1.50 marks per square meter. That is a price that would be appropriate for a major city or a fashionable spa. I can't imagine that such a piece of land, which is in danger of being flooded and can scarcely accommodate a garden, that this piece of land should carry such a monstrously high price tag.
>
> I have therefore become convinced that you or your representatives are motivated to give me a distaste for the property by demanding such a high price and delaying the transaction. For some reason, you do not wish my presence.
>
> I hereby inform you that I decline to buy the land and am already in negotiation for another piece of property in Schleswig-Holstein. I am very sorry that by your machinations you make it impossible for me to settle in the home of my wife.

Another problem was where the money for the property would come from.

Reinhard Heydrich's summer house on Fehmarn. (Courtesy Friedrich Wilhelm Klahn)

But a guardian angel appeared, the Consul Willy Sachs (called "Bayernwilli [Bavarian Willy]")," and the Heydrichs had their house.

They selected an architect, Gustav Rall, who turned out a set of plans that proved more costly than Lina Heydrich had anticipated, forty-two thousand reichsmarks. Yet Lina recalled the construction with pride. In early 1935 the carpenters began to build — a big event. Heinrich Himmler came as a "patron" to witness the laying of the foundation.

Heinrich Himmler and Fehmarn

Heinrich Himmler was born October 7, 1900, in Munich. The second most powerful man in the Third Reich, he controlled the police, the SS, and, toward the end of World War II, even parts of the army.

The son of a Catholic secondary schoolmaster, Himmler received a diploma in agriculture after World War I and soon joined militant rightist organizations. As a member of one of these, the Reichskriegsflagge, he participated in Hitler's abortive Munich ("Beerhall") Putsch in November 1923. Himmler joined the Nazi party in 1925 and rose steadily in the party hierarchy, but the foundations of his future importance were laid with his appointment as Reichsführer of the SS, Adolf Hitler's elite bodyguard nominally under the control of the Sturmabteilung (SA). After Hitler's accession to power (January 30, 1933), Himmler became head of the Munich police. He established the Third Reich's first concentration camp at Dachau and soon began to organize the political police all over Germany. In April 1934 he was appointed assistant chief of the Gestapo (secret police) in Prussia, and, from this position, he extended his control of police forces over the whole Reich, assuming full command of them in 1936. In the June 30, 1934, purge, Himmler's SS eliminated the SA as a power factor, thus strengthening Hitler's control over his own party and the German army, which had viewed the SA as a serious rival. Himmler then began to build the SS into the most powerful armed body in Germany next to the armed forces. Until World War II, its tasks ranged from the security service of party and state, known as the Sicherheitsdienst (SD), to studies and campaigns designed to protect the purity of the "Aryan race." After the mass murder of European Jewry began in 1941, Himmler organized the extermination camps in eastern Europe that were to wipe out all but a fraction of Europe's Jewish population by the end of the war.

The small, diffident Himmler looked more like a humble bank clerk than Germany's police dictator. His pedantic demeanor and "exquisite courtesy" fooled one English observer into stating that "nobody I met in Germany is more normal." He was a curious mixture of bizarre, romantic fantasy and cold, depraved efficiency. Described as "a man of quiet unemotional gestures, a man without nerves," he suffered from psychosomatic illness, severe headaches, and intestinal spasms. He almost fainted at the sight of a hundred eastern Jews, including women, being executed for his benefit on the Russian front. After this experience, Himmler ordered a more "humane" method of execution, the use of poison gas in specially constructed chambers disguised as shower rooms.

For the Heydrich house on Fehmarn, Himmler had a metalsmith handcraft a big door lock, which was supposed to shield the place from unwanted guests. Today the lock still adorns the door of a resident of the district. Lina Heydrich lived on Fehmarn until her death in 1985 at age seventy-four.[1]

Heinrich Himmler journeyed to Fehmarn a second time, on June 22, 1935, to take part in the housewarming. The next day, Sunday, a large detachment of SS enlivened the festivities, including a ceremony celebrating the equinox. A local historian, Peter Wiepert, a cousin of Lina Heydrich, was on hand to show Himmler the archeological and scenic high points of the island and the Katharinenhof. One day later, June 24, 1935, Reichsführer Himmler returned to Berlin.

Shortly after Himmler visited in June 1935, he suddenly ordered Wiepert to Berlin. In Himmler's office, Wiepert greeted the Reichsführer with "good day" rather than the customary Heil Hitler! Immediately Himmler replied, "Just as I suspected: another Fehmarn numskull. But never mind! You must continue your archeological researches. I give you thirty minutes to think it over and decide!"

Whether the meeting between the two men really happened this way, Himmler soon returned to Fehmarn. Wiepert gave him an extensive tour of the island and his own collection of its artifacts, which the Nordhav Foundation subsequently acquired. In 1970 Wiepert apologetically acknowledged his further contacts with Himmler.

The "Vitzbyer Steenkiest" deeply impressed Himmler during his 1935 tour of Fehmarn. Discovered in 1420, this prehistoric mass grave is southeast of the Katharinenhof. It is forty meters long, fifteen meters wide, up to two meters deep, and concealed by the numerous stones lying around it. There are five similar grave sites near the Katharinenhof, all partly destroyed.

Heinrich Himmler had a lively interest in popularizing early German history, and in 1935 he had organized the Stiftung Ahnenerbe (Ancestral Heritage Foundation), to fund archeological and anthropologic studies. Thus, excavations in Schleswig-Holstein fell within the purview of the Stiftung

---

[1]*After the war, to the annoyance of some Germans, the Fehmarn house became a gathering place for many former Nazi officials; the house burned down in the 1960s. Also controversial was Lina Heydrich's substantial postwar government pension, granted because she was a war widow with small children. Reinhard Heydrich's daughter now lives in the Johannisberg section of Fehmarn.*

Ahnenerbe; so did the ghoulish human studies later conducted in the concentration camps.

Adolf Hitler was quite contemptuous of Himmler's interest in early German culture. As he commented to his architect Albert Speer, "Why do we call the whole world's attention to the fact that we have no past? It isn't enough that the Romans were erecting great buildings when our forefathers were still living in mud huts; now Himmler is starting to dig up these villages of mud huts and enthusing over every potsherd and stone ax he finds. All we prove is that we were throwing stone hatchets and crouching around open fires when Greece and Rome had already reached the highest stage of culture. We really should do our best to keep quiet about this past. Instead Himmler makes a great fuss about it all. The present-day Romans must be having a laugh at these revelations."

Undeterred by Hitler's sarcasm, Himmler funded Wiepert's excavations, with the aim of ultimately creating a great Nordic museum on Fehmarn. The amount of money, in fact, was much larger than Himmler had doled out to anyone else. Wiepert had certain additional minor duties; for example, in the summer of 1939, he was instructed to research the question of increasing the fresh water supply of the region. This work was classified as a measure important to the war effort. But Wiepert's main job was the collection of Fehmarn antiquities.

Further talks regarding the proposed museum took place in July 1939.[2] Reinhard Heydrich, Lina Heydrich, and SS Sturmbahnführer (Major) Albert Sievers visited Wiepert to let him know that funds would be provided to acquire the Katharinenhof, where the Steenkiest was situated. But this acquisition was not envisioned as part of the museum or a German historical site; rather, the twenty hectares of land, near Heydrich's own vacation home, were simply to be state property.

In his history of the Wannsee Villa, Johannes Tuchel concludes that the endowing of the Nordhav Foundation, the purchase of the Katharinenhof in 1939, and the acquisition of the house Am Großen Wannsee 56–58 a year later were solely for Heydrich's own benefit. The rising SS official wanted the Katharinenhof as part of his vacation home and the Wannsee Villa for official functions. As Chief of the Reich Security Main Office, Heydrich believed that he was commencing a brilliant political career.

In years past, Heydrich would have had considerable difficulty obtaining the money for the two pieces of property. Lutz Graf Schwerin, the Reich

---

[2] *Today the Peter Wiepert Museum is one of the main tourist attractions in Burg, the largest town on Fehmarn. Located in a former schoolhouse, the museum houses the reconstruction of an old farmhouse room, objects related to fishing and seafaring, antique clothing, old documents, weapons, war souvenirs, a rock collection, and coins and paper money.*

Finance Minister, often objected to the financial demands of the SS and the Gestapo. But now Heydrich had access to the "black cash box," money plundered from deported German Jews. His foundation purchased the Katharinenhof and the Wannsee Villa, thus disguising his own use of the stolen money, since the SS was not supposed to control disposition of these funds. This situation is an example of how the SS sought to extend its control over state funds.

While the newly acquired property on Fehmarn was, in the long run, to be for Heydrich's personal and official use, he also permitted high SS officials to use Fehmarn Island as a relaxation spot. Perhaps Heydrich was simply trying to be certain that Himmler would accept his real estate transactions. Nevertheless, both men were pleased that the old Germanic term "Nordhav" was being revived.

On July 30, 1939, three weeks after his visit to Fehmarn, Reinhard Heydrich had established the Nordhav Foundation with one hundred fifty thousand reichsmarks, to be controlled by the SS. Heydrich named five close associates as directors: SS Brigadeführer (Major General) Werner Best, SS Brigadeführer Wilhelm Albert, SS Oberführer (Brigadier General) Dr. Herbert Mehlhorn, SS Sturmbannführer (Major) Walter Schellenberg and his Chief adjutant, Security Police Captain Kurt Pomme.

State Secretary Wilhelm Stuckart, a later participant in the Wannsee Conference, gave his approval for the creation of the Nordhav Foundation on August 3, 1939. A few days later, at Heydrich's request, SS Sturmbannführer Schellenberg appeared on Fehmarn and arranged for purchase of pieces of the Katharinenhof. Schellenberg was authorized to pay eighty thousand reichsmarks for eleven hectares of land owned by three individuals. The land included beachfront, a manor house, a smaller residence, a forest house, stables, a rear house, an apiary, and a chicken house.

The Nordhav Foundation set very stringent conditions for the sellers, who remained on Fehmarn: "The sellers are required to keep the road leading to the manor house clean and worthy. Dungheaps in the vicinity are forbidden. No new plantings may be made on any surrounding land which will disturb the view of the sea from the manor house."

Heydrich named Peter Wiepert to assume total control over all the SS property on Fehmarn. Wiepert was quite restrictive; in his guide to Fehmarn, he wrote: "Courtyard, forest, and beach on the island of Fehmarn may only be entered with permission of the proprietor," whom he identified as "SS Stiftung Nordhav."

After buying the Katharinenhof, the Stiftung Nordhav was inactive for the next six months, no doubt because the invasion of Poland necessitated changes in Heydrich's organization. But in the fall of 1940, the Stiftung Nordhav began negotiations for the Haus Am Großen Wannsee 56–58, the

Reinhard Heydrich's Berlin home. From 1937 until his assassination in 1942, Reinhard Heydrich lived in this house at Augustastraße 14 (now Reifträgerweg 14), in the Schlachtensee suburb of Berlin. In the basement of the house is a large room that housed Heydrich's SS bodyguards. The room has its own outside entrance and bathroom; it could be closed off with a heavy steel door, and had a direct phone line to Heydrich's Berlin office. The house has been considerably renovated, and the current occupants use the former bodyguard quarters as a children's playroom.

Wannsee Villa. Heydrich probably chose this property because it was an easy ten-minute drive from his own house at Augustastraße 14 (now Reifträgerweg 14), in the Berlin suburb of Schlachtensee, for which he had paid forty-nine thousand reichsmarks in 1937.[3]

While Reinhard Heydrich again made use of the Stiftung Nordhav, he did not employ the same officials who bought the Katharinenhof on Fehmarn. There had been a change of management because of the manpower needed in occupied France, which the Germans had overrun in June 1940.

Two officials represented the Stiftung Nordhav, Regierungsdirektor Dr. Hans Nockermann and Regierungsrat (Privy Counsel) Dr. Rudolf Bergmann. The two men carried a notarized document certifying that they were authorized to represent the foundation and were empowered by the appropriate state

---

[3] *Reinhard Heydrich's close friend, Admiral Wilhelm Canaris, lived just around the corner from Heyrich at Waldsängerpfad 17. Canaris was implicated in the July 20, 1944, Hitler assassination plot and was hanged by the SS in the Flossenbürg concentration camp on April 9, 1945, shortly before the arrival of American troops.*

officials to acquire the Wannsee Villa. But because the price was well over the one hundred fifty thousand reichsmarks that, according to the civil code, a foundation would be allowed to pay, Heydrich himself had to warrant the purchase.

Bergmann made quick work of the entire transaction, which was completed in November 1940. Part of the contract required a promise to the district of Wannsee that there would be no alterations in the building or surrounding landscape. The final purchase price was 1.95 million reichsmarks, delivered to a savings account in the Dresdner Bank, the preferred bank of the SS.

After acquiring the Wannsee Villa, the Nordhav Foundation enlarged the grounds, in case Heydrich should want the house for his own use. On June 17, 1941, the president of the city of Berlin was notified "that the Foundation intends to acquire the lot at Zum Heckeshorn 16/18 in Berlin Wannsee at a price of 120,000 RM. The funds for the purchase are at the disposal of the Chief of the Security Police and Security Service [Heydrich]. The lot will be used to expand the property Am Großen Wannsee 56/58." The Zum Heckeshorn 16/18 lot had belonged to Ernst and Martha von Simson, living in Oxford, England. The Gestapo had simply confiscated this land.

Directly west lay another piece of property, Am Großen Wannsee 43/45. This lake-front lot had once belonged to Franz Oppenheim, one of the directors of I. G. Farben, the giant chemical manufacturer. On August 15, 1940, the land was transferred to the Nazi party in a forced Aryanization. Kurt and Margarete Oppenheim, the owners of record, had long since moved to Switzerland. Neither the Oppenheims nor the Simsons, of course, ever received a pfennig for their land.

In the summer of 1941 the Wannsee House was renovated. The SS took over the dining room, and there was construction on the second and third floors; also, two refrigerated cells were built behind the kitchen, at a price of 5,785.10 reichsmarks. Heydrich declared that these improvements were intended to turn the building into a guest house for SS officials and their representatives stationed outside the country.

"The hotels in Berlin are mostly overfilled and exceptionally expensive," declared the *Befehlsblatt*, an SS newsletter. "To prevent visiting SS officials from enduring the tedious ordeal of finding a hotel, to provide them with an affordable, respectable place to stay, and to furnish them with the opportunity to enjoy the companionship of their fellow officers, the guest house *Am Großen Wannsee* was built."

What did the guest house offer?

"Completely new visitors' rooms, rooms for socializing, a music room, billiard room, a great hall and conservatory, a lakeside terrace, central heating, running water, and all other comforts. There is a good kitchen serving lunch and dinner. Wine, beer, and tobacco products are available. Although the guest house is outside the city center, accessibility is no problem, since a car is available for transportation to and from the Wannsee train station at any hour, telephone 80 57 60.

"Overnight stays cost 5 Reichsmarks, including service and breakfast. The guest house is intended for the widest possible use, so that it will become a centerpoint for collegial interaction of SS officials in Berlin."

Eight weeks after this issue of the *Befehlsblatt* had been published, the "centerpoint for collegial interaction of SS officials in Berlin" became the site of the Wannsee Conference.

6

Planning to Murder the Jews of Europe

There is one common misconception regarding the Holocaust. Many people believe that the final decision to destroy the Jews of Europe was made at the Wannsee Conference. In fact, mass murder of the Jews had begun well before the Conference.

Yet for decades, the ultimate enigma among historians of the Holocaust has been, how can anyone prove that Hitler ordered the annihilation of Europe's Jews, and when did he do so?

Despite a half century of research, no single document has provided evidence that Hitler gave a written order for the Holocaust. Without that crucial piece of paper, generations of historians have veered from the right-wing revisionism of David Irving of Britain, who fought to discount Hitler's role, to a belief, embraced by American scholars like Richard Breitman and Daniel J. Goldhagen, that Hitler made the decision in early 1941—a thesis supported by the systematic killing of Jews later that year. In contrast, the German historian Hans Mommsen has cast Hitler as a "weak dictator" and the Holocaust as the result of a horrendous bureaucratic process unfolding with its own momentum.

But now a German scholar, Christian Gerlach, has set off a debate among historians with a new and contentious theory, based on a notation by Heinrich Himmler, discovered in previously secret Soviet archives, and on other documents. The documents supposedly establish that Hitler did, indeed, make a personal decision to put to death German and all other European Jews, and that he announced it to his most senior Nazi followers on December 12, 1941.

In addition, Gerlach argues that the decision was touched off in part by America's entry into World War II after the Japanese attack on Pearl Harbor on December 7, 1941. According to Gerlach, Hitler decided it was time to redeem a prophecy he made that a new world war would mean the annihilation of all Europe's Jews, not just those in the Soviet Union. On January 30, 1939, he had told the Reichstag:

64

And one more thing I would like now to state on this day memorable perhaps not only for us Germans. I have often been a prophet in my life and was generally laughed at. During my struggle for power, the Jews primarily received with laughter my prophecies that I would someday assume the leadership of the state and thereby of the entire Volk and then, among many other things, achieve a solution of the Jewish problem. I suppose that meanwhile the then resounding laughter of Jewry in Germany is now choking in their throats.

Today I will be a prophet again. If international finance Jewry within Europe and abroad should succeed once more in plunging the peoples into a world war, then the consequence will be not the Bolshevization of the world and therewith a victory of Jewry, but on the contrary, the destruction of the Jewish race in Europe.

In his table talk, taken down by a stenographer at Wolfsschanze (Wolf's Lair), his east Prussian military headquarters, on October 25, 1941, Hitler had more to say about his prophesy: "From the rostrum of the Reichstag, I prophesied to Jewry that, in the event of war's proving inevitable, the Jew would disappear from Europe. That race of criminals has on its conscience the two million dead of the First World War and now already hundreds of thousands more. Let nobody tell me that all the same we can't park them in the marshy parts of Russia! Who's worrying about our troops? It's not a bad idea, by the way, that public rumor attributes to us a plan to exterminate the Jews. Terror is a salutary thing."

Gerlach argues that Reinhard Heydrich called the Wannsee Conference to make clear that German Jews, many of whom had already been deported to concentration camps in Eastern Europe, were to be destroyed. If borne out, the theory would provide new proof of Hitler's direct responsibility for the Holocaust and, therefore, overturn many postwar attempts to minimize his role in it.

Gerlach's findings seem to conflict with other historical versions. In November 1996, for instance, Professor Breitman, of American University in Washington, disclosed newly discovered documents from the National Archives showing that, as early as July 1941, after the German invasion of the Soviet Union, Jews were being systematically massacred, indicating that the decision to embark on the Holocaust was made earlier than December.

Gerlach argues that the behavior of German authorities toward Jews in occupied countries was uneven, suggesting that there was at that time no master plan. In mid to late 1941, Gerlach wrote in an article in the journal *Werkstatt Geschichte* (History Workshop) that "a general order for the murder of German Jews had not yet been made," even though thousands of German Jews had been deported to concentration camps in eastern Europe, some had been killed, and Soviet Jews were already being methodically massacred.

On December 18, 1941, Gerlach argues, Himmler met with Hitler and later noted that the discussion had covered "the Jewish question/to be exterminated as partisans," according to a document found in Soviet archives. But some historians believe that Himmler's remarks could have alluded to the way Hitler wanted to publicly depict the systematic killing of Jews. At the same time, the discovery of the Himmler note in the Soviet archive is significant because of the overwhelming lack of documentary evidence connecting Hitler to the Holocaust.

Certainly, Hitler's role in some murders is clear. He ordered the first killings in an edict of October 1939, which he back-dated to September 1, 1939, the date he invaded Poland. In this edict, he decreed the so-called "euthanasia" of all inmates of asylums. He also wanted to murder institutionalized children, whom he called "useless eaters." Destroying their own children was too much for even the obedient Germans to stomach, so Hitler subsequently withdrew this order, though the killing continued covertly.[1]

When the murder of Jews in German-occupied Soviet territory began, Einsatz groups and Einsatz commandos carried out shootings, subsequently described in the regular bulletins of the Reich Security Main Office. The bulletins, called "incident reports," were widely distributed.

One report, for example, from Einsatz group 1, dated July 31, 1941, tells of German collaboration with bumbling Rumanian police troops: "The Rumanians attacked the Jews in a totally unplanned manner. Their shootings of numerous Jews was lacking in technical preparation. They left the executed Jews where they fell, most without burial. Our *Einsatz*-commando leader then gave the Rumanian police some instruction. On account of not following security police orders, and as a payback for attacks on German soldiers, the Jewish leader of Belzy and other Jews were liquidated, a total of 45." A report from Einsatz group 5 describes the destruction of Ukrainian Jews: "In Radomyschl an action was carried out against Jews who were dirtying the area, potentially endangering our troops with an epidemic. 1,688 Jews were shot. The special commandos of the security police and the security service have liquidated a total of 11,328 Jews as of September 6, 1941." A 1941 report from Einsatz group 6 depicts other executions: "The Ukrainian people are quite angry at the Jews and blame them for the explosions in Kiev. Also the Ukrainians perceive the Jews as Soviet agents, who have terrorized the local people. To get even for fires set in Kiev, numerous Jews were arrested September 29 and 30, and a total of 33,771 Jews were executed. Money, valu-

---

[1] *In its March 10, 1941, issue, TIME printed a letter from a reader in Altus, Oklahoma, named Tom Hamilton: "You state as rumor ... that a large number of cripples and lunatics are being slaughtered by the German state [Feb. 3]. Be it fact or fiction, here's hoping they don't overlook Goebbels and Hitler!"*

ables, and clothing were collected and made available to native Germans and to the city government for distribution to the needy."

Further high-level decisions in August and September 1941 widened the scope of victims.

- On September 18, 1941, Heinrich Himmler informed district leader (Gauleiter) and governor Arthur Greiser of Hitler's instruction to deport sixty thousand Jews from Austria, Bohemia, and Moravia to the Polish Lodz Ghetto. The Main State Security Office would organize the deportations.
- In October 1941, building of a death camp began in Belzec, a little town now under German rule.
- At the same time, another death camp was built in Chelmno, which the Germans called Kulmhof. The Nazis asphyxiated their victims with diesel exhaust fumes inside of trucks. In the beginning of December, the murderers killed Jews from the surrounding villages and later from the Lodz Ghetto.

By the time of the Wannsee Conference in January 1942, the Einsatz groups, operating behind the army front lines, had murdered more than half a million people. Thus there was no need of a decision at the conference to commit mass murder.

The Einsatz groups were not the only murderers. In 1945, shortly after the defeat of Nazi Germany, the German generals began the fabrication of a legend — the legend of the "clean Army," according to which "the soldiers kept their distance from the Nazi regime and Hitler, and fulfilled their military duties with decency and dignity."

In reality, from 1941 to 1944 the German Army in the Balkans and the Soviet Union conducted not a "normal war" but a war of destruction against Jews, prisoners of war, and civilians that claimed millions of victims. This conclusion is supported by a 1997 exhibit in Germany. The exhibit, sponsored by a private foundation run by the tobacco heir Jan Philip Reemtsma, was called "War of Destruction — The Crimes of the German Army, 1941–1944." In grainy black-and-white photographs, some taken as grisly souvenirs, ordinary German soldiers — not SS goons — are shown humiliating Jews and conducting summary executions by firing squad and hanging. A letter a young soldier wrote home boasts that his unit had killed one thousand Jews — "and that was not enough."

The Wannsee Conference facilitated the killing. In the months before Reinhard Heydrich called for the conference, three problems arose during the organization of mass deportations and shootings.

- High SS and police officials had made many short trips to the occupied areas of the Soviet Union. They realized that the number of murders requested of them could not be carried out with firearms. They informed Himmler that shooting was inadequate to the task at hand, was a great psychological burden to the execution commandos themselves, and could not be kept secret from the local population. In addition, the Einsatz troops and the civil authorities often had fierce fights over the property of the murdered Jews.

• With the support of the Wehrmacht and local authorities, the German governor of Lodz steadfastly refused to accept another sixty thousand Jews for the Lodz ghetto. To be sure, the protests of the civil authorities had no effect, but the problem of where to send the next shipment of Jews still vexed Himmler and Heydrich.

• The German officials in the occupied territories and the civil authorities were unclear whether all Jews should be killed or whether Jews capable of work should be spared and exploited.

More problems arose in November and December 1941, during deportations to Minsk, Kowno, and Riga:

• The general commissar for White Ruthenia (the western Ukraine), former Gauleiter Wilhelm Kube, inspected the Minsk Ghetto. He found Jews who had fought for Germany during World War I or who had relatives currently serving in the German Army (Wehrmacht) deported from Berlin, Bremen, Brünn, Düsseldorf, Frankfurt, and Hamburg. Local Gestapo officials had wrongly deported these Jews, who should have been left alone according to Reich Security Main Office guidelines.

• Officials in the hometowns of deportees wanted to be able to strike names from the Gestapo lists; these officials were profiting from their "work-Jews" and did not want to lose them.

• Jews from Berlin, Breslau, Frankfurt, Munich, and Vienna were deported to Kowno at the end of November. There was no room at Riga, which had originally been scheduled to receive them. Because of this bungle, Einsatz commando group 3 decided to shoot all five thousand Jews in fortification trenches around Kowno on November 25 and 29, 1941.

• Latvian Jews from the Riga ghetto were shot in the woods around Riga on November 30 and December 8, 1941. These murders were to make room for an arriving transport. The one thousand Berlin Jews in the transport got to the Skirotowa railroad station in Riga at a bad moment, just when the shooting had begun, and were murdered with the Latvian ghetto Jews. This annihilation had not been centrally planned; indeed, in a telephone message the same day, Himmler had said, "Berlin Jews not to be liquidated."

Obviously, there was a large discrepancy between what Berlin had planned and what happened in a distant town or village. Mass murder was difficult to arrange and coordinate with the usual German passion for order and precision. The Wannsee Conference was necessary in order to deal with this problem, especially since the situation was bound to get worse, as more territory and more Jews came under Nazi control.

The Wannsee Conference

On November 29, 1941, Adolf Eichmann sent Reinhard Heydrich's letter inviting thirteen participants to the proposed conference. The topics to be discussed were well established. At the beginning of the month, Eichmann had gotten in touch with the statistical division of the Reich Union of Jews, to find out exactly how many Jews were in Germany. The numbers, compiled since the Nazi takeover and institution of anti-Jewish laws, were to inform the measures Heydrich would suggest.

The first invitation to the conference referred to a "collective solution of the Jewish question in Europe." The stated goal of the conference, the attainment of a consensus by the central authorities, was in keeping with the fact that "since October 15, 1941, Jews from Germany, Bohemia, and Moravia were being evacuated to the east."

The persons invited were not the same persons who attended, mainly because of protocol. Heydrich did not initially invite a representative of the security police from the occupied Baltic, probably because the mass shootings in Riga had already created a sensation. Also, Riga only became a preferred deportation spot after November 29. SS Sturmbahnführer (Major) Rudolf Lange, head of the security police in Riga, was finally asked later.

Heydrich's conference, a breakfast meeting, had originally been scheduled for December 9, 1941, in the offices of the International Criminal Police Commission, at Kleiner Wannsee 16. Heydrich had been the director of this organization, the precursor to Interpol, since 1940.

The Kleiner Wannsee address might have been included in the invitation letter inadvertently, but it was definitely not valid after the cancellation of the conference on December 8. The first known correction of the meeting place is in the margin of SS Gruppenführer (Lieutenant General) Otto Hofmann's invitation: "phone conversation with Sturmbahnführer [Rolf] Günther on December 4. Street altered." This handwritten correction follows the Kleiner Wannsee address in Hofmann's invitation letter. Nevertheless, one still occasionally sees the statement that the Wannsee Conference met at the Interpol House.

Why had the conference had been canceled? Why had a new date not been set? After the war, these questions puzzled investigators. The presumption is that Hitler's December 11th declaration of war against the United States pushed the conference to the back burner.

On January 8, 1942, Heydrich issued a new invitation from his office in Prague to the same officials, rescheduling the breakfast meeting for January 20 in the Wannsee Villa. The twelve-day delay probably was due to the need to calculate revised statistics regarding the number of Jews remaining in Germany after the massive deportations to Riga. In addition, the conference had more to deal with. How were the deportations and mass murders of Jews throughout Europe to be handled? How could all of Europe be made Jewfree?

Careful examination of the Wannsee Protocol suggests that Heydrich must have been the only speaker for most of the conference. According to Adolf Eichmann's later recollection, the whole gathering lasted an hour and a half, in a very relaxed atmosphere. In contrast to the euphemistic phrases of the protocol, the participants spoke quite openly about mass murder. No one expressed any misgivings or raised any objections.

Heydrich began by referring to Reichsmarschall Hermann Göring's letter to him of July 31, 1941, asking that Heydrich prepare the final solution for the European Jewish question. Heydrich had included a copy of Göring's letter with the conference invitations. The Reichsmarschall had given Heydrich

Dining room, Wannsee Villa, 1922. This room served as venue for the Wannsee Conference. The photograph is from the magazine *Die Dame* (The Lady), Ullstein No. 21/1922. When the SS bought the Wannsee Villa in 1940, they also bought Friedrich Minoux's dining room furniture, including the Gobelin tapestry (right). (Ullstein Bilderdienst)

the job of "working out a design for the organizational, factual and material aspects" of the final solution. Obviously, Heydrich was emphasizing his role as primary planner, as the protocol indicates: "The control of the treatment of the final solution of the Jewish question resides centrally with the Reichsführer-SS and chief of the German police (chief of the security-police and the security service), regardless of geographical borders." Heydrich was doubtless eager for the job, and after the war he was often referred to as "the evil young god of death." But as boss of twelve main offices of the SS, Heydrich could only organize deportations through Eichmann and direct the Einsatz groups from Berlin. The actual killing lay outside of his authority. Himmler had ordered the mass murders of August 1941 in the Soviet Union and the building of extermination camps in Belzec and Chelmno.

Heydrich derived his authority over forced emigration from a section of the extensive discrimination and disenfranchisement laws. His remarks in the Wannsee Protocol suggest that the forced Jewish emigration was only the beginning: "To carry out these measures, the accelerated emigration of the Jews from Reich territory is regarded as a temporary solution.... Everyone was aware of the disadvantages that such a forced emigration entailed. Yet they must be accepted, in view of the absence, for the moment, of other solutions..." Heydrich described the current situation and mentioned protests in Lodz, Minsk, and Riga. Then he continued: "In place of emigration, with the Führer's authorization, forced evacuation of the Jews to the east is another possible solution. Emigration and forced evacuation are only alternatives, however. Other practical experiences have been gathered, and these will be of great importance in the coming final solution of the Jewish question." What were these other practical experiences? One was the murder of six thousand Jews from Berlin, Breslau, Frankfurt am Main, Munich, and Vienna. The other was the transport of Jews to Chelmno, if they could not be integrated into the forced labor of the Lodz ghetto.

Heydrich proceeded to reveal the scope of his proposed European deportations. He envisioned eleven million deportees, with no country escaping the "combing-out," even countries not occupied by Germany or under German influence in January 1942. English Jews, Finnish Jews, Irish Jews, Portuguese Jews, Swedish Jews, Spanish Jews, and Turkish Jews were all slated for deportation. Estonia was now Jew-free as a result of the murderous efficiency of the police actions in the summer of 1941.

Heydrich mentioned the principle of working deportees to death: "In the course of the final solution, the Jews should be brought under appropriate direction in a suitable manner to the east for labor utilization. Separated by sex, the Jews capable of work will be led into these areas in large labor columns to build roads whereby doubtless a large part will fall away. The inevitable final remainder which doubtless constitutes the toughest element will have to be dealt with appropriately, since it represents a natural selection which upon liberation is to be regarded as a germ cell of a new Jewish development. (See the lesson of history.)" But Heydrich did not refer to the disabled; their fate was so clear to the conference participants that no mention was necessary.

Not everyone thought that Jews were important to the work force. Dr. Josef Bühler, of the Office of the Generalgouvernement (Polish territories), commented that forced labor of Jews would produce very little, and the deportations would cause few problems. Probably the venue for the final solution was also mentioned at this point. Although the western European Jews would be transported to the execution sites in the east, the Jews from Poland, the Baltic States, and the Soviet Union would be dispatched locally. The closed trucks using diesel fumes for asphyxiation could take care of these groups, and no transport would be necessary. In the protocol, this discussion appears as follows: "Finally there was a discussion of the various possible solutions, with both Gauleiter Dr. Meyer and State Secretary Dr. Bühler expressing the view that they could carry out certain preparatory measures in their territories on their own, provided, however, that any disturbance of the [non-Jewish] population had to be avoided."

In the course of his address, Heydrich referred to the sequence of the deportations. He affirmed that, to accomplish the final solution, there should be forced evacuations from Germany, Austria, Bohemia, and Moravia. He said that these were justified because of the need for apartments in individual cities. Indeed, in advance of the deportations from Berlin, Munich, Stuttgart, and Vienna, many local housing officials had been asked which apartments belonged to Jews.

Heydrich was vague about deportations from the rest of Europe: "The start of major individual evacuation operations will depend in large measure on military developments. With regard to the treatment of the final solution in European areas we occupy or influence, it was proposed that the appropriate specialists of the Foreign Office get together with the experts having jurisdiction in these matters within the Security Police and Security Service."

European states had differing attitudes toward the final solution. Croatia and Slovakia were regarded as partners because of their adoption of German anti-Jewish laws; whereas Heydrich thought Hungary and Rumania were unknown quantities, although their military and police units participated in the mass murders of Jews in the southern part of the Soviet Union. While Italy and France were probably mentioned as an aside, only for the sake of completeness, Dr. Martin Luther, the representative of the Foreign Office, noted that the implementation of the final solution in some countries, especially the northern ones, would be difficult, and therefore he recommended ignoring them for the moment.

Finally, Heydrich was forced to address an unpleasant problem, which Adolf Eichmann and Gestapo Chief Heinrich Müller had already brought up: The local Gestapo officials didn't always adhere to official guidelines when deciding whom to deport. Heydrich declared that an important prerequisite for carrying out the deportations was defining the rules clearly to everyone involved. Erich Neumann, representative of the Office of the Four Year Plan, declared that Jews working in war-related industries should not be deported if they could not be replaced. Heydrich thereupon promised that these Jews would not be deported under the guidelines he had established.

With regard to the German and Austrian Jews who had fought for the fatherland in World War I, Heydrich clarified the rules he formulated in October 1941, to be instituted as of June 1942: "It is intended not to evacuate Jews over 65, but to transfer them to an old people's ghetto (the plan calls for Theresienstadt). In addition to these age groups — some 30% of the 280,000 Jews who lived in the Old Reich and Austria on October 1, 1941, are over 65 — the old people's ghetto will receive badly injured Jewish war veterans and Jews with war decorations (Iron Cross First Class). Many problems will be eliminated in one blow by means of this definitive solution." None of the high officials present offered any objection to the deportation of eleven million human beings. Eighteen years later, Eichmann recounted that after the meeting, Heydrich felt relieved; the two men sat together, drank French cognac, and had a pleasant meal.

The next point discussed was the racial definition: Who was a Jew? Since the Nuremberg laws had explicitly addressed this question in 1935, should the laws be applied unequivocally?

Heydrich did not expect final instructions from Hitler clarifying the definition, and so he could only introduce his own suggestions. Point by point, he described the individual "mixed-breed" (Mischling) categories and mixed-breed variations, and declared that a "first degree mixed-breed" who agreed to sterilization could be spared deportation. Heydrich knew that mixed breeds, or non-Aryan spouses of mixed breeds, could not be included in the deportation guidelines without the agreement of other officials. In August 1941, there had been two conferences to address the problem, which was often a terrible one for the tens of thousands of mixed breeds in Germany. One sad example is the case of Hannah, uncovered by mark Rigg, an American research fellow at Cambridge University in England.

It was 1938 in Berlin, and nineteen-year-old Hannah was shocked to hear that her father had been arrested by the Nazis. She had been raised in the Lutheran faith of her mother, and her father's being a Jew had never been an issue, much less a crime. So she went to the Gestapo to complain.

Officers said they couldn't help her and told her to go to the Jewish community center. Once there, she told people what had happened and was questioned about her upbringing. "We don't help your kind," she remembers being told. Determined, she went back to the Gestapo to protest. This time the officer in charge took her into a back room and asked two leering junior officers if they "liked what they saw." The commander left, and the two men raped her.

Rigg' s study began with a chance encounter in a movie theater in Berlin with an elderly man of Jewish parentage who had fought for the Germans. The meeting led him to explore similar cases and in the process discover that he himself, a Bible-belt Protestant, had a Jewish great-grandmother and twenty-two relatives who had disappeared during the war.

Over the next four years, Rigg discovered documents called "declarations of German blood" that Hitler had personally signed to keep valuable officers with Jewish forebears in the Wehrmacht. The existence of such people had been known — one was Field Marshal Erhard Milch, deputy chief of the Luftwaffe (air force) — but Rigg found many unknown cases.

Helmut Schmidt, the West German chancellor from 1974 to 1982, kept secret the existence of a Jewish grandfather to remain a lieutenant in the Luftwaffe. Mr. Schmidt told Rigg he had always thought his own case was rare; he was startled to learn that the young researcher had unearthed a previously unknown 1944 German personnel document listing seventy-seven generals and colonels "of mixed Jewish race or married to a Jew" whom Hitler had declared "of German blood." Rigg confirmed the existence of more than eighty additional individuals formally exonerated for having Jewish forebears.

Some people considered themselves Jews but hid their backgrounds to survive, sometimes serving in the army of the regime that was annihilating their relatives. The great majority were raised as Christians and had never thought of themselves as Jews or people of Jewish heritage.

Only after the 1935 Nuremberg Laws for the "protection" of German blood did thousands of Germans find out that the Nazis considered them "quarter Jews" (people with one Jewish grandparent), "half Jews" (people with two Jewish grandparents) or "full Jews" (people with at least three Jewish grandparents). To protect German blood even further, the Nuremberg Laws declared intercourse between a Jew and an Aryan German, "racial desecration," to be a crime.

But by this time, assimilation in Germany was far more a fixture of the culture than the Nazis anticipated. Hitler, who may himself have had a Jewish paternal grandfather, was not only fighting against the Jews, he was fighting against hundreds of years of assimilation.[2]

[2]*Alois Hitler (1837–1903), Adolf Hitler's father, was the illegitimate son of Maria Anna Schikl-gruber (1795–1847). In Linz, Maria Anna had become pregnant while working as a servant in the house of a wealthy Jew named Frankenberger, and his young son might have been the*

Rigg encountered feelings of shame among those who falsified papers to survive while their relatives were being killed in death camps. He also met former officers who believed their families were spared by Gestapo officials who intruded in a Jewish household, only to spot a framed picture of a son in full uniform fighting at the front.

Some serviceman of Jewish parentage, on learning of the treatment their relatives were receiving, raised objections. After the French campaign in 1940, many petitions came to Hitler from these officers saying, "I have an Iron Cross, and I come home to find my mother and my grandmother being persecuted." Hitler had to decide to either protect the parents or kick the soldiers out. So there was a huge discharge in 1940.

One of Rigg's discoveries allowed the Lubavitcher movement to answer a question. Lubavitcher legend has always held that the grand rebbe, Joseph Schneersohn, and his followers were spirited through German lines by a Jew in a German uniform after being trapped in Warsaw in September 1939. Rigg established the truth of the story and identified the officer as Major Ernest Bloch, whose father was Jewish and who obtained a declaration of German blood signed by Hitler.

But the number of such declarations was small, probably no more than thirteen hundred, according to a recent issue of the *Vierteljahresheft für Zeitgeschichte*. Mixed breeds had the best chance of obtaining one. For example, Hitler declared the half-Jewish chemist Artur Imhausen a "full-Aryan," because Imhausen had developed a process for extracting fatty acids from cabbage ("If the man has actually discovered this thing, we'll make him an Aryan"). Hitler also Aryanized his diet cook, Helene Maria von Exner, and her entire family. Exner, who had a Jewish grandmother, prepared the Führer's special vegetarian meals.

Another Hitler Aryanization ended badly. On October 14, 1936, Hitler declared the part-Jewish jurist Hans von Dohnanyi an Aryan, at the request of Dohnanyi's boss, justice minister Franz Gürtner. A few years later, the Nazis killed both Dohnanyi and his brother-in-law, the theologian Dietrich Bonhoeffer, for their involvement in the anti-Hitler resistance.

(continued from previous page) *father. In 1842 she married Johann Georg Hiedler, who never adopted or legitimized the stepson. Hiedler's brother, Johann Nepomuk Hüttler, executed this legal nicety in 1876, when Alois was thirty-nine years old. The name "Hitler" probably arose through a hearing error of the pastor filling out the document. The German Hitler scholar Werner Maser has identified Hüttler as the natural father of Alois, and thus the grandfather of Adolf Hitler. But Maser also asserted that Adolf Hitler fathered an illegitimate son named Jean Loret in France during World War I, a claim Anton Joachimsthaler later debunked. In fact, Joachimsthaler wrote an entire book correcting errors in Maser's Hitler biography. For a detailed account of the various theories about Hitler's paternal grandfather, see* Explaining Hitler *by Ron Rosenbaum.*

The Wannsee Protocol and the Historical Record of the Conference

The Wannsee Protocol is a fifteen-page typewritten document which does not carry the name of an individual author. (See Appendix C.) While in prison in Jerusalem, Adolf Eichmann stated many times that he had written the protocol after the conference, based on the stenographic notes of a secretary who was present. Heydrich and Heinrich Müller had then extensively edited Eichmann's draft to produce the final version.

Heydrich sent the one copy of the protocol to survive the war to the Foreign Office with a cover letter carrying a handwritten date, January 26, 1942. In the letter, Heydrich invites Under State Secretary Martin Luther to a follow up conference to be held on March 6, 1942. In the last sentence, he asks Luther to make contact with his representative, SS Obersturmbannführer (Lieutenant Colonel) Eichmann. Historians assume that the cover letter, originally undated, must have been written before the Wannsee Conference to accompany the anticipated protocol.

Foreign Office Under State Secretary Luther wrote a note on the cover letter to Franz Rademacher, his authority on Jewish matters: "Pg [*Parteigenosse,* Party comrade] Rademacher, please inform me that you will attend the conference as an expert."

An official Foreign Office stamp attests to a March 2, 1942 receipt of the cover letter and classifies it g.Rs (geheime Reichssache, secret Reich material). The stamp also indicates that the letter and protocol were received by DIII, Luther's Deutschland department (D) and Rademacher's office (III). Rademacher informed Eichmann on the same day that he would attend the March 6 conference.

The Foreign Office copy of the protocol was numbered sixteen, of thirty that had originally been made. Each conferee probably was to receive two copies of the protocol, one for personal use and one for an official record.

What happened to the other twenty-nine copies?

Eichmann may have sent a copy to propaganda minister Joseph Goebbels, because Goebbels refers to it in a March 1942 diary entry: "I read an extensive analysis of the SD [security service] and the Police dealing with the final solution of the Jewish question. The document raises a large number of issues. The Jewish question must be solved throughout Europe." Heydrich mentions only one enclosed copy of the protocol in his cover letter to Martin Luther. Perhaps the Goebbels copy and the Luther copy were the only ones sent. The reason may have been the abandonment of the so-called Madagascar Plan.

The Nazis had devised this plan to solve the Jewish problem by forcing emigration to Madagascar. The world's fourth largest island (228,000 square miles), lying 250 miles off the southeast coast of Africa, Madagascar was a

French colony. The plan required that France cede the island to Germany. The German navy would then choose sites for military bases, while the rest would become a Jewish ghetto, under the jurisdiction of Heinrich Himmler. The Nazis preferred Madagascar because Palestine "belonged to the Christians and Muslims." In addition, the Jews deported to Madagascar could be held hostage, to ensure the good conduct of their "racial comrades" in the United States. The Jewish resettlement on Madagascar would be financed by the expropriation of Jewish property in Europe. But the Madagascar plan became unworkable after Britain declared war on Germany.

On February 10, 1942, Rademacher had informed colleagues of Hitler's decision that the Soviet Union, not Madagascar, would be the place of exile for the Jews. The Madagascar plan was officially dead.

Ernst Woermann, head of the Foreign Office Political Department, was worried. "Because of the implications of this decision, I would like to know its source." No doubt his colleague Luther told Woermann about the Wannsee Conference, but Luther himself may have wanted written confirmation of the new Jewish policy of murder rather than resettlement. Therefore, Heydrich might have sent Luther a single copy of the Wannsee Protocol in order to mollify him, according to a theory proposed by Peter Klein, a holocaust scholar. Indeed, during the postwar criminal trials of the Wannsee Conference participants, all steadfastly denied ever receiving a copy of the protocol. New documents emerging from former Soviet archives may one day shed additional light on this matter.

The Foreign Office copy of the protocol was filed in a folder labeled "Final solution of the Jewish question." Because of the air raids on Berlin, the Foreign Office decided to leave only important documents in the city. Most of the other files were moved to Krummhübel in the Riesengebirge, the Harz Mountains, and a facility near Lake Constance. On April 10, 1945, a telephone order was given to destroy all documents, but because of the rapid advance of the American First Army, very little was touched. The Allies recovered more than three hundred tons of records, which were first stored in a castle near Marburg, then brought to Berlin.

Though the Wannsee Protocol was among these records, it was not discovered immediately. In fact, the first allusion to the Wannsee Conference appeared in the multi-volume diaries of Hans Frank, Hitler's governor-general of Poland. Frank also mentioned the name of his representative at the conference, State Secretary Josef Bühler.

On March 20, 1946, Robert Jackson, Chief American Prosecutor at the Nuremberg war crimes tribunal, cross examined Hermann Göring. Acknowledging his signed letter to Heydrich of July 31, 1941, mandating the solution of the Jewish question, Göring complained vociferously about errors in the translation.

When Hans Frank was cross examined, the subject of the Wannsee Conference arose, and the tribunal called Frank's subordinate Bühler as a witness. On April 23, 1946, Bühler acknowledged being present at the Wannsee Conference. He said that Heydrich had discussed the future resettlement of the Jews in a territory in the northeast of the Soviet Union, with the Theresienstadt ghetto a possible alternate site for those Jews who could not withstand the rigors of Soviet resettlement.

These statements quite obviously contradicted the real fate of the deported Jews and also the wording of the Wannsee Protocol. However, the prosecutors were unable to challenge them because the protocol had not yet been found. Moreover, the prosecution never asked Bühler who else attended the conference. Another witness, former Reich minister and chief of the Reich Chancellery Hans-Heinrich Lammers, mentioned the conference but said little else. There the matter stood for the next year.

The breakthrough came in March 1947. Robert M. W. Kempner, an assistant prosecutor at the Nuremberg Trials, was searching the Foreign Office records for evidence to be used in further war crimes trials. Kempner suspected that these records might be of value, because he had seen letters from Heydrich's Reich Security Main Office to the Foreign Office. To Kempner's astonishment, the secret documents of the foreign office had all been

Robert M. W. Kempner. An assistant prosecutor at the Nuremberg Trials, Kempner searched the Foreign Office records for evidence to be used in further war crimes trials. Kempner suspected that these records might be of value, because he had seen letters from Heydrich's Reich Security Main Office to the Foreign Office. After two weeks of sifting through the material, one of Kempner's aides turned up the Wannsee Protocol. In its very first sentence, Kempner discerned the importance of the now famous document: "On January 20, 1942 in Berlin, Am Großen Wannsee Nr. 56/58, the following persons took part in a discussion about the final solution of the Jewish question...." (Ullstein Bilderdienst)

retained and brought to Berlin. They had been meticulously microfilmed, so that nothing would be lost.

After two weeks of sifting through the material, one of Kempner's aides turned up the Wannsee Protocol. In its very first sentence, Kempner discerned the importance of the now famous document: "On January 20, 1942 in Berlin, Am Großen Wannsee Nr. 56/58, the following persons took part in a discussion about the final solution of the Jewish question..."

Today, the original Wannsee Protocol is in Koblenz, in the Bundesarchiv (Federal Archives), in the Foreign Office section, filed under the heading "Acts Inland IIg, Volume 177, pages 165–180." A color reproduction is on permanent exhibit in Room 6 of the Wannsee Villa in Berlin.

Holocaust Revisionists and the Wannsee Conference

Many guilt-burdened Germans, among others, have tried to use the euphemistic wording of the Wannsee Protocol to rewrite history. These individuals would like to turn the evil deeds of the Nazi past into well-intentioned acts.

The first revisionist was, in fact, Heydrich himself. When he described the conference to his wife, he put quite a positive spin on it. As Lina Heydrich wrote in her memoirs:

> [The Wannsee Conference] dealt, as he [Heydrich] said, with organizing the migration of the European Jews to central Russia. "You're not saying," I asked, "that all Jews are to be deported to Siberia?" His answer: "Yes, I am saying that. Siberia is not such a horrible place. It's only the Russian prisons there that give it a frightening reputation. Think of father von Pomme." What was he saying, I thought? Major Pomme's father (Pomme was Reinhard's chief police adjutant) was a prisoner of war during World War I and was sent to Siberia. He had always said to his son, "I would like once more to live in Siberia as a free man. It's a wonderful place."
>
> Siberia, Reinhard told me, had everything: fertile land, ore, minerals, and coal. When I asked him skeptically whether the Jews would be able to adapt to these new conditions, he said: "Certainly. They are intelligent, and they need a new beginning. Things can't go on the way they have. We want to get rid of this problem once and for all. Now, during the war, a one-time opportunity presents itself!" Then he sketched out for me his detailed plan, that included the deportations. Naturally a large percentage would not survive the resettling, especially the elderly Jews. One had to accept some attrition. "The Jews we bring there," he continued, "will adapt." And when I asked where the proposed state should arise, he said, "In the north, in the south, in front of or behind the Urals. Behind the Urals and in their middle." Then he showed me the area on the map. The "thing" had only one

drawback. The area first had to be conquered. Why, I asked myself afterward, should such a human relocation not be possible? Reinhard's men would be able to do it.

One popular method modern revisionists use to put a benign face on the Wannsee Conference is to isolate key statements in the protocol from context, then subject them to intense scrutiny. For example, Holocaust scholar Peter Klein quotes a self-appointed "Professor," operating under the pseudonym "Ernst Gauss," who said the following during his "Lectures on Contemporary History": "This Protocol deals with, for example, the difficulties in the definition of half and quarter Jews and the question of the number of Jews in German territory. Further, it speaks of Jews transported to build roads in the east, where a natural reduction will occur because of the harsh conditions. The hardy Jewish seed which survives will provide the nucleus for a lively future Jewish state." Another historical revisionist presents the same text as follows: "Under corresponding leadership, in the course of the final solution, the Jews will fulfill work missions in the east. In large work colonies, separated by sex, the Jews capable of work will build roads. Doubtless a large part will perish, a result of natural diminution. The further text of the Protocol can be ignored." Here is the way a third revisionist jiggered the same protocol text. First the author quotes the initial two sentences: "Under corresponding leadership, in the course of the final solution, the Jews will fulfill work missions in the east. In large work colonies, separated by sex, the Jews capable of work will build roads." He explains, "If the WP [Wannsee Protocol] were to serve as proof of a 1941 destruction plan, it was naturally necessary to formulate the plan in concrete terms." He quotes another sentence from the protocol: "The remainder must be handled appropriately, because these are the hardiest..." Then he adds, "The Protocol does not state the nature of this appropriate handling. Is it the building of roads? This was undoubtedly a central question for one more conference, at least, which would deal with clarification, planning, and coordination."

Other opportunities exist for revisionists in the form of variant Wannsee Protocol texts. In his book *Eichmann and his Accomplices*, prosecutor Robert M. W. Kempner cites the protocol, but occasionally with a variant word. The revisionists have pounced upon these small discrepancies to declare that the protocol itself is a forgery.

Reinhard Heydrich's protocol cover letter to the Foreign Office has been a boon for the revisionists. They point out that the handwritten date on the document, January 26, 1942, antedates by four weeks the March 2 date of the Foreign Office's receipt stamp. Therefore, was the document in the mail for four weeks? The revisionists also dispute the fact that the conference was held in the Wannsee Villa, rather than in the offices of the International Criminal Police Commission, at Kleiner Wannsee 16. (As was mentioned, Heydrich used the Kleiner Wannsee address in his first conference invitation letter of November 29, 1941.)

Right-wing radicals have even subjected the grammar of the Wannsee Protocol to intense scrutiny. The phrase "Bezüglich der Frage der Auswirkung der Judenevakuierung..." (With regard to the question of the carrying out of the Jewish evacuation...) is an example. The radicals assert that this phrase is an "un-German multiply, consecutively used genitive." In other words, the German equivalent (*der*) of the words "of the" appears three times. This is an American grammatical construction, they claim, and so the protocol must be an American forgery.

Revisionists find other evidence of forgery on page six of the protocol, which gives estimates of the number of European Jews. The phrase "Italien einschl. Sardinien (Italy including Sardinia)" must be an American forgery, they say, because "everyone in Europe knows what belongs to Italy."

Other self-proclaimed "specialists" have seized on the following sentence from the protocol: "Um den deutschen Devisenschatz zu schonen, wurden die jüdischen Finanzinstitutionen des Auslandes durch die jüdischen Organisationen des Inlandes dazu verhalten, für die Betreibung entsprechender Devisenaufkommen Sorge zu tragen." Literally translated, the German is not entirely logical: "In order to spare German foreign exchange reserves, the local Jewish organizations held back the foreign Jewish finance institutions to take care of managing of an appropriate amount of foreign currency." The "specialists" dwell on the words *verhalten* (hold back) and *Betreibung* (managing), maintaining that they are simply part of a clumsy translation of an American forgery. But the author of the protocol, Eichmann, was Austrian. And an unabridged German dictionary would immediately reveal that the phrase "*jemanden verhalten zu...*" is the widely used Austrian equivalent of the German "*jemanden verpflichten zu...*" (obligate someone to...). Also, *Betreibung* is a synonym for *Einziehung* (collecting). Thus the meaning becomes clearer: "In order to spare German foreign currency reserves, the Jewish financial institutions abroad were obligated by Jewish organizations at home to take care of collecting an appropriate amount of foreign currency."

Revisionists like to point out discrepancies between the postwar testimony of the surviving Wannsee Conference participants and the text of the Wannsee Protocol. The participants all tended to put a more benign face on the event than did the protocol, with the notable exception of two participants, Adolf Eichmann and Friedrich Wilhelm Kritzinger. Some revisionists ignore the disturbing testimony of Eichmann and Kritzinger entirely. Others claim the Israelis brainwashed Eichmann in his Jerusalem prison cell, and simply disregard Kritzinger.

Another revisionist tactic has been to debase each statement the perpe-trators made before the courts, saying the admissions were coerced by threat of torture. Surely, the revisionists argue, if the authorities had known the truth, the sentences they imposed would have been much lighter.

For decades, revisionists have tried to present their theses as serious his-torical research. There is, of course, an enormous mass of documentary and photographic evidence refuting these pseudohistorians. Alas, they are unde-terred, and probably will never stop churning out their wild distortions of the truth, even though it is a crime in Germany to deny the reality of the Holocaust.

Reinhard Heydrich's Second Conference

In his March 2, 1942, cover letter sent with the Foreign Office copy of the Wannsee Protocol, Heydrich announces a second meeting to hash out the practical details of how to dispose of the Jews. The meeting was to take place in Berlin on March 6, 1942, in Kurfürstenstraße 116. Heydrich requests the men he invites to get in touch with his representative, SS Obersturmbann-führer Eichmann, for further details.

The same fifteen men who attended the Wannsee Conference attended the March 6 meeting. Also present were Franz Rademacher, the Foreign Office official, and Leopold Gutterer, State Secretary in the Reich Ministry for Pro-paganda and National Enlightenment. Gutterer had been unable to attend at Wannsee and, inexplicably, had not sent a representative.

At the meeting, two issues were discussed: the mixed-breed problem and the mixed-marriage problem.

Dr. Wilhelm Stuckart insisted that only grade I mixed breeds be sub-ject to compulsory sterilization, after which they should be allowed to remain in Germany. Here is Stuckart's rationale: "I have always maintained that it is extraordinarily dangerous to send German blood to the opposing side. Our adversaries will put the desirable characteristics of this blood to good use. Once the half Jews are outside of Germany, their high intelligence and education level, combined with their German heredity, will render these individuals born leaders and terrible enemies." Other participants suggested that after the grade I mixed breeds had been sterilized, all other grades of mixed breeds should be neutered in order to effect a complete solution to the problem. If the Führer should then decide, on political grounds, that compulsory steril-ization was indicated, the sterilized grade I mixed breeds could be sent to the Jewish old-age ghetto. One participant suggested that the living conditions of all mixed breeds be regulated. But there was doubt that existing Reich laws mandated such regulation.

The conference resolved that all divorces in the case of mixed marriages should be handled quickly. Any objections from the Jewish partner should be steadfastly ignored. But appearances were important, and no impression should be given that the divorce was compulsory. The partner of German blood should have a specific time period in which to institute proceedings. After this period had elapsed, state officials could step in. These regulations would apply only to a marriage in which one partner was a full-blooded Jew or a first-degree mixed breed. The chief of the security police or security service would be responsible for determination of Jewishness. After divorce, a full-Jewish former spouse would be deported and probably murdered.

Yet mixed marriages remained a thorny problem for the Nazis. When the final round-up of Berlin Jews began on Saturday, February 27, 1943, some four thousand seven hundred Jewish men who were partners in mixed marriages were segregated from the others and taken to a building in the Rosenstrasse. On Sunday morning, their non-Jewish wives banded together and went out to find them. They converged on Rosenstrasse and mobbed the building where their husbands were being held. There they stood, refusing to leave, shouting and screaming for their men, hour after hour, throughout the day and the night and into the next day.

Worried SS leaders assembled in their nearby Burgstrasse headquarters, not knowing what to do. They had never been faced with such a situation. Would they have to machine-gun nearly five thousand German women? All night the arguments raged, until at noon on Monday a decision was reached: All men married to a non-Jewish wife could return home. "Privileged persons," the official announcement said, "are to be incorporated in the national community." The four thousand seven hundred Jewish men remained in an uneasy state of limbo until the end of the war, as did the mixed breeds whose fate had been debated at Heydrich's March 6 conference.

Needless to say, the conference raised more issues than it settled. On the following day, March 7, Foreign Office official Rademacher sent a memorandum to Martin Luther and two other under state secretaries: "Certain difficulties are bound to arise during the sterilization of 70,000 mixed breeds. According to the Reich Medical Office, 700,000 days of hospitalization would be required. But there is a war going on, and the hospital beds are needed for the wounded. Therefore, regarding point IV/1 in the [Wannsee] Protocol of January 20, all First Grade mixed breeds should be sent to a single place in Germany or German occupied territory, and the sterilization question postponed until after the war."

The Assassination of Reinhard Heydrich

Heydrich did not have long to live after the Wannsee Conference. In 1941, Himmler, eager to put some distance between his ambitious subordinate and the center of power in Berlin, got Hitler to name Heydrich Reich Protector of Bohemia-Moravia (Czechoslovakia), replacing the ineffectual diplomat Konstantin von Neurath (later, after his Nuremberg trial, the oldest prisoner at Spandau).

Heydrich's brief governorship, during which he managed to persuade a surprisingly large number of Czechs to cooperate with him, was triumphantly successful. He highlighted his rising status by an act of homage to his father, a suspected Jew, who was never quite accepted by polite old-German society. On the evening of May 26, 1942, Reinhard Heydrich inaugurated the Prague music festival with a concert of Bruno Heydrich's chamber works, performed by a quartet of Bruno's former pupils from the Halle conservatory. Heydrich himself wrote the program notes. According to Lina Heydrich, this event was the fulfillment of an old dream. The musical establishment of Prussia had disdained Bruno Heydrich's talent, but his son, a member of the new Nazi elite, had recognized it.

The following day, Heydrich was to depart Prague for a bigger job in Germany. But two young Czechs, Jan Kubis and Josef Gabcik, sent from London to assassinate him, ambushed his open Mercedes as he drove the twenty kilometers from his residence, the castle of Jungfern-Breschan, to his Prague office in the Hradcin Palace. In *The Killing of Reinhard Heydrich,* Callum MacDonald describes what happened.

Gabcik raised his gun and pulled the trigger at point blank range, but the weapon failed to fire. Heydrich then made a fatal error. Instead of ordering his driver, Oberscharführer (Technical Sergeant) Klein, to speed away from the ambush, Heydrich stood up, drew his pistol, and ordered that the car be stopped. Neither Heydrich nor Klein had seen Kubis and thought they were dealing with a lone assassin.

Kubis stepped forward and tossed a bomb at the two men in the Mercedes. But his aim was poor, and instead of landing in the open car, the bomb exploded against the right rear wheel. Shrapnel flew back into Kubis's face and shattered the windows of a trolley which had stopped on the other side of the road. Passengers screamed as they were hit by shards of flying glass and metal. The Mercedes lurched violently, coming to rest in the gutter, belching smoke. The blast hurled upward two SS jackets folded on the back seat of the car; they landed over the trolley power lines.

Heydrich and Klein jumped from the wrecked car, brandishing pistols, to fight it out with their assailants. The strapping six-foot Klein made for Kubis, who was staggering away, half-blinded by blood. Klein tried to shoot Kubis with his automatic, but inadvertently pressed the magazine release catch, jamming the gun. Kubis grabbed a bicycle, fired his Colt pistol into the air to scatter the crowd of shocked passengers pouring out of the trolley, and pedaled away furiously.

Heydrich, meanwhile, lurched towards Gabcik, weaving like a drunk. Gabcik ducked behind a telephone pole, trading shots with Heydrich, who took cover behind the stalled tram. Suddenly Heydrich, wounded and in pain, doubled over and staggered to the side of the road. The bomb had broken one of his ribs and had driven fragments of horsehair and wire from the upholstery of the car into his spleen. Heydrich collapsed against a fence, supporting himself with one hand against the railing, as Gabcik sprinted away. As Klein returned from his unsuccessful pursuit of Kubis, Heydrich, his face etched with pain, gestured with his free hand and gasped, "Get that bastard!" Klein dashed after Gabcik while Heydrich staggered along the pavement, finally falling against the hood of the wrecked Mercedes. Although the crowd of trolley passengers observed his desperate struggle, no one stepped forward to help the badly wounded man in SS uniform.

Finally, a young blond woman recognized Heydrich and shouted for a car to take him to a hospital. An off-duty Czech policeman, who had been a passenger in the trolley, hailed a passing baker's van. The driver, hesitant to get involved, argued heatedly with the policeman. Heydrich remained slumped against his car as a dark bloodstain spread across his uniform.

A small truck carrying a load of floor polish was finally commandeered, and the policeman helped shoehorn the wounded Heydrich into the cramped cab. The ride in the jolting truck quickly overwhelmed Heydrich, and he asked the driver to stop. He was moved into the back of the truck, where he flopped on his belly among the boxes of wax and floor polish, one hand across his face, the other pressed against his wound. At eleven o'clock, he arrived at Bulkova Hospital.

In the emergency room, a young Czech physician, Vladimir Snajdr, cleaned Heydrich's wound. "I took forceps and a few swabs and tried to see whether the wound was deep...he did not flinch although it must have hurt him." A Dr. Dick, the German hospital director, ordered x-rays of what appeared to be only a superficial wound. The films showed the broken rib, a ruptured diaphragm, and metal fragments in the region of the spleen.

Dr. Dick recommended immediate surgery, but Heydrich did not want to trust his life to a Prague surgeon and demanded someone from Berlin. After some arguing, Heydrich agreed to an operation, but only if the top Nazi surgeon in Prague, Dr. Holbaum of the German Clinic, was called in. Shortly after noon, Heydrich was wheeled into an operating room.

Himmler sent his friend, Dr. Karl Gebhardt, and Hitler's doctors, Dr. Karl Brandt and Dr. Theodor Morell, to Prague to look after Heydrich. At first, Gebhardt was optimistic and believed Dick and Holbaum had done good work. But in a few days, Heydrich's condition deteriorated. He developed peritonitis and septicemia, his temperature soared, and he was in great pain. Gebhardt refused to operate to remove Heydrich's infected spleen.

Instead, he gave the patient large doses of morphine, blood transfusions, and an antibacterial sulfa drug to control infection.

On June 2 Himmler flew to Prague to visit the mortally ill Heydrich. During their conversation, Heydrich quoted from his father's fourth opera, *Amen*: "The world is just a barrel organ which the Lord God turns himself. We all have to dance to the tune which is already on the drum." Heydrich slipped into a coma and died at 4:30 A.M., June 4, 1942. He is buried in Section A of the Invalidenfriedhof in Berlin's Scharnhorststraße.[3] His grave is now unmarked. Cemetery authorities have removed the tombstones of many other prominent Nazis, because they became gathering points for neo-Nazi rallies.

The SS was ruthless in pursuing Heydrich's assassins. The Gestapo searched the home of Marie Moravec, who had helped the conspirators. Mrs. Moravec asked if she could go to the toilet. Once she had locked herself in, she swallowed a cyanide capsule. The Gestapo took her son, Ata Moravec, to the cellars of the Pecek Palace, where he was tortured for half a day. Then he was stupefied with alcohol and presented with his mother's head floating in a fish tank. Finally breaking down, he told his interrogators that the assassins might be in the catacombs of the Karel Boromejsky Church.

To force Kubis, Gabcik, and their accomplices from the church crypt, the Prague fire brigade pumped in water. The conspirators used their last bullets to kill themselves rather than be taken alive.

Nazi revenge against the Czechs followed swiftly. On June 9, the SS surrounded the village of Lidice, on the pretext that it had provided refuge for the assassins, and razed it; 199 adult males were shot; 191 women were sent to Ravensbrück concentration camp, where 50 of them were to die; and the village's 98 children were deported to Germany, where only 25 survived.

But this atrocity was not Heydrich's most terrible legacy to the twentieth century. Heydrich is also credited with the concept of the extermination camps, in particular the creation of the Sonderkommandos, groups of strong young Jews who on arrival in the killing centers were temporarily kept alive to clean, sort the victims' possessions, burn the corpses, bury the ashes, and efface the traces until, burnt out or at the Germans' whim, they too were gassed. Heydrich boasted that he had drawn the idea from his study of Egyptian history, where a similar need to preserve the secrets of the tombs of the Pharaohs found the same solution: the immediate death of all those who had

---

[3] *Other military leaders lie in the Invalidenfriedhof, among them Colonel General Max Hoffmann (1869–1927). Hoffman planned the 1914 Battle of Tannenberg, which resulted in the crushing defeat of the invading Russian army, the only significant German military victory of World War I. At the time, Field Marshal Paul von Hindenburg got the credit. But when Hoffmann later took vistors over the field of Tannenberg, he would tell them, "This is where the Field Marshal slept before the battle; here is where he slept after the battle; here is where he slept during the battle!"*

Top: Heinrich Himmler eulogizes the fallen Heydrich in the Mosaic Hall of the New Reich Chancellery, June 9, 1942. (Ullstein Bilderdienst)

Left: Reinhard Heydrich's grave. Heydrich was buried with military honors in Section A of the Invalidenfriedhof in Berlin's Scharnhorststraße. He lies next to General of the Infantry Count Tauentzien von Wittenberg, who fought against Napoleon in the wars of liberation. Heydrich was to have had a monumental tomb, designed by the architect Wilhelm Kreis and the sculptor Arno Breker. Because of the downhill course of the war, the tomb was never built. Heydrich's grave is now unmarked. The marker disappeared at the end of World War II. Cemetery authorities have removed the tombstones of many other prominent Nazis, such as Rudolf Heß, because they became gathering points for neo-Nazi rallies. (Bildarchiv Preußischer Kulturbesitz)

built them. In June 1942, a few weeks after Heydrich's own death, Himmler named the organization in occupied Poland, which administered the four extermination camps in which two and a half million Jews were to be gassed over the next sixteen months, the Aktion Reinhard in Heydrich's honor.

The British journalist Gitta Sereny interviewed Heydrich's nephew and godson Thomas, a well-known German cabaret artist who sings and recites, mostly from works by Jewish poets. Thomas Heydrich was eleven years old when his father's much-loved older brother was killed.

"I was very angry because at that time I was of course a passionate *Pimpf* [junior Hitler Youth]," he told Ms. Sereny, when she met him in 1990.

"He was a hero to us; we didn't know anything about politics, we only knew that he was a fantastic sportsman. And of course he was always in the papers, standing next to our idol, the Führer. I was sad because I knew my father would be very unhappy. My uncle was a very good, tender father," he said, thoughtfully. "It's almost a cliché now, isn't it, about these appalling men? But that doesn't make it any less true. One just doesn't like to think of it. Can you imagine? Tender?" He repeated the word bitterly.

Thomas Heydrich's family lived on the exclusive Prinzregentenstrasse in Berlin when he was small. The large house next door — "It had lovely big steps on which I played as a child" — belonged to Jews. "It was burned down during the Kristallnacht," he says. "I watched furniture being thrown out of a window, including a piano — imagine, a piano! I remember wondering why anybody would do this rather than calling the fire brigade. I mean, our family was musical, and I knew those neighbors were too. I asked, but was told to hush."

Thomas noticed placards on shops and park benches: Juden Verboten (Jews Forbidden). He despises the Nazi generation of Germans who insisted, to the end of their lives, that they knew nothing, saw nothing, and even suspected nothing reprehensible during the Nazi time.

"I saw all this, and everybody else did too. They are all liars," he said.

Thomas thinks his father, who was a journalist, began to have doubts in 1941. "He suddenly asked for a posting to the eastern front as a private in an army information unit," he said. "He was by nature a very happy, jolly sort of man. I adored him. Every time he came home on leave after this, he was more depressed. My mother often asked why he was so sad, and he would invariably answer, 'We'll talk about it after the war.'"

Thomas believes his father only found out the worst things his uncle had been responsible for after Reinhard Heydrich's assassination.

"There is a photograph of my father at my uncle's state funeral in June 1942, standing in his sergeant's uniform between Hitler and Göring. Later that day an officer came, bringing my father a thick letter from my uncle that had been found in his safe. He took it and went to his study. Hours later he came out, ashen-faced, with this sheaf of pages.

"He went into the kitchen, which still had an old wood stove, and burned them one by one, very slowly, almost like a ceremony. There must have been a hundred pages. We all stood there watching, and at the end, when he looked as if he was about to drop and my mother put her arms around him and asked him what was in the letter, he said, 'Don't ever ask. I can't talk about it, ever, not until it's all over.'"

Thomas feels sure that in the letter his uncle explained to his father everything he was planning and offered justification for everything he had done. Thomas's conviction stems from the fact that his father became as of then an active anti-Nazi, using the printing facilities available to him to produce passports and other papers to spirit people — most of them Jews — out of Germany. In late 1944, believing himself discovered, he wrote a good-bye letter to his family and shot himself.

The family never learned about his father's anti-Nazi activities until after the war, when a man who had worked with him told them. "We never knew whether he'd really been discovered," Thomas said, "but a prosecutor had come that evening and they'd spent all night in his study, talking. Soon after the man left, he killed himself." A trade-off, Thomas thinks: the suicide and the family's safety, rather than a scandalous treason trial of Reinhard Heydrich's brother. A few weeks after the end of the war, Thomas read what had been done and saw the photographs. As of that moment "and forever," he says, he carried his family's guilt. "I was, if you like, deputizing for all the others," he said, "my aunt, who, inconceivable as it is, felt proud of her husband; his three children, who, incomprehensibly to me, claim to feel nothing; my mother, who, having always instinctively disliked my uncle, was able to hide comfortably behind that early rejection.

"My father, who would have helped me shoulder this guilt, was no longer there. Somebody had to feel guilt for the devilish things my uncle had done."

Adolf Eichmann

Among the men who attended the Wannsee Conference, Americans and Israelis are most familiar with Adolf Eichmann. While Eichmann was incarcerated in Jerusalem, he was the subject of meticulous interrogation and study. His name will forever be synonymous with the mass murder of European Jews.

Eichmann was born in Solingen on March 19, 1906, the son of a bookkeeper for the Solingen Light and Power Company. The family moved to the Austrian city of Linz, where Eichmann grew up. Eichmann attended a vocational secondary school, where he studied engineering but never received a degree. From 1925 to 1933 he worked as a traveling salesman, his last employer being the Vacuum Oil Company (today the Mobil Oil Company).

On April 1, 1932, Eichmann joined the Austrian Nazi party as member number 889,895, and the SS as member 45,326. When the Austrian government banned these organizations on June 19, 1933, Eichmann decamped to Germany, where with other Austrian SS members he received military training. He was assigned to the SS camps in Lechfeld and Dachau, but he soon found them dreary.

His prospects improved when on October 1, 1934, he was assigned to the SD (Security Service) in Berlin under Reinhard Heydrich. The SD was the original Nazi organization and was becoming more influential. Eichmann's job was keeping track of Jews and Jewish organizations, both inside and outside of Germany, and planning the expulsion of the Jews from the Reich.

In 1937 Eichmann traveled with his superior, Herbert Hagen, to Alexandria and Cairo. Their mission was to evaluate the possibility of deporting German Jews to Palestine and to develop contacts with anti-Jewish Arab circles.

When Hitler annexed Austria in 1938, Eichmann became leader of the newly formed Central Office for Jewish Emigration in Vienna. His mission was to plunder Austria's Jews, rendering them destitute before forcibly expelling them. So effective were his tactics that Heydrich considered them a model to be used in other countries.

The eighty-two-year-old Sigmund Freud received the attentions of Eichmann's office. On their first visit to his home, Gestapo officers looted six thousand Austrian shillings from a safe, prompting Dr. Freud to observe that he had never taken so much for a first visit. Just before leaving Vienna for London on June 4, 1938, Freud remarked, "I can heartily recommend the Gestapo to anyone." Freud's four elderly sisters stayed behind and were murdered at Auschwitz.

In April 1939, Franz Walter Stahlecker, a former superior, summoned Eichmann to Prague. Eichmann's task was to oust Jews from Bohemia and Moravia. In the following months, Eichmann shuttled between Prague and Berlin, but he left his family in Austria, where they remained until the end of the war.

After Hitler overran Poland in September 1939, he determined to Germanize the conquered territory, converting it into a district of the Greater German Reich. Eichmann was put in charge of organizing the effort to drive out Jews and Poles. His first plan, submitted February 5, 1940, entitled "Emigration and Evacuation," later became infamous under the designation "IV B 4." By March 1, 1941, the plan bore the title "Jews and Evacuation Issues." In the meantime, the war had turned the trickle of emigrants into a torrent.

Eichmann's authority continued to broaden. He was responsible for depriving all forcibly evacuated German Jews of their citizenship, which was immediately forfeited when they were deported. Their money went to the Reich Treasury. Eichmann's large offices were now in the center of Berlin, on the Kurfürstenstraße. He was the boss of five SS officers of varied ranks, as well as secretaries and assistants.

As the leader of IV B 4, in 1940 and early 1941, Eichmann worked together with German railway officials to arrange for the transport of huge numbers of people, to whose fate Eichmann was completely indifferent. Among these people were tens of thousands of Poles and Jews, forcibly evacuated to the east under deplorable conditions. Eichmann made official trips to the conquered territories and knew, by his own observation, the results of his work.

A decisive turn in Eichmann's duties occurred after Hitler invaded the Soviet Union on June 22, 1941. Eichmann learned of Hitler's decision to begin murdering Jews, and he received the "Incident Reports" describing the massacres. He knew also that the transports he was organizing served to deliver the victims to their killers.

Before the Wannsee Conference, Heinrich Müller, Eichmann's boss, had sent him to inspect the murder sites. Eichmann witnessed shootings and, in Kulmhof, December 1941, the killing of Polish Jews from the Lodz ghetto in gas trucks.

"I saw the following," Eichmann testified in Jerusalem, "a room.... There were Jews in it. They had to undress, and then a sealed truck drove up. The doors were opened, it drove up to a kind of ramp. The naked Jews had to get in. Then the doors were closed and the truck drove off.... The whole time [the truck] was there, I didn't look inside. I couldn't. The screaming and.... I was much too shaken.... I drove after the truck...and there I saw the most horrible sight I had seen in all my life. [The truck] drove up to a fairly long trench. The doors were opened and corpses were thrown out. The limbs were as supple as if they'd been alive. Just thrown in. I can still see a civilian with pliers pulling out the teeth...."

Back in Berlin, Eichmann made a new determination of the number of Jews living in the Reich territory, to decide how many should be deported to the east or Theresienstadt. He hoped that by having an accurate census, he would be able to employ the available rail transport most efficiently. His success, in the case of victims not living in the Soviet Union, would depend on access to enough trains, careful preparation of timetables, and efficient Gestapo roundups. The killing in the death camps would also need to be accomplished with dispatch. Eichmann had no real desire to inspect the camps, but he had to understand the intricacies of the entire murder process. In 1944 he became more intimately involved when he went to Budapest to oversee special commandos, in league with Hungarian fascists, who were deporting Hungarian Jews to Auschwitz.

During the first Nuremberg trials in 1946, Eichmann's name came up many times, but the prosecutors thought he had died at the end of the war. In reality, he had acquired the uniform of an SS officer and also a pilot's outfit. He moved from Austria to Bavaria to a detention camp, where some of his fellow inmates recognized him. Nevertheless, he managed to escape to the Lüneburg Heath, near Hamburg, where he was a wood worker for the forest superintendent's office.

In 1950, Eichmann decided to leave Germany because he wanted to be reunited with his family, who were still living in Austria. He chose Argentina as his place of exile because many other Nazi criminals had hidden there. He traveled from Germany, through Austria to Genoa, to Italy, to Argentina along the "route of the rats," a well-trodden path followed by thousands of Nazis and their collaborators after the war. He sailed from Genoa to Buenos Aires with a passport identifying him as Ricardo Klement.[4] Two years later, his wife and sons joined him.

Eichmann worked in a Mercedes-Benz factory in central Buenos Aires and lived quietly in a suburb, Villa San Fernando. A neighbor, Cecilio Guillermo, remembered him as "a polite German who bought lots of pastries but didn't like to talk much. When they told us that he was a Nazi who had killed all those people, we didn't believe them."

Israeli Mossad agents kidnapped Eichmann on May 11, 1960, a chilly, rainy night, as he walked home from his commuter bus stop. One agent, Peter Z. Malkin, approached Eichmann and said, "One minute, sir." Suddenly, Malkin spun his quarry around by the shoulders, pinning his arms behind his back. Eichmann screamed. The two men fell into a ditch, where other agents grabbed Eichmann, shoved him into a car, and sped away. Years later,

---

[4] *Other émigrés were Dr. Josef Mengele, notorious for his horrifying human experiments at Auschwitz, and Erich Priebke, responsible for the massacre of 355 civilians in the Ardéatine caves north of Rome in 1944. Bishop Alois Hudal and the Argentine government under its president, Juan Peron (1946–1955), were the organizers.*

The Austrian-born Alois Hudal was director of the German College of Priests in Rome. When the Nazis deported more than one thousand Roman Jews to Auschwitz in 1944, Bishop Hudal, along with Axis diplomats in Rome, had discouraged Pope Pius XII from mounting even a mild protest. Hudal, not surprisingly, had been a great proponent of the Nuremberg laws.

Convents and other Catholic religious institutions received the fleeing former Nazis. They received passports from the International Red Cross at the recommendation of the Vatican, or from the Argentine government, which had issued more that eight thousand blank passports. Argentine consulates in Switzerland, Italy, or Spain processed the visas according to lists Buenos Aires had furnished.

An ex-Nazi, Walter Rauff, opened a center in Genoa for receiving the émigrés in 1945. Rauff, a former specialist in mobile gas chambers, finally emigrated to Chile in 1949.

In Buenos Aires, a special division of the bureau of immigration, called the Peralta Commission, received the ex-Nazi fugitives. Three close associates of Juan Peron—Carlos Fuldner, an ex-Nazi officer; Jacques de Mahieu, a Frenchman, formerly of the Charlemagne Division; and Branko Benzon, a Croat—chose the candidates for immigration from lists the Vatican furnished. The Argentines were eager for scientists and specialists who could participate in economic expansion of the country.

Malkin commented, "All I was thinking was, don't let him get away, because then you'll be known as the guy who had his hands on Adolf Eichmann and let him slip away."

The Mossad agents hid Eichmann in a house, handcuffed to a bed. There Malkin interrogated him, as he recounted in his book, *Eichmann in My Hands*:

> "I love children," [Eichmann] put it to me one night early on, smiling almost dreamily.
>
> "You love children?" I shot back, unable to help myself. "You must mean some children."
>
> "No, I love all children."
>
> "Do you?" Once again I found myself struggling for self control in his presence.
>
> "Look," he replied evenly, daring to broach the subject himself, "perhaps to you it seems as if I hate Jews. I don't. I was never an anti-Semite. I was always repulsed by Streicher and the *Sturmer* crowd." The reference was to the most primitive racist ideologue at the top echelons of Nazism and his venomous magazine. In fact, he continued, "I have always been fond of Jews. I had Jewish friends. When I was touring Haifa, I made a point of finding Jewish taxi drivers. I always liked Jews better than the Arabs...."
>
> I paused, almost unable to contain myself. "My sister's boy, my favorite playmate, he was just your son's age. Also blond and blue-eyed, just like your son. And you killed him."
>
> Perplexed by the observation, he actually waited a moment to see if I would clarify it. "Yes," he said finally, "but he was Jewish, wasn't he?"

Eleven days after the abduction, the Israeli agents spirited Eichmann out of Argentina illegally in an El Al airplane. The Israeli action led the Argentine government to mount a vigorous protest in the United Nations Security Council, June 22, 1960. The lively debate engendered considerable controversy over old Nazis still living in West and East Germany.

Eichmann in Jerusalem

An Israeli captain, Avner Less, interrogated Eichmann and recorded the proceedings on tape. Born on Prager Straße in Berlin in 1916, Less had been educated in German schools until he fled to Paris in 1933. He emigrated to Palestine with his Hamburg-born wife in 1938. His father was deported to the east in January 1943, in one of the last transports to leave Berlin.

Less was disappointed when he first saw Adolf Eichmann at 4:45 P.M., May 29, 1960. The prisoner was a thin, balding, utterly ordinary-looking man in a khaki shirt, trousers, and open sandals. (German men have a preternatural fondness for open sandals.) Eichmann looked nothing like a Hollywood movie Nazi.

Moreover, he was a bundle of nerves. The left half of his face twitched. He hid his trembling hands under the table. Because he was a heavy smoker, Less made sure Eichmann had plenty of cigarettes. The jailers had taken away his glasses, and Less had to arrange for a new pair with plastic lenses.

After about a week, Eichmann recovered his composure. But he did have one moment of panic a few days later, when he thought his last hour had arrived. The officer of the guard had stepped into the room and informed the prisoner that he had come to escort him to the judge. Terrified, Eichmann rose to his feet. As one of the guards blindfolded him, to prevent his getting an overall view of the prison compound, his knees buckled. "But Herr Hauptmann [captain]," he bleated, "I haven't told you everything yet." Less reassured the frightened man that he was only being taken to a justice of the peace for renewal of his order of detention, after which the interrogation would continue. Eichmann immediately recovered his soldierly demeanor and marched out of the room flanked by two guards.

Eichmann's German was atrocious. Although a native German speaker, Less had great difficulty understanding the jargon of the Nazi bureaucracy rendered in a mixed Berlin-Austrian accent, further garbled by Eichmann's fondness for endlessly complicated sentences, in which he himself occasionally became lost.

Even Eichmann's German attorney had difficulty understanding his client. Because no Israeli lawyer would defend Eichmann, the parliament ordered that a foreigner be engaged. The eventual choice was a lawyer from Cologne, Dr. Robert Servatius. During the Nuremberg trials, Servatius had defended Fritz Sauckel, who went to the gallows for his treatment of slave laborers.

After Servatius's first visit, Eichmann told Less: "Herr Hauptmann, do you know what Dr. Servatius said? He objected to my German. He said, 'You'll have to relearn your language. Even the best translator won't be able to find his way through those convoluted sentences of yours.' Is my German actually that bad, Herr Hauptmann?" When Less agreed that it was, Eichmann was offended.

Less was struck by Eichmann's complete lack of humor. On the rare occasions when Eichmann's razor-thin lips broke into a smile, his eyes remained mirthless. His expression was sardonic, often aggressive.

Eichmann's cell, which measured ten by thirteen feet, was furnished with a cot, a table, and a chair. Every day the prisoner cleaned the cell and the adjoining toilet and shower room with thoroughness and dedication.

Elaborate precautions were taken to prevent Eichmann from committing suicide. A guard sat in the cell with him day and night. Outside the cell door sat a second guard, who watched the first guard through a peephole and made sure there was no contact between the guard and Eichmann. A third guard, in a vestibule outside the door, constantly watched the second guard. An electric light was left on all night. When the light disturbed his sleep, Eichmann would pull his woolen blanket over his head, whereupon the guard would pull it back, to be certain the prisoner was not trying to kill himself under the blanket.

None of the guards spoke either of Eichmann's two languages, German or Spanish, but their officers spoke at least one. To prevent any act of revenge, no one who had lost family members in the Holocaust was chosen for the guard unit.

When Less interrogated Eichmann, the officer responsible for Eichmann's transfer from his cell to the interrogation room entered first, followed by two guards with Eichmann between them. Eichmann stood at attention behind his chair until Less asked him to be seated. Though Less had told Eichmann that there was no need to stand at attention, Eichmann went on doing so throughout his incarceration.

Eichmann's military formality didn't stop there. When on January 1, 1961, Less mentioned that a new year had begun, Eichmann replied, "Herr Hauptmann, may I take the liberty of wishing you a happy New Year?" And he performed a sort of seated bow and clicked his heels under the table.

Eichmann was indicted on February 1, 1961. The chief prosecutor, Gideon Hausner, initially introduced thirteen hundred documents in evidence, to which three hundred were later added.

Eichmann's prosecution in Jerusalem was the world's first televised trial.

The rapt courtroom spectators, mostly Israelis, found it hard to listen to the gruesome details of their families' fates but were unable to turn away. Occasionally there was an outburst from an onlooker who couldn't bear any more. A prosecutor broke off his examination of a man who had just told of his last glimpse of his young daughter, a speck of red in a mass of women and children marked for extermination; the prosecutor was silenced by thoughts of what it would be like to watch his own daughter vanish.

Seated in a bulletproof glass booth, Eichmann showed no reaction to the horrors he was hearing. Head tilted, lips tight, twisted mouth moving as though he were tasting something very disagreeable, he looked to the *New York Times*' Walter Goodman like a silent movie actor playing a vil-

Adolf Eichmann on trial in Jerusalem. (Ullstein Bilderdienst)

lain. Was this really the man in SS uniform witnesses remembered, hand on pistol, barking orders?

During the trial's climax, when Eichmann took the stand, his testimony was a grim travesty of what had happened. He "sought peaceful solutions acceptable to both parties," he said. He complimented himself on having paid a rabbi to teach him Hebrew, rather than forcing the rabbi to give him free lessons.

After the Wannsee Conference, Eichmann testified, he sat "cozily around a fireplace" with Heydrich and Gestapo chief Heinrich Müller, drinking French cognac and chatting. "At that moment, I sensed a kind of Pontius Pilate feeling, for I was free of all guilt.... Who was I to judge? Who was I to have my own thoughts in this matter?" He, Heydrich, and Müller were only carrying out the law, decreed by the Führer.

Eichmann sought to portray himself as an uninfluential shipping clerk who had no responsibility whatsoever for the fate of his human freight. In fact, he controlled the final solution from a desk in Berlin. But he insisted that he was upset by the sight of blood. "I was not the right man for these things." The exasperated prosecutor replied, "If you want to be a laughing-stock, do so." Undeterred, Eichmann averred that he was "on the lowest rung," that his "position was too insignificant." His oft-repeated mantra was, "I had to obey."

"Humanity does not know how to punish people like this," remarked one Israeli.

Convicted and sentenced to death by hanging, his plea for mercy rejected by the court, Eichmann was executed in Rameleh Prison, Tel Aviv, May 31, 1962. He was cremated and his ashes scattered in the sea. An Auschwitz survivor, watching the dispersal of the remains, remembered that the heaps of human ashes from the camp crematoria were spread over the icy paths so that the guards would not slip on patrol.

Hannah Arendt (1906–1975), the German-born U.S. political philosopher, covered the trial for *The New Yorker* and later produced a book about it, *Eichmann in Jerusalem: A Report on the Banality of Evil.* In her epilogue, she wrote: "The trouble with Eichmann was precisely that so many were like him, and that the many were neither perverted nor sadistic, that they were, and still are, terribly and terrifyingly normal. From the viewpoint of our legal institutions and of our moral standards of judgment, this normality was much more terrifying than all the atrocities put together."

In addition to Heydrich and Eichmann, historians have extensively chronicled the life of Under State Secretary Martin Luther. The Foreign Office, which Luther represented, was chiefly responsible for the annihilation of millions of Jews living outside of Germany. Although there is no formal biography of Luther, many details of his surprising career are recorded. He was a little entrepreneur with organizational talent who rose to occupy a high diplomatic post in the Nazi regime before ending up in a concentration camp.

Details of the lives of some of the other officials who attended the Wannsee Conference are known because they were arrested and tried. American, British, or Polish tribunals convicted and sentenced Josef Bühler, Otto Hofmann, Wilhelm Stuckart, Eberhard Schöngarth, and others.

Results of the Wannsee Conference

On January 30, 1942, ten days after the Wannsee Conference and nine years to the day since he had become German Chancellor, Adolf Hitler spoke to the Reichstag in the Kroll Opera House in Berlin. He had probably received reports of the Wannsee Conference as well as of the murder of Jews in the east. Expounding on one of his favorite topics, the fate of the Jews in the coming war, he said: "For the first time the old Jewish law will be applied: an eye for an eye, a tooth for a tooth. The more this war spreads, the more anti-Semitism will spread. Let world Jewry take note. In each prison, in each family which has made sacrifices, there will be nourishment from this explanation. The hour will come when the most evil world enemy of all times, at least a millennium, will have played out his role."

This passage, quoted in the *Völkischer Beobachter* the next day, is somewhat confused. Presumably Hitler was referring to unnamed Aryan families and jailed Aryans. But he was obviously trying to explain the mounting toll of battle deaths. According to Hitler, the fathers, brothers, and sons were falling in the war against the Jewish enemy. The helpless, pathetic figures Germans saw being herded into boxcars in their cities and towns were "the most evil world enemy of all times."

The deportations proceeded with clockwork efficiency. All households got written instructions as to what and how much a person was permitted to carry: one backpack with provisions, mess kit, spoon, two blankets, warm clothing, and heavy shoes, maximum total weight twenty-five kilograms, no knives or scissors. Valuables had to be turned in, other property registered, house keys surrendered. A waiting truck carried the Jews to a place of assembly or directly to the railroad station.

The trains had twenty freight cars, all windows fastened shut, two passenger cars for the guards. Carrying a thousand Jews, the trains left frequently from Berlin, Warsaw, Amsterdam, Paris, Prague, Budapest, Oslo, and Athens. Though exhausted from a journey that lasted several days, sleepless, thirsty, dirty, and desperate, the deportees were shown no mercy.

At first, people meekly complied with the order to present themselves with their baggage for "resettlement." The Reich Security Main Office made the arrangements. SS men combed through entire districts to fill the trains, using the ruse that the deportees were being sent to Poland to "work." But when rumors began to emerge from the camps, young people tried to hide, while many of the sick and elderly opted for suicide. In 1943 Martha Liebermann, the eighty-five-year-old widow of artist Max Liebermann, poisoned herself when she learned the Gestapo was coming for her.

Transit camps were the first stop for the Jews of western Europe. Here they were interned preceding deportation. Most of the camps had been built before the war to hold refugees from Germany. Even prior to the German invasion, they existed in Holland (Westerbork and Hertogenbosch), France, Hungary, and Romania. They were constructed later in Belgium (Malines), Italy (Fossoli), and Yugoslavia.

Many of the original camps were in France. The first internees were a half million refugees from Spain: Spanish soldiers, civilians, and members of international brigades, who sought asylum after Franco's victory. In late 1939 the French interned thousands of antifascists and all Jewish refugees from Germany and Austria as "enemy aliens."

At first, the Ministry of Defense and the Ministry of the Interior had jurisdiction over the French camps, but the French police soon took them over. The camp food was bad, drinking water scarce, accommodations inadequate, and hygiene poor. Epidemics were rife; in the camp at Gurs, twelve hundred people perished. The other French camps—Les Milles, Le Vernet, Rivesaltes, St. Cyprien, Compiègne, Pithiviers, Beaune-la-Rolande, and Drancy—were not much better. After Hitler's victory over France in June 1940, the French transferred more Jews to the camps before their shipment to extermination camps in Poland.

At the time of the Wannsee Conference, the gas chambers at Auschwitz, the largest extermination and concentration camp, were unfinished. The first ones had been built and tested on September 3, 1941, in the cellar of Block 11, the punishment block, in the main camp. A powerful insecticide, Zyklon B, was poured from metal canisters into airtight rooms. The guinea pigs were six hundred Soviet prisoners and sick concentration camp inmates. The murderers considered their experiment successful.

Between March and July 1942, the Germans built new Polish extermination camps at Belzec, Sobibor, and Treblinka. Himmler assigned Odilo Globocnik, SS and Police Chief of the Lublin District, the job of destroying Jews. Assisting Globocnik were four hundred fifty men, among them ninety-two "experts" who had already murdered seventy thousand sick adults and retarded children in Germany.

The Germans tried to disguise their crimes by setting up the death camps at a safe distance from nearby villages, but always adjoining a rail line. All of the death camps had gas chambers, but not all had crematoria. A special commando unit of twenty men ran each camp, with ninety to one hundred twenty

Ukrainian, Latvian, or Lithuanian guards and a work gang of several hundred Jews. The Jewish work gang dragged the corpses from the gas chambers, pulled gold teeth, buried the looted bodies, and collected clothing and baggage. Because they were witnesses, these Jews were killed after a few weeks and replaced by others. The Germans kept careful track of the value they extracted from each liquidated Jew.

Himmler designated Auschwitz in the summer of 1941 as the principal extermination site. Constructed in 1940 for political prisoners, the main camp was augmented by two additional camps, Birkenau and Monowitz. Eight thousand slave laborers died during construction.

Auschwitz was a true death factory. Four installations, with gas chambers and crematoria, transformed ordinary murder into industrialized killing. A rail connection to the camp delivered thousands of victims and transported their possessions back to Germany. Seven hundred inmates sorted out cash for the Reichsbank, clothing and shoes for winter relief. Even hair and bone ash were recycled.

The guards immediately killed the old, the handicapped, pregnant women, very young children, and anyone wearing glasses. SS doctors selected young men and women in good health for forced labor. But most people arriving were murdered immediately. By the end of the war, a million and a half people had died at Auschwitz.

The selection process did not determine life and death; rather, it determined the time of death. The men and women not killed immediately were slaves worked to exhaustion, a process the SS called "annihilation through labor." The slaves were hired out for three to four marks per diem to German companies. By late 1944, this labor was bringing in more than fifty million marks a month to the Reich treasury.

A minuscule fraction of this money went to the workers themselves. They were inadequately fed and subjected to fetid sanitary conditions, hours of roll calls in the harshest weather, and horrifying punishments. Sadistic guards withheld food and confined their prisoners in cells too small to sit in; they beat the captives publicly and whipped them on the way to the gallows.

Most people could survive three to six months at most. If they did not die of despair or commit suicide, they could be found incapable of work and killed with a phenol injection or sent to the gas chamber. The only chance of survival was a job in the camp administration, the infirmary, or the kitchen.

Besides their triage function, SS doctors carried out gruesome, lethal medical experiments on prisoners. They tried bone transplants and inflicted ghastly wounds. Dr. Josef Mengele infected twin children with typhus and later had them killed.

Especially controversial were the Dachau studies of hypothermia, done to establish the most effective treatment for crew members of the German air force shot down in the icy waters of the North Sea. Dr. Sigmund Rascher, an SS captain who did these bestial human trials, also collected prisoners' skin for making saddles, riding breeches, and ladies' handbags. Himmler, who strongly supported the hypothermia research, had Rascher executed in 1944 on charges of kidnapping, financial irregularities, and the murder of a German assistant.

Rascher's research was poorly designed, fraudulent, and riddled with errors. Nevertheless, to the consternation of biomedical ethicists, Rascher is occasionally cited in modern studies of hypothermia.

In October 1942 Himmler ordered that all concentration camps be rendered "free of Jews." But the deteriorating war economy forced the SS to send many Jewish prisoners back to Germany to work in armament production.

The Jews who remained behind were not always passive victims. In April 1943, the largest Jewish armed uprising broke out in the Warsaw ghetto. People who had lived through the deportations of the previous summer and had survived as factory workers found they were to be taken away with their families. The SS thought the fighting would last for three days, but in fact it went on for a month. When the battle was over, SS troops with machine guns, flame throwers, mortars, and field artillery had killed fifty-six thousand Jews. The SS commander, Oberführer (Brigadier General) Jürgen Stroop, wrote triumphantly in his final report, "The Jewish quarter of Warsaw is no more." Stroop was hanged March 6, 1952.

After the calamitous German surrender at Stalingrad on February 2, 1943, it was obvious that Hitler was losing the war. As a consequence, the murderers tried to efface all traces of their crimes. They razed the death camps at Belzec, Treblinka, and Sobibor. They destroyed the gas chambers, plowed up the grounds, built farm houses, and planted shrubs. Himmler created "Special Commando 1005" to eliminate all mass graves next to the camps. Jewish prisoners dug up the corpses, burned them on gigantic pyres, ground the remaining bones, and scattered the ashes. To get rid of witnesses, the SS then shot the prisoners. But Himmler's scheme failed. There were too many graves and the German retreat too precipitous. Advancing westward, the Red Army found pit after pit full of corpses.

As the German position on the battlefields deteriorated, the Nazi genocide increased swiftly. In June 1944, as the Allies landed on the Normandy beaches, the SS deported almost half a million Hungarian Jews to Auschwitz. By August, the U.S. Army was in Paris, but the Auschwitz gas chambers continued to consume victims until October, and the camp was not liberated by Soviet soldiers until January 27, 1945. The SS had already driven fifty-eight thousand Auschwitz prisoners on death marches west, but had no time to shoot the sick and those too weak to march. The Russians found 600 dead and 7,650 survivors, among them 100 children left alive for medical experiments.

With the Allied armies closing in from all sides, the SS herded the help-less camp inmates into Germany. Those unable to march were killed on the spot. In freezing weather, the brutal guards drove huge lines of captives along the roads in forced marches, shooting anyone who collapsed. Other prison-ers were transported by freight car from one camp to another, dying at an appalling rate from cold and starvation. Many ended up in the Bergen-Belsen camp, where there was no food and epidemics were rife. Tens of thousands died in the days just before liberation, among them the diarist Anne Frank.

The Allied soldiers who liberated the camps witnessed scenes of unmit-igated horror. Thousands upon thousands of the prisoners lay dead or dying. "Behind the barbed wire and the electric fence," wrote journalist Martha Gell-horn of Dachau, "the skeletons sat in the sun and searched themselves' for lice. They have no age and no faces; they all look alike and like nothing you will ever see if you are lucky."

Many of the dying, too weak to call out for help, perished among piles of corpses. All told, the Nazis had murdered six million Jews, a million in camps and ghettos, another million in mass executions, and the remainder in gas chambers. This appalling crime was the legacy of the Wannsee Confer-ence.

A Victim's Tale

The Nazis did not like to kill prominent Jews. They established the Theresienstadt ghetto for these Jews, as a showplace to impress and deceive visitors from abroad. Ernst Kaltenbrunner, head of the Reich Security Main Office, later confirmed at Nuremberg that "special care was taken not to deport Jews with connections and important acquaintances in the outside world." Less prominent Jews were murdered in droves, but those whose disappear-ance might create unpleasant inquiries were generally left alone. Anne Frank is probably Hitler's most prominent victim, but she did not become famous until her father, Otto Frank, published her diary two years after her death.

Jewish or Christian, almost all well-known German writers fled. So many ended up living in southern California that locals began referring to Pacific Palisades as Weimar by the sea. Vicki Baum (*Grand Hotel*), Erich Maria Remarque (*All Quiet on the Western Front*), Thomas Mann (*The Magic Moun-tain, Death in Venice*), Franz Werfel (*The Song of Bernadette*), Heinrich Mann (*The Blue Angel*), Bertolt Brecht (*The Three Penny Opera, Mother Courage*), and Lion Feuchtwanger (*Jew Süss*) all lived within a few miles of one another. But one eminent German writer, Else Ury, a beloved author of children's books, did not get out.

A recent survey of German women revealed that 55 percent had read Ury's Nesthäkchen books. Even more had heard them read over the radio or had seen the television serialization. But like the wild west books of Karl May, the Nesthäkchen books have not traveled well. An English translation in the late 1930s was a complete failure, and a Dutch translation a few years earlier was hardly more successful. Yet in German-speaking countries, the Nesthäkchen series is a perennial best seller. As of 1992, seven million copies were in print. German bookstores invariably reserve a special rack in the children's department for Ury's Nesthäkchen books.

Else Ury was born in Berlin, November 1, 1877, the third child of third-generation Berlin merchant Jews. Her large, well-to-do, close-knit bourgeois family provided a loving environment. The experiences of her own happy childhood, as well as her observation of the growth of her sisters, brothers, nephews, and nieces, inspired Else Ury to later write her family and youth books.

Her grandfather, Levin Elias Ury, was director of the synagogue in the Heidereutergasse in central Berlin. Her parents, who lived in Charlottenberg, were no more religious than most of the Christians in the neighborhood. But the Urys never hid their Jewish origins.

One older brother, Ludwig, studied law, while another, Hans, studied medicine, and Else's younger sister Käthe became a teacher. Although women's needs for education and a profession to secure independence were later a recurring theme in her books, Else Ury herself pursued no professional studies.

In 1900 Else Ury began publishing travel reports and stories in the *Vossiche Zeitung*, a Berlin newspaper, under a pen name. Because a father was supposed to support his unmarried daughters, if a girl still living at home earned money by writing, social convention forced her to disguise her identity.

Else's father, Emil Ury, was a tobacco products manufacturer who produced snuff and chewing tobacco. When cigarette popularity soared around the turn of the century, snuff and chewing tobacco sales declined precipitously. Faced with economic ruin, Emil Ury tried to prevail upon Else to marry the son of a rich cigarette manufacturer, with the hope that a merger of the two family companies would follow. But Else resisted this scheme and remained single her entire life.

In 1906 Else Ury had her first modest literary success with *Educated Girl*, a novel dealing with the very controversial subject of higher education for women. Indeed, regular women's university studies were first permitted in Prussia only in 1908. Although Emil Ury's business had gone bankrupt, Else was able to help support her family with book royalties.

Her breakthrough to best seller status came with her Nesthäkchen books. Germans call a spoiled child or family pet a Nesthäkchen. Else Ury's Nesthäkchen is a Berlin doctor's daughter, Annemarie Braun, a slim, gorgeous, golden blond, quintessential German girl. The ten-book series follows Annemarie from infancy (*Nesthäkchen and Her Dolls*) to old age and grandchildren (*Nesthäkchen with White Hair*). Despite Else Ury's Jewish background, she makes no references to Judaism in the Nesthäkchen books.

In the fourth and most popular volume of the series, *Nesthäkchen and the World War*, published in 1922, ten-year-old Annemarie returns home from a summer vacation in 1914 to find her family dispersed. Mother Braun, on a visit to England, cannot come back because of the outbreak of war. Dr. Braun has become an army doctor with the German troops in France. Grandmother has moved in to care for the three small children. Annemarie experiences the first thrill of victory when Ludendorff captures the Belgian fortress city of Liege. One night in her bed, she prays, "Dear God, let my dear mommy come back soon to Berlin, but not the hateful Russians. And please take care of my father in the war.... Please help us Germans, dear God. And if you don't want to help us, then please don't help the others either — at least stay neutral."

The book is not chauvinistic and is filled with Else Ury's quirky humor. An Asian man lives in Nesthäkchen's apartment building, and she takes him for Japanese. When Japan enters the war against Germany, she vows to avenge herself on this enemy. She stops saying hello to the man. When he sends her a little gift of chocolates, she spits on them. Then she discovers that her neighbor is from Thailand, not Japan.

Six years after publication, *Nesthäkchen and the World War* had sold 160,000 copies. Else Ury wrote the fifth and sixth volumes, *Nesthäkchen's Teenage Years* and *Nesthäkchen Flies From the Nest* in 1923. She intended to stop there, with Nesthäkchen's marriage, but her readers simply wouldn't let her. Distraught girls inundated her Berlin publisher, Meidingers Jugendschriften Verlag, with a flood of letters pleading for more Nesthäkchen stories. Else Ury obliged her young fans with four more Nesthäkchen books.

On November 1, 1927, Else Ury's fiftieth birthday, Meidingers Jugendschriften Verlag gave her a large reception and announced the publication of an expensively bound new edition of all ten Nesthäkchen books. The series had been an immense success, and even the head of the company, Kurt Meidinger, was on hand to praise Else Ury and her work. The Adlon Hotel, the most elegant in Berlin, catered the affair, which was attended by many reporters and chronicled in German newspapers the next day. In the meantime, Meidingers had established a special post office box for Nesthäkchen correspondence. Readers sent both letters and pictures they had drawn for the stories. Else Ury answered all mail monthly and, from time to time, held parties for her Nesthäkchenkinder, with cake and chocolate, in the garden of her house. Many of the parties were the subject of newspaper stories.

Despite her literary success, Else Ury lived very quietly and didn't consider the details of her own life to be especially noteworthy. In 1926, with money from her books, she bought a vacation house in the Riesengebirge area of Krummhübel, which she named "House Nesthäkchen." Here she and her family spent many summer and winter vacations.

In Else Ury's last book, *Youth to the Fore*, published in 1933, she tried to put a good face on Hitler's rise to power. The book dealt with overcoming the economic crisis and unemployment, restoring order with a firm hand, and strengthening Germany. No one is certain whether Ury was politically naive and had been seduced by Nazi propaganda, or whether her publisher, to please the regime, had obediently altered the text. But Else Ury had not depicted Nazi symbols in her book.

As a Jew, Else Ury was excluded from the Reich Chamber of Writers in 1935, which meant she was no longer allowed to publish. By 1936 most of her relatives had emigrated, and her brother Hans had committed suicide. She herself did not want to leave Germany, because she had to care for her ninety-year-old mother, Franziska, who in photographs bears a remarkable resemblance to Sigmund Freud's mother, Amalie. Else Ury traveled to London in 1938 for a short visit to her nephew, Klaus Heymann. She returned to Berlin and stayed until the Nazis deported her. Her mother died in 1940.

Until 1933 Else Ury lived in Kantstrasse 30, then at Kaiserdamm 24. In 1939 she was forced to move to a "Jew house," a former Jewish old-age home in Solingerstraße 10, where the Gestapo collected Jews for deportation. On January 6, 1943, she had to fill out a declaration of all her possessions and, with one valise and a few articles of clothing, report for resettlement. She was ordered to present herself at a collection point, Großer Hamburgerstraße 26, to wait for transport. On January 11, 1943, she signed a release, turning over all her property to the German Reich. German officials proceeded to sell off everything she owned.

On January 12, 1943, the sixty-five-year-old Else Ury was taken to the railroad station at Berlin Grunewald, along with 1,190 other Berlin Jews, and deported to Auschwitz-Birkenau. A day later, SS doctors selected 127 men from her transport for labor. SS guards murdered Else Ury and the other Jews in the gas chambers.

After 1945 Else Ury's books were heavily edited and many contemporaneous or historical references removed. In 1983 there was a six-part television serialization of the Nesthäkchen books. Finally, half a century after her death, her millions of women readers learned the details of her dreadful fate.

A group of high school students from the Robert Blum Gymnasium in Berlin-Schöneberg discovered the exact date of Else Ury's death on a visit to Auschwitz in 1995. They also found there her battered valise, labeled with her name and Berlin address. The valise, on loan from Auschwitz, and other objects and documents relating to her life were placed on exhibit in the Wannsee Villa in Berlin. They are heartbreaking to see.

Of all the millions of murders the Nazis committed, Else Ury's stands out. Could anyone imagine the British murdering A. A. Milne a few years after he had written *Winnie the Pooh?*

A Survivor's Tale

New York City is a Holocaust survivors' enclave. There were once so many German Jewish refugees living in the Washington Heights section of upper Manhattan that the neighborhood was known as the Fourth Reich. Henry Kissinger's mother lived there for fifty-eight years in the same apartment until her death at age ninety-seven in 1998. She refused to leave the neighborhood, even after her husband's death, when her son asked her to move in with him and his wife downtown.

Survivors have poignant stories. The director Steven Spielberg is videotaping every surviving one for his Shoah Foundation.

Sam Cohen, doyen of the Zabar's appetizing department store, told his story to New York *Daily News* columnist Vic Ziegel. Cohen was surrounded by rows of schmaltz herring, whitefish, baked salmon, sturgeon, brook trout, pickled lox, gefilte fish, matjes herring, smoked salmon, Greek olives, and tins of caviar. He was busily slicing and selling.

"That's all you want, a quarter-pound?" he said to one customer. "You wanna taste a little?" The customer, delighted, replied, "Sure," and Cohen handed her a small, pink morsel. Hooked and reeled in, she added a quarter pound to her order.

A reluctant buyer, a snowy-haired man, holding a prepackaged container of herring in sour cream very close to Cohen's face, demanded if it was fresh. Cohen was incredulous. "Is it fresh? What are you talking about?" he retorted. "It's all fresh. You're at Zabar's." The same man wanted the olives, but the price, $4.95 a pound, made him hesitate. "You wanna taste one?" Cohen asked.

Cohen was at Zabar's four days a week, twenty-six hours, always in the same place, never far from the lox. He used to work a sixty-hour week, but he doesn't need a full week anymore. His son is a doctor, his daughter a dentist, the tuition no longer a difficulty. He didn't need a new car because he never learned to drive.

In his forty-fifth year at Zabar's, the customers knew him and sought him out. A regular wanted "a big piece" of gefilte fish, and when her request ended there, Cohen, the gefilte maven, took over. "You want juice," he asked, "or you don't want?" She wanted.

It was difficult to picture him doing anything else, but, Cohen said, selling fish was never in his plans. He came to America from Poland in 1950 after what he called, almost casually, "eleven years of torture."

Before World War II, Cohen lived in Druskininkai, a summer resort known for its mud and salt baths and for being the birthplace of the sculptor Jacques Lipchitz. Druskininkai is two hundred eighty kilometers northeast of Warsaw, in southern Lithuania, near the Belarussian and Polish borders.

Cohen was a bookkeeper, the secretary of a small bank, an officer in the synagogue, and the president of a Zionist group. Also, he sold feed. Because the summer guests lived in wooden villas, a Warsaw insurance company used Cohen to help market their fire coverage. A brother and sister left for America in the mid-1920s, "but I wasn't anxious to go," he said. "I had a life, my literature, my culture. I wasn't a big shot, but I didn't have any complaints. Then came Hitler."

The Germans forced the Jews in Druskininkai to live in a two-block ghetto. Then they were moved to a camp. "A kind of concentration camp you don't hear so much about," he said. "It wasn't a death camp like Auschwitz. For me, Auschwitz would have been next."

He met a man in the camp, "a butcher, who knew the woods. He was a brave fellow, but a little crazy. Maybe that's what it takes to be brave." When the butcher used a pair of scissors to cut the camp's wire fence, he took Cohen with him into the woods.

"I was running, and the bullets were like this," Cohen said. He parted his hair. "Deep, deep into the woods. God knows where. Every day they followed us, and we walked 20, 25 miles a day. At night, we went out for food."

They found a cave and were living inside it with a third man, a tailor. "He didn't have boots," Cohen said. "But he was a tailor, so he let out his coat to keep his feet warm." When the Germans found their hiding place, "We had to run away, but the tailor couldn't run. He didn't have shoes, and his coat was too long. They caught him and killed him."

For a while, Cohen stayed with a Lithuanian family. "The son was a killer; he killed a neighbor," Cohen said. "He used to go out and ambush Germans. He liked to kill. Until they killed him."

The advancing Russian Army captured Cohen after two years in the woods. They sent him to Siberia. "My seven brothers and sisters died," he said. "From my town only five Jewish people survived."

Cohen came to the US with $3, and it wasn't long before he was behind a counter. "To sell fish, you don't have to know much English," he told columnist Ziegel. "You don't have to be an intellectual. I'm a very friendly person. I love people."

The people stood in front of him, across the glass, and enjoyed him. The packaged salmon on the shelves was much cheaper than the fish Cohen sliced and sold. But the package couldn't talk to customers, the way Cohen had for all these years: "I'm giving you the best cut. You wanna taste?" Sam Cohen died October 14, 1999, age 86.

War and Holocaust:
The View from the Berlin Morgue

At Hanoverstraße Number 6, adjacent to the Dorotheenstadt Cemetery, stands the century-old Institut für gerichtliche Medizin der Humboldt Universität zu Berlin, the Berlin Morgue. During the Nazi era, the morgue pathologists, staff members of the celebrated Charité Hospital, recorded autopsy protocols that offer a kaleidoscopic view of the darkest pages of German history.

By the end of the 1930s, rampant German anti-Semitism was clearly reflected in the protocols. Among the Jews, a devastating suicide epidemic broke out. With sleeping pills, nooses, and leaps, they evaded persecution and deportation. Even the Jewish pathologist, Paul Fraenckel, who was for a short time the Berlin coroner, committed suicide.

The pathologists did meticulous autopsies, as was their wont, on each suicide victim. The Jewish ones are simple to identify. After January 1, 1939, by Hitler's decree, all Jewish men had to adopt the middle name Israel, and women the middle name Sara.

"Walter Israel Weidenreich, merchant, born April 22, 1913, received January 8, 1942. Cause of death: overdose of sleeping pills."

On January 11, 1942, a randomly chosen day, of twelve bodies brought to the morgue, six were Jewish suicides. In August 1942, of three hundred eighty decedents, eighty-nine were Jewish, of which only four died of natural causes. But in the protocol books, there is no indication that Jews were ending up on the autopsy tables because they were Jews. Every case had only an identifying number.

While the trains rolled to Auschwitz, Berlin criminals continued to kill Jews. One miscreant murdered, robbed, and dismembered Vera Korn and her daughter Eva in November 1942. He was executed in 1944.

Sometimes the protocols indicate that Nazi officials were the murderers. For example, thirty-one slave laborers from the Netherlands and Belgium, working for the Steinruck Company in Berlin, were shot on June 4, 1943, in Tegel, a suburb now known for its airport. The corpses were sent to the morgue for documentation of wounds.

Bodies of concentration camp inmates from nearby Sachsenhausen ended up in the morgue. A frequent, euphemistic cause of death was "general bodily weakness." Prisoners were killed in police stations and Gestapo jails. But instead of trying to hide their deeds, the murderers sent the bodies to the morgue.

Meanwhile, bombs were falling on Berlin. After August 26, 1940, countless pages of the protocols record bomb casualties: "enemy action," "flying bomb," "bomb shrapnel injury."

The last Nazi-era entry in the autopsy protocol book is dated April 22, 1945. The Red Army had already occupied parts of Berlin. Shortly after midnight on the 21st, SS troops let prisoners out of their cells, promising to free them. The prisoners belonged to the July 20, 1944 conspirators who had attempted to assassinate Hitler. But instead of freeing their captives, the SS shot them in the back of the head.

After the entries of these deaths in the protocol book, a peculiarity occurred: a blank page. The pathologists had never before left such a page. The ruled columns indicate that many deaths had been omitted.

Outside, chaos reigned. The pathologists had retreated to a bunker, Hitler had committed suicide, the Wehrmacht had laid down their weapons, and the Red Army had marched in.

Four weeks later, the entries begin again, as they always had. The winter of hunger had arrived, as well as new ways to die, among them starvation and freezing.

7

Ordinary Germans, the Catholic Church, and the Holocaust

How did the holocaust happen? Why in Germany? And could the Catholic Church have effectively intervened? Historians have argued these questions for more than half a century.

Many scholars have taken a broad interpretation of the causes of the Holocaust, ascribing it to Hitler's maniacal anti-Semitism, the extermination program concocted by Nazi leaders and their fanatic followers, the climate of terror, the fear of resistance, the brutalities of war, and the need for slave labor. But the dissenting views of Hannah Arendt and Daniel Jonah Goldhagen have engendered highly vocal controversies. Indeed, Goldhagen's thesis, that ordinary Germans became Hitler's willing executioners, is supported by a new book about the execution of an elderly Jewish merchant for racial desecration and the malicious neighbors who turned him in. Finally, there has been considerable debate over what the Catholic Church and Pope Pius XII could have done to prevent the Holocaust.

In *Eichmann in Jerusalem*, Hannah Arendt argued that it was simplistic to pin all Holocaust guilt on Adolf Eichmann, despite his famous boast: "I will jump into my grave laughing, because the fact that I have the death of five million Jews on my conscience gives me extraordinary satisfaction."

Eichmann was not really a Nazi at heart, wrote Arendt, and was, all in all, quite a modest man. He did not know Hitler's program when he joined the Nazi party, and "there were no voices from the outside to arouse his conscience."

Arendt wrote that others besides Eichmann were equally responsible — fellow Germans, western countries, even the Jews themselves, who had assented actively or passively to the mounting evil. In her book she described in sickening detail how the Jewish elders of eastern Europe obediently turned over members of their communities to the Nazis.[1] Moreover, Arendt asserted

---

[1]*Another holocaust scholar, Raul Hilberg, has also chronicled this hideous activity.*

that the Gestapo helped the Jews immigrate to Palestine, that Himmler had a sense of pity, and that the extermination of the Jews was simply an outgrowth of Hitler's euthanasia program.

Arendt maintained that she was simply trying to make a calm assessment of the situation and get beyond the histrionics. But her book, needless to say, caused a howl of outrage. She retorted that people should not try to avoid unpleasant information and that the dictatorships dug "giant holes in which to bury unwelcome facts and events, a gigantic enterprise which could be achieved only by killing people who had been the actors or witnesses of the past."

"When the facts come home to roost," she concluded, "let us try at least to make them welcome; let us not try to escape into some utopias — images, theories, or sheer follies."

Three decades after *Eichmann in Jerusalem*, another book, *Hitler's Willing Executioners: Ordinary Germans and the Holocaust* by Daniel Jonah Goldhagen, jolted the world of Holocaust scholarship.

"The most committed, virulent anti-Semites in human history took state power in Germany and decided to turn private, murderous fantasy into the core of state policy," Goldhagen writes. They did so in a society where negative views of Jews were widely shared for centuries. And Germany's conquests allowed the killing to proceed unchallenged.

Goldhagen, an associate professor of government and social studies at Harvard, argues that many "ordinary" Germans, chosen at random, were involved in the murders. Most were not even Nazi party members and were not motivated by an inbred sense of obedience, as has often been claimed, or by peer pressure but by a "conviction" that what they were doing was "right." They hunted down Jews like wild animals, killing them in their homes, their hiding places, the streets, by the thousands at open trenches dug for their burial, and at the end one by one.

Few if any of the men were compelled to serve in the killing squads. Many actually volunteered. Few if any were ever punished for refusing orders. If some had refused, Goldhagen maintains, others would have willingly replaced them, for in their prejudice against Jews they were but a representative cross section of the German people. The Holocaust was a "national project," Goldhagen claims. To prove his point he cites the peculiar "eliminationist" tenor of anti-Semitism in Germany long before Hitler's rise to power.

During the mass shootings the killers proudly posed for photos and sent them home to their wives and children. The wives came out to visit their husbands in the killing fields; one wife was pregnant. After the killings the men held parties. Many were decorated for their deeds. They were so "average" that, with few exceptions, they were readily absorbed into civilian society after the war and peacefully lived out their unremarkable lives.

Others scholars have studied the same documents as Goldhagen, notably Christopher R. Browning, whose 1992 book, *Ordinary Men: Police Battalion 101 and the Final Solution in Poland,* is a chilling portrait of a police battalion which Goldhagen investigated. At least thirty-eight thousand murders are ascribed to this battalion. But while Browning calls the battalion members ordinary men, Goldhagen calls them ordinary Germans, a clear difference in point of view.

Goldhagen's book is a huge best seller in Germany. Why? *New York Times* writer Amos Elon was browsing the shelves of a large Berlin bookstore when an elegantly dressed woman rushed in and asked for four copies of the Goldhagen book ("gift-wrapped, please"). She appeared to be a regular customer. As the saleswoman wrapped the books, the lady told her that she was buying copies for her two sons and her two married daughters. With so much idle talk after German reunification of "We are finally able to turn the page," she said, it was proper that the "past" was in the news again and a hot issue on all the television talk shows. This Goldhagen, she declared, was "kolossal."

"Yes," said the saleswoman, "and he is so handsome and so sincere too! I can't stand those groaning old professors who attack him!"

But German historians and commentators have challenged Goldhagen's book on various points: Why does it pay so little attention to the Weimar Republic, whose collapse helped the Nazis come to power? Why does it offer no researched comparisons between German anti-Semitism and other forms of European vilification of Jews? Why does it not acknowledge the broader, European aspects of the Holocaust? Norbert Frei, a Berlin historian, says that much of Goldhagen's narrative draws on secondary research, and that even his central research into the murderous police units working behind Germany's eastern front "says little new" for people who had read *Ordinary Men.*

More criticism is contained in a book, *A Nation on Trial: The Goldhagen Thesis and Historical Truth,* which holds that Goldhagen has oversimplified. The book is based on two articles that appeared in two British journals and were written by two historians, Ruth Bettina Birn and Norman G. Finkelstein. Birn is chief historian of the War Crimes and Crimes Against Humanity Section of the Canadian Department of Justice and a former adviser to the Office of Special Investigations, the Nazi-hunting unit in the United States Justice Department. Finkelstein is adjunct associate professor of political science at Hunter College and professor of general studies at New York University.

Ms. Birn attacked the Goldhagen book in a twenty-one-page article in *The Historical Journal,* a publication of Cambridge University Press. Titled "Revising the Holocaust," her article says that Goldhagen based his conclusions on a small number of unrepresentative cases and used sources uncritically and selectively to overemphasize the motivating role of anti-Semitism in the atrocities. Birn criticizes Goldhagen for the statement that "the specific traits of German culture are the root causes of the Holocaust." She says his book abounds with such unfair generalizations as: "The German is generally brutal and murderous in the use of other peoples."

Finkelstein's forty-nine-page critique in the July-August 1997 issue of *New Left Review* in England characterized Goldhagen's book as contradictory and "worthless as scholarship." Finkelstein contends there was a conspicuous lack of anti-Jewish violence in pre-Nazi Germany. As for the social ostracism of Jews that Goldhagen depicted as part of an "eliminationist compulsion" ending with their slaughter, Finkelstein wrote that it "barely differed from the Jim Crow system in the American South."

As the war turned against Germany, Finkelstein wrote, "Germans grew increasingly insensitive to Jewish suffering" and demonstrated the "callousness toward human life typically attending war" and, under the terror of bombings, "occasionally lashed out at the weak."

Finkelstein found that Goldhagen had taken quotations out of context. For example, Goldhagen quotes the historian Max Domarus: "Hitler announced many times with passion that the war would end with extermination of the Jews, and people were generally understanding, if not in total agreement." But when Finkelstein checked Domarus, he found the sentence, "Even during the war, as his killing machine was running at full speed, [Hitler] mentioned the massacre of Jews solely in the form of threats. He knew only too well that most people, and a majority of his party colleagues, would reject the killing program he envisioned."

Reviewing the Finkelstein-Birn book for the *New York Times*, Max Frankel points out the duality in all human nature:

> So is there a beast wrestling an angel in each of us? Finkelstein and Birn seem convinced that there is, and my mother taught me that they must be right. She affirmed her belief one day in 1940 as she ran desperately around Berlin wondering how she and I — marked as Jews and also as Polish "enemy aliens" in wartime — might obtain a permit to escape from Nazi Germany at last. She came upon a commissioner of police who, though angered by her invasion of his office, nonetheless dared to close the door and whisper the name and location of the Gestapo chief to whom she should apply.
>
> As she thanked him and turned to leave, the commissioner suddenly asked,
> *Where did you say you want to go?*
> *To America.*
> *If you get there, will you tell them we're not all bad?*
> To her last day, she did.

Efraim Zuroff, director of the Simon Wiesenthal Center in Israel, has written an incisive commentary in the *Jerusalem Report* on the Goldhagen thesis: "Goldhagen presents a simple answer to a question that has puzzled scholars and non-scholars throughout the world. One has only to equate Germans with Nazis and the enigma of the twentieth century is solved. Who would not be thankful for such an elementary solution to a complex problem?"

The Jew and the Girl

Yet Goldhagen's elementary solution may have some merit. A new book by Christiane Kohl reconstructs the denunciation of a Jewish merchant in Nazi Germany, and it raises again the question of the responsibility of completely ordinary Germans for the Holocaust.

Researching the book, reporters from *Der Spiegel*, the weekly newsmagazine, ransacked the cellar of an old hall of justice. Coughing and wheezing from the thick dust, they dug through dirty piles of documents until they came upon a folder labeled Js 91/38 (GStA). The folder held unknown details about the case of Lehmann Katzenberger, a Nuremberg shoe merchant. The sixty-eight-year-old Katzenberger had committed the crime of "racial desecration" with Irene Scheffler, an Aryan photographer thirty-six years his junior. In 1942 Katzenberger was sentenced to death, and the pretty, vivacious Irene sentenced to two years imprisonment for perjury.

Irene steadfastly denied that any sexual relationship ever existed. But malicious neighbors had tattled to the authorities. The musty, yellowed legal documents paint an ugly picture of the behavior of ordinary Germans toward a Jewish fellow citizen. In Nuremberg, housewives, salesmen, and little shopkeepers became Hitler's willing executioners. Worked up by the party's exhortations and the Führer's oratory, these people had an intractable itch to dispatch the Jew Katzenberger. From their first whispers in the stairwell, to their gossip about a rumored kiss reflected in a mirror, they anonymously brought catastrophe down upon the head of an innocent man. Thus did neighbors become assassins in Nazi Germany.

Nuremberg was a perfect spot for the transformation. It was the city of the Reich Party Day, an annual celebration in which the Führer himself participated. Carnival wagons were emblazoned with the slogan, "Off to Dachau." Policemen whipped men dressed as Jews, to the great delight of the crowds. Nuremberg was also home to a corrupt Nazi clique, led by the rabid anti-Semite Julius Streicher, who went to the gallows in 1946 for his crimes against humanity.

Lehmann Katzenberger was the owner of a Nuremberg shoe wholesale business, in partnership with his brothers Max and David. The Katzenbergers ran thirty shoe stores in Bavaria, Hesse, and Thuringia; three were in

Nuremberg. The Katzenberger firm was one of the largest shoe dealers in southern Germany.

Lehmann Katzenberger, Leo to his friends, had lived in Paris as a young man, and he was a leading figure in the Nuremberg Jewish community. In 1932 he met the twenty-two-year-old Irene Scheffler when she moved to Nuremberg from the town of Gubin (now on the German-Polish border, 276 kilometers northeast of Nuremberg). In Spittlertorgraben 19, an apartment building the Katzenbergers owned, she took over a ground floor photo studio.

Oskar Scheffler, Irene's father, asked Katzenberger to keep an eye on his young daughter. A friendship quickly developed between the flirtatious Irene and the older shoe merchant. Other tenants in the building noticed. The neighbors' disapproval became a mortal threat with the passage of the 1935 Nuremberg Laws forbidding intimate contact between Jews and Aryan Germans.

The Katzenberger apartment house, Spittlertorgraben 19, was a pleasant five-story building on the edge of the oldest part of Nuremberg, the Altstadt. The colored tiles in the entrance hall were kept spotless, the wooden staircase always well waxed. On the fourth floor dwelt a door-to-door salesman named Östreicher and his wife. On the fifth floor a clerk named Heilmann lived under the sloping roof in a small apartment with his wife and young daughter. The building had a courtyard and a converted carriage house where another family named Mäsel lived.

Irene Scheffler wanted more from life than what she saw in the Spittlertorgraben apartment house. She didn't want to be another dowdy hausfrau who aired out her feather bed in the early morning, washed clothes, and cooked meals. Instead of waiting for customers in her apartment, which also served as her photo studio, she liked promenading through the shopping district. If a dress or blouse caught her fancy, she often bought on credit.

Irene enjoyed visiting the building across the courtyard, which housed the firm of D&M Katzenberger. Lehmann Katzenberger, her father's friend, was her only acquaintance in Nuremberg. And besides, she had a weakness for the stylish shoes he sold. As she carried shoe boxes through the courtyard, she never suspected that spiteful neighbors might be spying on her.

The attentions of his new tenant greatly flattered Lehmann Katzenberger. As his chauffeur Wilhelm Fabro remarked, the old bon vivant had quite an eye for the ladies. Irene thanked the shoe merchant effusively for gifts of pralines and cigarettes. When he took her on little afternoon business trips to Frankfurt or Regensburg, she threw her arms affectionately around his neck. "I really didn't think much about it," she told her judges later. "I'm frightfully impulsive."

The relationship between Irene Scheffler and Lehmann Katzenberger became an eyesore for Johann Heilmann, the fifth-floor tenant, who worked for the Katzenberger firm as a stock clerk. In 1941 he told the police, "The behavior of Scheffler and Katzenberger annoyed me." The Nazis had made Heilmann their "house observer" in 1936. Every month he went around with a sealed red metal money box from door to door, collecting for "National Socialist People's Welfare," a party organization.

Heilmann devoted himself to spying on Irene. Once, when he came around with his red box, Irene told him she would be able to donate money after her friend visited her. So Heilmann hid on the staircase to watch. By and by, Katzenberger came to the door, the nosy stock clerk reported to the police. Afterwards, Irene was able to come up with money for his box.

Heilmann was certain that Katzenberger was supporting Irene, and he let the neighbors know. The gossip got back to Katzenberger and infuriated him. He warned Heilmann to stop. When the stock clerk continued his tattling, Katzenberger fired him, thereby making an enemy of a Nazi collaborator.

"I have seen Scheffler and Katzenberger communicate through winks and signs," Heilmann told the police. "Then they go off together." Irene customarily "comes home later with a package under her arm," he added, perhaps a new fur coat, a new dress, or a piece of jewelry. Heilmann never found out exactly what was in the packages.

Hans Mäsel, who occupied the converted carriage house, could confirm Heilmann's suspicions. "Fräulein Scheffler lived beyond her means," he told the police. "She had two fur coats."

Reflected in a mirror that hung in the Mäsel apartment, Hans Mäsel's mother supposedly saw Katzenberger give Irene a kiss many years before. Mrs. Mäsel had died in 1933, but the kiss rumor lived on. Hans Mäsel also told the police he always saw "fresh flowers in the window" of Irene's apartment. Of course, Mäsel didn't know who had bought the flowers, but said that "most must have come from Katzenberger."

Before the war began, Lehmann Katzenberger could have emigrated. In the summer of 1938, Katzenberger's daughter, Käthe Freimann, visited her mother and father in their elegant villa in the Praterstraße, a few hundred meters from the Spittlertorgraben apartment house. Käthe had traveled to Nuremberg from Palestine with her husband and two oldest children. They had emigrated in 1934.

Katzenberger showered his grandchildren with candy and new shoes. He took them to Irene's photo studio for portraits. But when Käthe tried to convince her father to emigrate, he changed the subject. Emigrating to America would not have been more difficult than getting to Palestine. At the time of Käthe's visit, a travel agency, Braun and Gutmann, had moved to the third floor of the Spittlertorgraben apartment house. Braun and Gutmann specialized in American tours and advertised in Jewish publications. A ticket, Antwerp — New York in "comfortable class — good, cheap, agreeable," cost 251.25 reichsmarks. Lehmann Katzenberger knew the owners of the agency well but had no interest in their services. When his grandchildren left Nuremberg that summer of 1938, the elderly shoe merchant stood on the railroad platform and waved them off with a large handkerchief.

In September 1938, Paul Kleylein, his wife, and three children moved into a first-floor apartment at Spittlertorgraben 19. Kleylein had an orthopedic appliance shop in the Glockendonstraße. Katzenberger, plagued by foot problems, was one of his customers. Kleylein needed the apartment in a hurry, and Katzenberger readily accepted him as a tenant.

Before he moved, Kleylein had known one other tenant in Spittlertorgraben 19. Heinrich Besold, a government inspector, worked in the office for disabled war veterans, a source of referrals for Kleylein. Besold was the first neighbor to give Kleylein the scuttlebutt about Katzenberger and Irene Scheffler. First the Jew and the girl would communicate with gestures, said Besold, then Katzenberger frequently disappeared into Irene's apartment.

Soon the gossip had spread from Spittlertorgraben 19 throughout the neighborhood. Everyone knew what was going on. Babette Gilger, the owner of a tobacco shop on Plärrer, was a first-rate tattletale. "Just think, the Jew gave the girl a bouquet," she would gush. Because Katzenberger was her customer, she was able to provide more "evidence" about the reputed affair. "Irene and Katzenberger both smoked the same brand of cigarette. When she would change, he would change." Kleylein went to the disabled war veterans office looking for business, and officials asked him if he knew any more gossip. "They're shouting it from the rooftops," he replied.

The constant chatter made the one Jewish family living in the Spittlertorgraben apartment house, on the second floor, very uneasy. This family, named Weglein, increasingly withdrew from the neighbors. The Katzenberger firm employed Leo Weglein as a buyer. Walter Weglein, then eight years old, today remembers only Irene, "a very friendly, beautiful woman," and Katzenberger's chauffeur Fabro, who liked to ride a motorcycle.

When Irene met her future husband, Hans Seiler, her relationship with Katzenberger became less flirtatious. Seiler was a blond, well-dressed charmer, a car salesman with a twin brother, and the two often visited Irene's apartment. The visits of the fiancé and the future brother-in-law gave the neighbors even more to prattle about.

Toward the end of 1938, Hans Seiler showed up at Spittlertorgraben 19 in a car. Irene, not one to keep her own counsel, told her neighbor, Betty Kleylein, that Seiler had been short five hundred reichsmarks for the purchase. Betty Kleylein thought she knew where the money came from. "Katzenberger gave it to her," she told the police.

In fact, there were many good opportunities to obtain automobiles, housing, furniture, carpets, fur coats, and jewelry in Nuremberg. The financial pressure on Jews was so intense that they were forced to sell everything they owned. On February 21, 1939, Jews who had anything left were ordered to bring all gold, silver, and jewelry to the Nuremberg pawn shop, now called the Reich Party Day City Lending Office. Soon there was a line of people at the front door dragging sacks, trunks, and carts.

On March 27, 1939, Lehmann Katzenberger joined the line. Lending office officials carefully recorded what he turned in. Among his possessions were a twelve-piece fish-silverware set, two saltcellars with spoons, a five-piece silver toilet set, two candlesticks, silver goblets, napkin rings, a breadbasket, a diamond ring, a pearl necklace, his wife Claire's gold wrist watch, and his own beautiful pocket watch with chain. In all, Katzenberger handed over 103 objects, which he never saw again.

Many Jews now took the hint and decided to get out, though emigration was becoming more difficult every day. At the beginning of 1939, the Jewish community organization in Nuremberg counted 3,800 remaining members, of 10,000 in 1930. By the beginning of the war in September 1939, 2,700 Jews were left.

After the Kristallnacht pogrom, November 9, 1938, the Jewish stores in Nuremberg lay in ruins. The police arrested Lehmann Katzenberger and accused him of currency manipulations, of which he was completely innocent. His two brothers, Max and David, were interrogated in the office of the German Workers' Front. On November 17, the brothers' real estate was Aryanized. Lehmann Katzenberger's villa in the Praterstraße, for which he had paid 115,000 reichsmarks, was sold for 45,730 reichsmarks to a local Nazi official. The Spittlertorgraben apartments, which the brothers had bought in 1919 for 185,000 reichsmarks, went for 65,234 reichsmarks.

The Katzenbergers were virtually wiped out. The money from the sale of their property went to an escrow account, not to them. Reichsmarschall Herman Göring had declared that the money in the account would pay for the sins the Jews had committed.

Lehmann Katzenberger decided to emigrate after Kristallnacht. In November 1938, he asked his son-in-law in Jerusalem to do "everything to get us out of here as soon as possible." The elderly merchant also traveled to Berlin to petition the Palestine Office for help.

At first, his chances seemed good. He knew the leaders of the Zionist movement. A relative in Jerusalem put up one thousand pounds as security, and Katzenberger bought ship passage. But then many other people got emigration permits and left for Palestine. Nuremberg was far from Berlin, where the precious documents were distributed. "My contacts failed me," wrote the disappointed merchant to his family abroad.

Ludwig Rosenzweig, the Nuremberg Jewish community leader, emigrated, and Katzenberger was named his successor. At the same time, the old merchant was having less and less contact with Irene Scheffler and her husband, having visited their apartment only a few times to help with a tax matter. After Kristallnacht, he told Irene that it was dangerous to remain on friendly terms.

Paul Kleylein sealed Lehmann Katzenberger's doom. The orthopedic technician blabbed to officials about the rumored relationship between the merchant and Irene Scheffler. Yellowed court documents reveal that Kleylein had tattled some time in late autumn 1939 to the "block observer," a man named Klein. Herr Klein alerted his superior, who filed a formal report. Finally, the Nazi boss in Nuremberg, Georg Haberkern, told his party comrade Irene Scheffler that she "could no longer meet or speak" with Katzenberger. But she did see her old friend once more and kissed him when they parted.

On August 16, 1940, Irene discovered her neighbors' hostility during an air raid. Everyone had crowded into a vaulted underground shelter, Irene wearing "a thick swastika," Kleylein later testified. Suddenly there was a dull thud and something fell. Very nervous herself, Irene told Östreicher, the door-to-door salesman from the fourth floor, that he shouldn't behave like an idiot. He screamed back, "You Jewgirl, I'll help you anyhow."

The next day Irene met Katzenberger on the street in front of the Ludwigstor gate. The snoop who saw the encounter couldn't hear what the two were saying but from their gestures surmised that they were talking about what had happened in the air raid shelter. Before the air raid, Irene thought she had good relations with her neighbors. Afterward, as she naively told interrogators, she knew that "the people in the building [were] angry at [her]."

No one was surprised when Herr Klein, the block observer, visited Kleylein in his apartment. Kleylein began telling Klein about the contretemps in the shelter, but "he already knew more than I did," Kleylein later testified. The block observer visited other tenants, and it was obvious to everyone that trouble was brewing. Only Irene Scheffler remained blissfully oblivious to the gathering storm.

Her detachment may have been partly due to immersion in her newly booming photo business. "People were sending pictures to the front, and were making many snapshots of the fallen. During the war, all the photo shops were doing well," Irene testified later.

There was another cause for her prosperity. Besides wearing a yellow star sewn to their clothing, Jews were required to carry special identification cards, which they had to display on many occasions, even when buying stamps at the post office. (Mischlinge did not have to wear the yellow star.) The so-called "J-identification cards" carried a photo, a fingerprint, and personal details. Irene made many of the photos and also did a good business with SS men from a nearby barracks.

Katzenberger seldom saw Irene. Once in the autumn of 1940 he met her in the Dennerstraße, when her husband was on leave. Despite all of his troubles, the old gentleman was smartly dressed, in dark suit and vest. He gave Irene a bouquet, according to the report of a witness.

In 1940 Irene Scheffler moved to new rooms in the Pfannenschmiedgasse. In early 1941, Oskar Scheffler came for a visit with his daughter. The retired accountant invited his old friend Katzenberger to call on him in Irene's apartment. Toward evening, Irene arrived, then was joined by her husband. Hans Seiler was stationed in a Nuremberg barracks and was permitted to sleep at home. Irene greeted Katzenberger perfunctorily, and the old merchant hurried off to beat the 8:00 P.M. curfew.

The police arrested Katzenberger a few days later. A photograph — his last — shows him dressed, elegantly as ever, in pin-striped suit, vest, and tie, his hat pulled down over his forehead at a rakish angle.

The police proceeded to interrogate the tenants of the Spittlertorgraben apartment. At first Frau Östreicher, the wife of the door-to-door salesman from the fourth floor, professed to know nothing. She referred investigators to the Kleyleins on the ground floor. Betty Kleylein, hearing of Frau Östreicher's reticence, marched off to the police station to denounce her. That woman Östreicher wouldn't talk, said Betty, because Katzenberger had sold her some furniture in 1938 after Kristallnacht.

Johann Heilmann and Hans Mäsel dished up the old story about Irene's carrying shoe boxes across the courtyard. Paul Kleylein said he had once seen Katzenberger coming out of Irene's apartment, and "he was shaken and left quickly." As Kleylein was leaving the police station, he ran into Irene on Ludwigstraße. "God in heaven," he muttered, "the woman thinks I have denounced her."

The chief district court judge, Oswald Rothaug, assigned himself to the Katzenberger case. Rothaug, who liked to patronize a nearby Nazi pub, the Blue Grape, was called "the executioner." He was determined to prosecute not only the old merchant but Irene Scheffler as well. And when he took on a case, "he was like a dog worrying after a bone," said Hermann Markl, the Nuremberg district attorney.

Rothaug, forty-four years old, could mete out severe punishment, even death, for petty crimes. He could execute a thief who had stolen a chicken in the night, since committing a crime under cover of darkness automatically called for a more severe penalty. Rothaug characterized Katzenberger's crime of racial desecration as having occurred "toward evening." It was thus more serious than desecration in broad daylight.

The trial began on Friday, March 13, 1942. Rothaug behaved in court like the demonic judge Roland Freisler. He gesticulated wildly as he spat out the surname of the accused, as well as his German and Hebrew given names. When Katzenberger's lawyer, Richard Herz, said that one name would suffice, Rothaug screamed back, "It doesn't make any difference to me what the man's name is." He then denounced Irene Scheffler with a flood of angry words.

Irene's persistent denial of trysts with Katzenberger unsettled Rothaug. "I can't confess something that never happened," she insisted. "Jawohl, you can also lie!" Rothaug shouted back, and "neutralized" her denial by charging her with perjury. Rothaug probed Irene's sex life. He asked if she had lived with her husband before marriage and whether she had other "gentleman acquaintances." Irene answered yes to both questions. Heinz Hugo Hoffmann and Karl Ferber, the two other judges on the bench with Rothaug listened with interest. Hoffmann thought Irene "an easy girl." Ferber, who conducted racial inquiries of couples who wanted to marry, thought Irene was "a barmaid type."

Before Katzenberger's trial, there had never been a death sentence for racial desecration, though *Der Stürmer*, the Nazi paper, had often demanded one. The worst penalty had been fifteen years imprisonment. But with the "under cover of darkness" charge added, Katzenberger was a dead man walking. Rothaug was indifferent to whether or not there had been sex. "It's enough for me that the Jew pig admitted he had a German girl on his lap," he told associates.

Katzenberger prepared a speech which his lawyer edited. "I am innocent," he told his judges, and "I ask to be exonerated." Then he turned to Rothaug. "You have branded me as a Jew throughout this trial," he said softly. "I would like to add that I am also a human being." When he tried to quote Frederick the Great, Rothaug cut him off. He would not let a Jew "dirty" the King's name.

"Only righteousness ennobles a people," said Frederick the Great, who nevertheless detested Jews and declared them detrimental to Christian civilization.

The court handed down a death sentence quickly. But Rothaug insisted the penalty was humane because Katzenberger would at least be better off than the deported Jews in the hands of the SS. Irene was given two years in prison for perjury.

Far from the Nuremberg courtroom, Adolf Hitler sat at Wolf's Lair, in a bunker from which he had directed the Russian campaign since 1941. The building, with walls five meters thick, was situated in the marshes of northeastern Poland, near the town of Rastenburg. During the entire winter the Führer had been receiving bad news from the front.

Yet a newspaper story stimulated his interest. Under a banner headline, "Racial Desecrator Sentenced to Death," the March 18, 1942, *Berliner Illustrirte* reported the Katzenberger-Scheffler case.

Adolf Hitler was displeased. When the racial laws were formulated in 1935, Hitler had specified that only the man should be punished for racial desecration, not the woman. He believed that during sex the male played the active role, while the female was only the innocent object of manly lust. Of course, the statutes as written had the practical effect of encouraging "desecrated" women to snitch.

Disturbed by the sentence given to Irene, Hitler dispatched his adjutant to intervene. When the adjutant arrived in Nuremberg and communicated the Führer's unhappiness, the senior state prosecutor left for Berlin in such a hurry that he had to shave in the train station lavatory. But Hans Heinrich Lammers, the Reich Chancellery Chief, was able to settle the matter. Hitler had thought that Irene was sentenced for racial desecration. When Lammers explained that the two years were for perjury, "the Führer was satisfied."

Lehmann Katzenberger was transferred to a cell in Stadelheim Prison on March 20, 1942. Prison officials would not allow him to have the special orthopedic shoes which his betrayer Paul Kleylein had made for him. The elderly merchant was forced to endure considerable discomfort from his bunions and flat feet. After a few weeks, his jailers finally permitted him to have his special shoes. But they would not allow a group of orthodox Jews to bring him his Bible.

Katzenberger wrote many letters to his wife, though they may not have reached her. Claire Katzenberger and her brother-in-law Max Katzenberger were deported on March 24, 1942, to a town named Izbica, near Lublin. "No word from my dear wife and the others?" Katzenberger wrote to his lawyer on April 14.

On Tuesday, June 2, 1942, at 6 P.M., a guard opened the heavy door to Katzenberger's cell to tell the old merchant he would die the next morning. Katzenberger wrote three letters that night, one to an old friend in Munich, another to his brother David in Nuremberg. The third was a Red Cross telegram to Palestine, which has been preserved in a shoe box for half a century. "I kiss you in my heart," he wrote to his daughter and her family, all of whom he mentioned by name. "May God bless and keep you all."

Next morning, just before 6 A.M., a guard took Lehmann Katzenberger from his cell. In the prison death chamber, an executioner beheaded the merchant with a guillotine.

After the war, a U.S. military tribunal investigated the Katzenberger case during the trial of the Nazi judges. In 1947 the tribunal convicted Oswald Rothaug of judicial murder and sentenced him to life imprisonment. But he was released after serving nine years, while nothing at all was done to his fellow judges Karl Ferber and Heinz Hugo Hoffmann. The German courts later took up the matter and spent forty years with it, on and off. Irene Scheffler told her story to one judge after another and was always confronted with the same question: Was Katzenberger a friend or a lover?

Robert M. W. Kempner was involved in prosecuting Katzenberger's Nazi judges and describes them in his 1983 book, *Ankläger Einer Epoche* (*Prosecutor for an Epoch*). Christiane Kohl, a reporter for Der Spiegel, later published an entire book on the Katzenberger case. Ms. Kohl starkly portrays the barbaric mistreatment of the German Jews in her chronicle of one tragic family. Her excellent study lends considerable credence to Daniel Jonah Goldhagen's thesis that many ordinary Germans were Hitler's willing executioners.

The Church and the Holocaust: "What a Disgrace"

Since the end of the war, there has been considerable debate over what the Catholic Church, in particular Pope Pius XII, could have done to prevent the Holocaust. On October 31, 1997, Pope John Paul II spoke in Rome to a group of sixty Christian theologians of different denominations on the origins of anti-Semitism, and he introduced the subject of the historic role of certain Christian teachings.

As Celestine Bohlen reported in the *New York Times*, the Pope said that these teachings, based on "wrong and unjust" interpretations of the New Testament, had contributed to the Holocaust and the persecution of Jews in Europe over the centuries.

As he had done several times, the seventy-seven-year-old Pontiff strongly denounced anti-Semitism as "totally unjustifiable and absolutely condemnable" and called it a pagan refutation of the essence of Christian doctrine. In the text of the Pope's comments made public by the Vatican, John Paul joined other Roman Catholic theologians in acknowledging that by blaming the Jews for the death of Jesus, certain Christian teachings had helped fuel anti-Semitism.

"In the Christian world—I do not say on the part of the church as such—the wrong and unjust interpretations of the New Testament relating to the Jewish people and their presumed guilt circulated for too long, contributing to feelings of hostility toward these people," he said.

"These interpretations soothed consciences," the Pope remarked, "to the point that when a wave of persecutions swept Europe fueled by a pagan anti-Semitism—which in its essence was equal to anti-Christianism—next to those Christians who did everything to save the persecuted at the risk of their own lives, the spiritual resistance of many was not that which humanity expected from the disciples of Christ."

The Pope added that any form of racism is "a negation of the deepest

identity of the human being, who is a person created in the image and like-
ness of God." He also emphasized the common heritage that binds Christians and Jews. Those who consider Jesus' Jewish heritage as a "simple cultural
accident," he said, do a disservice to history and to Christianity.

But the Pope did not make the direct apology that many Jews still hope
to hear from the Vatican, both for its muted protests during the Holocaust
and for its centuries-old tolerance of anti-Semitism in its ranks and, until
thirty years ago, in its liturgy. As part of the reforms adopted during the Second Vatican Council in the 1960s, the church finally removed references to
"perfidious Jews" and, in a document issued in 1965, deplored anti-Semitism
and condemned references to Jewish guilt for the death of Jesus.

Expectations that the Pope would make a public apology to Jews arose
in the fall of 1987, after the public repentance of French bishops for the silence
of the Catholic Church in France during the Nazi deportation of French Jews.
Germany's Roman Catholic bishops made a similar apology several years ago
on behalf of their church.

On March 16, 1998, the Vatican released a document, in the works for
eleven years, examining the behavior of the church and Pope Pius XII during the Holocaust. Entitled *We Remember: A Reflection on the Shoah,* the document concludes that church teachings, though often hostile to Jews, did not
contribute to the crude anti-Semitic ideology of the Nazis, whom the Vatican calls "neo-pagan." The document does not even mention the Pope's failure to speak out against Nazi atrocities. Instead, it offers evidence of church
efforts to save Jews and recalls the thanks Pius XII received from Jewish leaders after the war. "It is regrettable that the Vatican has not yet found the
courage to discard this defensive, incomplete depiction," wrote the *New York
Times* in an editorial.

The Vatican has always been reluctant to come to grips with the attitude of Pius XII toward the Jews. Because of the explosive nature of the matter, the Holy See would prefer to avoid it entirely. When Rolf Hochhuth
dramatized the Church's relationship to the Holocaust in his 1963 play, "The
Deputy," Pope Paul VI denounced the drama more heatedly than any other
literary work in recent memory.

In September 1997, the American professor and rabbi David Blumenthal lectured in Rome at the Church's Gregoriana University. In his lecture,
Blumenthal described how intervention by Pope Pius XII, Eugenio Pacelli,
could have saved at least a third of the murdered Jews.

Blumenthal maintained that the Pope would not have been able to totally
restrain Hitler and other prominent Catholic Nazis, even though Hitler
himself was raised a Catholic and had tithed regularly to the Church until he
came to power. But Rudolf Augstein, founding editor of *Der Spiegel,* took
issue with Blumenthal, pointing out that Hitler had never renounced his

Church affiliation and advised his many Catholic associates to remain Church members.

Long before he took power, Hitler had two clear goals: a war of annihilation against the Soviet Union and the murder of the European Jews. He must have known instinctively that he could never achieve these goals if both the Lutheran Church, and above all the Roman Catholic Church, opposed him.

Therefore, on July 20, 1933, Germany concluded a concordat with the Vatican. In Rome, one man, the fifty-seven-year-old Cardinal and State Secretary Pacelli, played a key role. With the nominal imprimatur of Pacelli's predecessor, Pius XI, the concordat ultimately facilitated Hitler's attainment of his cherished goals.

Signed by Pacelli and German Vice-Chancellor Franz von Papen in an elaborate ceremony at the Vatican, the concordat stated that the two signatories, led by "their reciprocal desire to consolidate and develop amicable relations between the Holy See and the German Reich," had decided to conclude a solemn agreement. Article One guaranteed "freedom of the profession and public exercise of the Catholic Religion," as well as the right of the Church to regulate and administer freely its own affairs independently within the limit of laws applicable to all and to issue, within the framework of its own competence, laws and ordinances binding on its members. Other clauses reaffirmed diplomatic representation, the legal status of the clergy, the appointment of bishops, guarantees for the property of the church, the ecclesiastical right of veto over the appointment and continuation of Catholic teachers of religion, Catholic education, the appointment of a bishop for the armed forces, Catholic organizations, and the exclusion of the clergy from politics. A secret annex concerned the treatment of the clergy in the event that the government should introduce universal military training.

World opinion regarded the concordat as a great diplomatic victory for Hitler. In return for the assurance from Rome that it would not meddle in German politics, the Führer granted Catholics freedom to practice their religion. He made the agreement to undermine the strength of the Catholic Center party in German politics, to cut the influence of the Catholic labor unions, and to win public recognition for his new regime. He probably did not intend to abide by the concordat. In the end, the Church, and many other organizations, were subject to the government's total control.

Years before the concordat, Eugenio Pacelli had come to know Germany. In 1917 he was Nuncio in Munich to the state of Bavaria and, from 1925 to 1929, Nuncio in Berlin. When he was recalled to Rome, the master diplomat Pacelli could hardly have imagined that he would end up in the middle of the worst crisis for the Holy See of the twentieth century. But when he was elected Pope, March 2, 1939, he must have sensed that trouble lay ahead.

Pacelli was an extremely intelligent man, dry, skeptical, and realistic. He was suspicious, cool, and given to sarcasm in conversation. One devout Catholic who visited him remarked, "He radiated friendly concern for me in a way that made me almost sorry; it seemed so touching and pathetic that I shouldn't be more concerned about the concern."

In his memoirs, the pope's personal physician describes Pacelli's mania for hygiene. After every audience, the Holy Father disinfected his hands. His physical repugnance for daily contact with pilgrims fueled his passion for hand-washing. He also liked to rinse his mouth with hydrochloric acid, a practice which eventually caused stomach disturbances and hiccups.

Could Pacelli, as Pius XII, have saved many of the Jews from their awful fate? Could he have saved half of them? There are no incontestable answers to these questions, only indications. The official Church response is that open Papal intervention in the Jewish situation would have made matters worse. In the Netherlands, protests from the church had only spurred even more murderous measures.

Asked by American and other diplomatic missions to intercede, Pius XII did not object. As he must have realized, as "Representative of Christ on Earth" he certainly had a role to play. And as a human being, he must have abhorred Hitler's heathen leanings.

Indeed, one of his predecessor Pius XI's most passionate encyclicals, issued March 14, 1937, addressed the disturbing aspects of National Socialism. *Mit brennender Sorge* (With Burning Concern) was the first and only papal encyclical in the German language "concerning the situation of the Catholic church in the German Reich." Based on a draft by Cardinal Michael Faulhaber, the encyclical was secretly rushed to Germany and read from the pulpits of Catholic churches on March 21. It offered strong criticism of the "new heathenism" of National Socialism and its "idolatry" of race, *Volk,* and state. It further regretted that the "tree of peace planted in German earth," represented by the Concordat, had not borne the desired fruits because of the guilt of others (i.e. the Nazis). Pius XI warned in the encyclical against "corrosive religious struggles" and admonished the government to fulfill the terms of the concordat, but he carefully avoided any reference to the concentration camps or to the persecution of Jews in Germany.

On March 19, 1937, Pius XI issued another encyclical, *Divini Redemptoris,* commemorating the common anti-Bolshevik mission of the Church and National Socialism against atheistic communism. This second encyclical did not, however, dampen the Nazi urge for retribution against the earlier one. A wave of priest trials for morals and currency infractions, restriction of religious instruction in public schools, and the final liquidation of the Catholic workers' associations were among the measures that considerably exacerbated the church's problems in Germany.

A year after *Mit brennender Sorge*, Pius XI began work on a draft of a third encyclical, *Humani Generis Unitas* (The Unity of Mankind). Racism, according to the document, runs counter to Catholic belief and teachings. Repression of the Jews was a heaping of injustice upon injustice.

On September 6, 1938, Pius XI spoke in private to a group of Belgian pilgrims. With great emotion, apparently in tears, the pope declared: "It is impossible for Christians to participate in anti-Semitism. We recognize that everyone has the right to self-defense and may take the necessary means for protecting legitimate interests. But anti-Semitism is inadmissible. Spiritually, we are all Semites." The increasingly infirm Pius XI never finished The Unity of Mankind, and he died on February 10, 1939.

Pius XII did not complete the encyclical, though as cardinal and state secretary he had sharpened the language of *Mit brennender Sorge*. The Jesuit general Wladimir Ledóchowski, a Pole, is said to have discouraged the Pope, always sensitive to diplomatic nuance, from publishing. Ledochowski was a fanatical anti-Communist, who hoped that some political rapprochement with Nazi Germany remained possible.

Also, the Holy See did not view laws discriminating against Jews as contradictory to Catholic teachings, at least in peacetime. To the Vatican, the Jews were simply not "in a proximal sphere of interest."

World War II confined the Church to a straitjacket, and, given his exquisite political sensitivity, Pius XII was not the person to act as liberator. The Pope, the Curia, and the Holy See determined to maintain a rigid neutrality.

Indeed, during the entire war, Pius XII intervened in only one instance. When Hitler invaded the three neutrals, Holland, Belgium, and Luxembourg, the Pope expressed his regret, though he did not name the invader. In this way he was able to justify his sentiments to the German Bishops, who supported the invasion.

Remarkably, after even the mere expression of regret, Pius XII was forced to back and fill. Since the Vatican recognized all three neutral states and had Nuncios in each, the Pope had the option to speak out in their favor. But the fascist Italian government threatened to forbid the sale of *L'Osservatore Romano*, the Vatican newspaper. The Pope had to announce over the Vatican Radio and in *L'Osservatore Romano* that henceforth only strictly neutral material would be broadcast and published.

Pius XII adhered religiously to this pronouncement. He was silent about SS atrocities in Poland, even though many Catholic priests were eyewitnesses. No doubt the atrocities horrified the pontiff, but, as Rudolf Augstein has written, to be horrified was just not enough.

In his first Christmas address, the Pope sought to formulate his conception of his august station: "For our office and for our times, we are obliged to be a strong apostolic witness to truth: *testimonium perhibere veritati* [testimony brings forth truths]. This duty includes exposing and contradicting errors and human failings." But a Christmas address two years later did not mention as errors and human failings the barbaric murders the SS Einsatz groups were committing in the Soviet Union: "Like a light house with its rays, Christian teachings must direct the workings of men, who will heed the healing, useful reminders." Yet the Pope could have intervened to prevent the murders. Germany was almost 25 percent Roman Catholic. The power of the Church is illustrated by the fate of the only mass murder order Hitler signed, which mandated extermination of persons unworthy to live — the mentally ill and retarded.

Clemens August Graf von Galen, Bishop of Münster, spoke out against this order, after other clergy had sent letters of protest to Hanns Kerrl, Reichsminister for church affairs. In a sermon on August 3, 1941, six weeks after the German invasion of the Soviet Union, the Bishop warned that soon all "unproductive fellow citizens" would be destroyed, including the elderly, invalids, the sick, and even disabled war veterans.

The regime considered arresting the Bishop of Münster, even liquidating him. Yet Joseph Goebbels wrote in his diary that all of Westphalia would be lost to National Socialism if anyone touched the churchman. Bishop Galen became known as "the lion of Münster," a resistance fighter, which he was not. But he had guts. The case of Bishop Galen shows the clear constraints upon the Hitler government. The Pope may have had no divisions, as Josef Stalin remarked, but he did have clout.

Sadly, church officials such as Galen cared mainly about the souls in their parishes. The plight of the deported Jews did not especially move them, except for those few Jews who had converted to Catholicism. Like almost all Catholic Bishops at the beginning of the war in 1939, Galen preached in support of Hitler, especially when German armies invaded the atheistic Soviet Union. Although he did not refer to Russians as having "degenerated to animals," as did his colleague Archbishop Lorenz Jaeger von Paderborn, Galen did mention the "threatening red flood." At the end of the war, Galen regretted that Hitler had lost.

Archbishop Gröber von Freiburg did not stand by the Führer as long as Galen had. The Roman Catholic Church had always been minimally tolerant of the Nazis, but Freiburg's attitude changed drastically after the calamitous German defeats at Stalingrad and Kursk, when it was obvious that Germany would lose the war.

Among the German Bishops, only Konrad Graf von Preysing, Bishop of Berlin, would have liked to oppose the regime, which he disdained. Pius XII seems to have put great stock in Preysing's opinions, but he would not allow him to engage in anti-Nazi activity.

The Pope himself had mixed feelings about the war. Initially, he wished for a German victory over the godless Soviet Union, although he never would have announced this preference. Hitlers came and Hitlers went, he believed, but if nothing was done about Bolshevism it would infect all of Europe. Pius XII did not learn of the mass murder of European Jews until the summer of 1942, at latest. He is said to have wept when the following report reached him, written in Latin for security purposes by an Italian priest in Poland: "We have been robbed of all humanity by witnessing the bestial behavior of people devoid of any human feeling. We live in a state of constant, horrible terror, always in danger of ending up in a concentration camp." Certainly a papal encyclical was now imperative. But Pius XII was silent. No doubt the preservation of Catholic institutions was foremost in his mind.

Other Catholic officials had already recognized the ultimate damage that the Pope's politics would cause. In June 1940, Cardinal Eugène Tisserant, a high official of the Vatican Library, had sent a letter to Cardinal Emmanuel Suhard, Archbishop of Paris, shortly before France capitulated. By this time, high level diplomats knew of the Nazi atrocities in Poland. In his letter, Tisserant wrote: "I fear history will accuse the Holy See of following a policy of comfort for itself, and not much more. This is very sad, especially when one had lived under Pius XI. And everyone knows that after Rome is declared an open city, no one from the curia will suffer. What a disgrace." Cardinals Tisserant and Suhard had no idea of what worse disgrace was in store. They did not know that the Nazis intended to murder all the European Jews and that almost every bystander would excuse himself from intervening. Everyone anxiously awaited a pronouncement from the Pope. Would he express regret for the murders or not?

A key question is whether the Nazis would have arrested Pius XII if he had denounced them openly. There was, after all, a precedent. Napoleon had abducted Pope Pius VII from Rome in 1809 and had held him in Savona.

Yet one must not underestimate the power the Vatican commanded, a power it does not possess today. How could Catholic clergymen have refused to acknowledge publicly a papal encyclical condemning the massacre of the Jews? What effect would the condemnation have had on the million Catholic Wehrmacht soldiers? Undoubtedly Hitler would have had to rein in the Einsatz groups, especially after the 1942 reverses on the Russian front, if he had wished to continue his war. And even if only a quarter of the Jews had then been saved, what a shining hour it would have been for the Roman Catholic Church.

But Pius XII was not ready to offer himself up as a martyr. The Church revered the martyrs from the stories in the New Testament, yet it didn't want to see more martyrs come from within the Vatican.

Would Hitler have martyred Pius XII? Certainly if he had, the Pope's fate could not have been kept secret from the large contingent of Catholic soldiers in the Wehrmacht. As long as Pius XII remained in the Vatican, he could have saved Jews. On October 18, 1943, the Nazis rounded up Jewish women and children in Rome and sent them directly to Auschwitz. What would have happened if the Representative of Christ on Earth, accompanied by six Swiss guards, had gone to the debarkation point?

Pius XII did help to hide Jews in cloisters, churches, even the Vatican. But no one knows whether the number of Jews he saved was equal to the number of Nazis that the Austrian-born bishop, Alois Hudal, Director of the German College of Priests in Rome, smuggled to South America after the war. New evidence suggests that the Vatican may even have directly handled funds the Nazis and their allies stole from Jewish victims. Some of the stolen wealth was apparently used to help Croatian fascists flee to South America. So far, the Vatican has flatly refused to allow investigators access to its archives, despite repeated pleas from several nations and from Jewish groups.

The Nazis' opportunity to comb through the Eternal City for Jews was due to differences within the Allied leadership. These differences let Hitler take Rome and hold it for half a year. During this time, the Nazis sent more than a thousand Roman Jews to Auschwitz. Only fifteen survived.

Although Pius XII was indignant at the arrest of the Roman Jews, he did nothing. Bishop Hudal, along with Axis diplomats in Rome, discouraged the Holy See from mounting even a mild protest. Hudal, not surprisingly, had been a great proponent of the Nuremberg laws. Ernst von Weizsäcker, German ambassador to the Vatican, reported on the situation to his bosses in Berlin: "Though besieged by appeals, the Pope has permitted no protests against the deportation of the Roman Jews. Still, he must reckon with the fact that our enemies and the Protestant circles in Anglo-Saxon countries will use his behavior in anti-Catholic propaganda. But in dealing with this difficult matter, he has decided not to damage his relations with the German government or German officials in Rome. We can reckon with the fact that German actions related to the Jewish question will no longer be possible, and that this unpleasant question for Vatican-German relations has been liquidated." On the basis of this letter, and other documentary evidence that he initialed "illegitimate orders," an American military tribunal sentenced von Weizsäcker to seven years imprisonment in 1949, but he was released during a general amnesty in 1950. His son, Richard von Weizsäcker, later president of the German Federal Republic, wrote: "No one knows whether Hitler's original intention was, possibly, to occupy the Vatican or to abduct the Pope, and if he had, what world wide commotion might have ensued."

German Catholic officials and clergy solidly supported Hitler's war and the sacrifice of German soldiers for Führer and fatherland. But the clerics' enthusiasm became more muted as the war continued, and they mourned the innocent civilians, Catholic and Protestant, killed during bombing raids. They never mentioned the fate of the Jews.

When the Vatican learned of the murders the Hitler regime was committing, his advisors urged Pius XII to recall his fascist friend and successor in Berlin, Nuncio Cesare Orsenigo. But the Pope, always the diplomat, worried that his relationship with the German Reich could deteriorate drastically if another nuncio were in Berlin. So he did nothing, thereby sending a signal to the Catholic clergy. Although Hitler had officially withdrawn his signed order mandating the "euthanasia" of the mentally ill and retarded, the killing went on covertly. The silence of Pope and clergy gave the Nazis carte blanche to continue murdering the helpless.

After the war, Romans ignored the moral failings of their Church and exhibited unbridled enthusiasm for their Pope. Despite his ethical lapses, Pius XII had not left the Eternal City, as had King Victor Emmanuel III and his transition government chief, Pietro Badoglio.

But the Church of Jesus Christ had demeaned itself by virtue of its hypocritical diplomacy. Henceforth, no one would know whether a Pope was really the Representative of Christ on Earth, or whether he was merely the head of a rich and powerful philanthropic enterprise. During his widely awaited lecture of October 31, 1997, and in the Vatican document of March 16, 1998, John Paul II carefully avoided addressing this painful question.

8

The Wannsee Villa After the Wannsee Conference

The War Years

The Czech partisans who attacked and mortally wounded Reinhard Heydrich in Prague on May 27, 1942, derailed further expansion plans for the Wannsee Villa. After Heydrich's death on June 4, 1942, the Nordhav Foundation no longer needed the large villa, which was costly to maintain. On January 29, 1943, the foundation sold the Wannsee Villa to the German government and the SS for the same price it had paid Friedrich Minoux. Until the end of the war, the SS continued to use the Villa as a guest house.

The Nordhav Foundation acquired smaller properties to turn into SS guest houses, among them buildings in Lenzenberg, Keilberg, Bad Altheide, and Attersee. But when the Third Reich collapsed, so did the Nordhav Foundation.

One noteworthy wartime guest at the Wannsee Villa was SS Oberführer (Brigadier General) Georg Klein, who arrived from Nuremberg on July 2, 1944. After Claus von Stauffenberg tried to assassinate Hitler on July 20, 1944, Klein was named to a special commission which would interrogate Field Marshall Erwin von Witzleben and other prominent conspirators.

In December 1944, after the execution of most of the conspirators, there was a meeting of government officials in the Wannsee Villa. The bureaucrats had assembled to talk about "the plans for state and government reform" of the July 20th conspirators. The discussion was based on a memorandum written by Fritz-Detlof Count von der Schulenberg, who had been executed on August 10, 1944.

Thus, from Friedrich Minoux's 1923 meetings to establish an authoritarian regime, to Reinhard Heydrich's 1942 conference to organize the mass murder of the Jews, to the meeting to analyze the plans of the anti-Hitler conspirators in the final days of the Third Reich, the Wannsee Villa had witnessed the unfolding and dénouement of the greatest of all disasters in German history.

Joseph Wulf and the Creation of the Wannsee Memorial

In May and June 1945, Soviet soldiers occupied the Wannsee Villa, followed by American troops, who used the house as an officers' club. When the German borders were established, the Villa ended up in West Germany.

In 1947 the August Bebel Institute established in the Wannsee Villa a college which educated functionaries of the Social Democratic Party. The ground floor was divided into lecture rooms, dining rooms, and a reading room. There were bedrooms and a library on the second floor and work rooms on the third floor.

In March 1952, the August Bebel Institute vacated the Wannsee Villa. Maintenance costs were high, and the building needed a new roof. In April 1952, the district of Neukölln made the house into a youth hostel. Local schoolchildren spent their summer vacations playing on the park-like lawn and in the lake-front garden. The historian Joseph Wulf was responsible for reawakening public awareness of the Wannsee Villa's notorious past.

Joseph Wulf was born in Chemnitz (later Karl Marx Stadt) in 1912, son of a well-to-do merchant. When he was five years old, his family moved to Krakow. His father wanted him to be a rabbi, but Joseph Wulf aspired to be a writer. When he was age twenty-seven, he published his first book, *Critical Miniatures*, in Yiddish. But the year was 1939, and Hitler's attack on Poland brought Wulf's writing to an abrupt halt.

In 1941 Joseph Wulf joined the resistance, while his wife and son hid in the home of a Polish farmer. Two years later, the Gestapo captured Wulf and, after a month of cruel interrogation, sent him to Auschwitz. There, SS guards tattooed his arm with his inmate number, 114866. He survived two terrible years and a death march before the Red Army freed him. He found his wife and son miraculously still alive, but the Germans had murdered his father, mother, brother, sister-in-law, and niece.

Wulf was one of the founders of the Central Jewish Historical Commission in Poland in 1945. He left Poland for Paris in 1948, where he worked at the Centre pour l'Histoire des Juifs Polonais. In the 1950s he moved to Berlin to continue his historical studies. He was driven by the conviction he developed at Auschwitz, that he must do everything to prevent the world from forgetting the millions of murdered Jews.

His first in a series of books on the Holocaust was entitled *The Third Reich and the Jews*. He subsequently wrote books on the Nuremberg Laws,

Joseph Wulf. In 1965, Wulf, a historian and Holocaust survivor, urged the creation of an international Holocaust document center in the Wannsee Villa. He wanted the documents to be available to everyone. A library would house references in all languages, and the remainder of the building would be open to scholars doing research studies, as well as to conferences and seminars. But the German politicians did not want a Holocaust monument, and spurned Joseph Wulf. At the end of his life, Wulf believed all his efforts had been in vain. "I have published 18 books about the Third Reich," he lamented, "and they have had no effect. You can document everything to death for the Germans. There is a democratic regime in Bonn. Yet the mass murderers walk around free, live in their little houses, and grow flowers." Distraught over the collapse of his plans for a document center, Joseph Wulf committed suicide on October 10, 1974, by jumping from the window of his Berlin apartment, Giesebrechtstraße 4, Charlottenburg. (Ullstein Bilderdienst)

the history of the Warsaw and Lodz ghettos, and biographies of Heinrich Himmler, Martin Bormann (Hitler's private secretary and close associate), and Raoul Wallenberg, the Swedish diplomat who rescued Jews and disappeared in Russian captivity. The German publishers Rowolt and Ullstein issued many of Wulf's works in paperback editions, which are still in print. He received the Leo Baeck Prize in 1961 and the Carl von Ossietzky Medal in 1964.[1] But German historians criticized his writing as poorly organized, unreadable, and biased. Wulf responded, "I am objective, but not neutral."

[1]*Leo Baeck (1873–1956) was a rabbinical scholar and leader of the Jewish community in Berlin during the Third Reich. He declined all offers from abroad and announced that he would stay in Berlin until the last minyan (prayer quota). Baeck was arrested in 1943 and sent to There-*

Strolling down the Kurfürstendamm in Berlin, Joseph Wulf cut an unmistakable figure, and a casual observer could easily have taken him for a boulevardier. He dressed impeccably, carried a walking stick, and held a long cigarette holder clenched between his teeth at a jaunty angle.

In 1965 Wulf urged the creation of an international Holocaust document center. He wanted the documents to be available to everyone. A library would house references in all languages, and the remainder of the building would be open to scholars doing research studies, as well as to conferences and seminars. On August 29, 1966, Wulf, Friedrich Zipfel, and Peter Heilmann founded the International Document Center Organization for the Study of National Socialism and its Aftermath. The three men advocated that the document center be located in the Wannsee Villa.

Senator Heinrich Albertz and the Berlin Senate were not thrilled. As Albertz replied: "The Senate's view is that the past will not be overcome by setting aside a house, worth more than a million marks, which is now a domicile for schoolchildren. One would have to set aside many houses to isolate every building that was a venue for horrors. One should be more concerned with the people responsible for the horrors committed in these houses." The mayor of Neukölln, Klaus Schütz, was more blunt. In his district he wanted "no macabre cult site."

Joseph Wulf suggested a compromise. The Wannsee Villa would be used for the document center, while the World Jewish Congress would provide money to build school buildings on the grounds. The Berlin Senate refused this trade-off, instead suggesting two other pieces of property in Berlin that could be used for a document center. But these two spots weren't even available, and the World Jewish Congress did not wish to pay for any location other than the Wannsee Villa.

In fact, the German politicians did not want a Holocaust monument, and they spurned Joseph Wulf. At the end of his life, Wulf believed all his efforts had been in vain. "I have published 18 books about the Third Reich," he lamented, "and they have had no effect. You can document everything to death for the Germans. There is a democratic regime in Bonn. Yet the mass murderers walk around free, live in their little houses, and grow flowers."

(continued from previous page) *sienstadt. Yet he never abandoned his faith and tried to console fellow prisoners, most of whom were doomed to die. When the camp was liberated in 1945, he prevented the lynching of the Nazi guards by embittered inmates. In 1954 he founded and became the first presiding officer of the Leo Baeck Institute, New York and London, which was devoted to research on the history of Jews in Germany.*

Carl von Ossietzky (1889–1938) was a German journalist, pacifist, and critic of the army, arrested and tortured in 1933 after Hitler came to power, then interned in two concentration camps as an enemy of the state. While an inmate he was awarded the Nobel Peace Prize for 1935, but the Nazi government did not let him accept it. Ossietzky died in Berlin on May 3, 1938, of tuberculosis, which he had contracted in the concentration camps.

Distraught over the collapse of his plans for a document center, Joseph Wulf committed suicide on October 10, 1974.

There was no further consideration of Wulf's document center until September 1, 1986, when Eberhard Diepgen, mayor of Berlin, announced the intention of the Senate to place a memorial at Wannsee. Diepgen recalled that when he had first learned of nazism as a young student in the 1950s, nothing shocked him more than the Wannsee Protocol, which he described as "so cool and dispassionate in its form, so immensely evil in its content."

"There have been many cases of government-sponsored mass murder," said Diepgen. "But that a highly modern state, working with such brutal success, killed all the members of a race that it could capture, including mothers, children, and old people — that is unique and without any historical parallel."

In 1989 the Berlin schoolchildren finally moved out of the Wannsee Villa, and renovation began. Three years later, fifty years to the day after the Wannsee Conference, the Wannsee Villa was inaugurated as a monument to the millions of Jews who had perished at the hands of the Nazis. "In this house, on January 20, 1942, a barrier of civilization was broken and the abyss of barbarism was opened," said Heinz Galinski, an Auschwitz survivor and head of Germany's largest Jewish organization, at the dedication.[2]

The permanent exhibition in the Wannsee Villa is a powerful collection of photographs and texts that document not just the conference itself, but also its background and aftermath. Visitors pass large photos of Jews being arrested, herded into trucks and railroad cars, and then marched to their deaths in the gas chambers. One room of the exhibit is devoted solely to the murders at Auschwitz-Birkenau. On the walls of the former dining room, where the conference was held, hang photographs and short biographies of the fifteen men who attended the conference. The Joseph Wulf Mediothek on the second floor holds thousands of books on nazism, anti-Semitism, and the Jewish genocide, along with many videos, microfilm texts, and original Nazi era documents.

"Let us not deceive ourselves about what we have done," said Rita Süssmuth, President of the German Parliament, in a speech at the opening of the Wannsee memorial. "Experience tells us that whatever we repress catches up with us. No one can flee from their history."

---

[2]*Heinz Galinski died on July 19, 1992, age seventy-nine. On December 20, 1998, a bomb destroyed Galinski's marble tombstone in the Charlottenberg Jewish Cemetery. Vandals had already damaged the stone three months earlier. German authorities attributed the desecration to anti-Semitism.*

Appendix A

A Jew Defined

(*Reichsgesetzblatt [Reich Legal Gazette]* 1935, I:1333.)

First Ordinance to
the Reich Citizenship Law

November 14, 1935

On the basis of article 3 of the Reich Citizenship Law of September 15, 1935 *(Reich Legal Gazette I:* 1146) the following is ordered:

Article 1

1. Until the issuance of further regulations for the award of citizenship, nationals of German or related blood who possessed the right to vote in Reichstag elections at the time when the Reich Citizenship Law entered into force or who were granted provisional citizenship by the Reich Minister of Interior acting in agreement with the Deputy of the Führer, are provisionally considered Reich citizens.

2. The Reich Minister of Interior acting in agreement with the Deputy of the Führer may revoke provisional citizenship.

Article 2

1. The regulations of Article 1 apply also to nationals who were part Jews [jüdische Mischlinge].

2. Partly Jewish is anyone who is descended from one or two grandparents who are fully Jewish [volljüdisch] by race, in so far as he is not to be considered as Jewish under article 5, section 2. A grandparent is to be considered as fully Jewish if he belonged to the Jewish religious community.

Article 3

Only a Reich citizen as bearer of complete political rights may exercise the right to vote in political affairs or hold public office. The Reich Interior Minister or an agency empowered by him may make exceptions with regard to an admission to public office during the transition. The affairs of religious communities will not be affected.

Article 4

1. A Jew cannot be a Reich citizen. He is not allowed the right to vote in political affairs; he cannot hold public office.

2. Jewish civil servants will retire as of December 31, 1935. If these civil servants fought for Germany or her allies in the World War, they will receive the full pension to which they are entitled by their last position in the pay scale, until they reach retirement age; they will not, however, advance in seniority. Upon reaching retirement age their pension is to be based on pay scales which will prevail at that time.

3. The affairs of religious communities will not be affected.

4. The provisions of service for teachers in Jewish public schools will remain unaltered until new regulations are issued for the Jewish school system.

Article 5

1. A Jew is anyone who is descended from at least three grandparents who are fully Jewish by race. Article 2, paragraph 2, sentence 2 applies.

2. Also considered a Jew is a partly Jewish national who is descended from two fully Jewish grandparents and

a) who belonged to the Jewish religious community, upon adoption of the Reich Citizenship Law, or is received into the community thereafter, or

b) who was married to a Jewish person upon adoption of the law, or marries one thereafter, or

c) who is the offspring of a marriage concluded by a Jew (as defined in paragraph 1) after the entry into force of the Law for the Protection of German Blood and Honor of September 15, 1935 *(Reich Legal Gazette* I, 1146), or

d) who is the offspring of an extramarital relationship involving a Jew (as defined in paragraph 1) and who is born out of wedlock after July 31, 1936.

Article 6

1. Requirements for purity of blood exceeding those of article 5, which are made in Reich laws or regulations of the National Socialist German Workers' Party and its organizations, remain unaffected.

2. Any other requirements for purity of blood, exceeding those of article 4, may be made only with the consent of the Reich Minister of the Interior and the Deputy of the Führer. Insofar as requirements of this type exist already, they become void on January 1, 1936, unless they are accepted by the Reich Minister of the Interior acting with the agreement of the Deputy of the Führer. Acceptance is to be requested from the Reich Minister of the Interior.

Article 7

The Führer and Reich Chancellor may grant exemptions from the stipulations of implementory ordinances.

Berlin, November 14, 1935
The Führer and Reich Chancellor Adolf Hitler
The Reich Minister of the Interior
Frick
The Deputy of the Führer
R. Hess
(Reich Minister without Portfolio)

Appendix B

Letters

Reinhard Heydrich Writes a Letter About the Jews of Poland

Berlin, 21 October 1939,

To the chiefs of all participating groups of the security-police
Involves: Jewish-question in the occupied area.

I make reference to the discussion which took place in Berlin today and point out once again that the planned total measures (and therefore the ultimate goal) are to be kept strictly secret.

I distinguish between

1. the ultimate goal (which needs a longer grace period) and

2. the sections of the ultimate goal (which need a shorter time).

The planned measures necessitate a most thorough preparation, in both the technical and economic senses.

It is obvious that the necessary tasks cannot be fixed in all details. The standing instructions and guidelines serve the purpose of guiding the chiefs of the participating groups regarding practical considerations.

I.

The first step to the ultimate goal is transporting and concentrating the Jews in the country into the bigger cities.

This step is to be enforced with dispatch...

Concentration points will only be cities with rail links or hubs.

It is fundamental that Jewish communities with under 500 heads are to be dissolved and led to the next concentration point...

II.

Jewish elders.

1. In each Jewish community, a Jewish elder is to be identified.

He is to have full-responsibility for the carrying out of all instructions.

2. In case of the sabotage of such instructions, the elders are to announce the harshest measures.

3. The elders will provide a makeshift census of the Jews by sex in the following age-classes: a) below 16 years, b) from 16 to 20 years and c) over 20 years, and after segregation by main occupations, the elders will report the results in the shortest possible period.

4. Dates, means, and routes of deportation are to be determined by the elders. The elders are personally responsible for the deportation of the Jews of their communities.

The reason to be given for the concentration of the Jews in the cities is that Jews have taken part in sniper raids and looting-actions...

III.

All necessary measures are always to be coordinated with the German civil authorities and responsible local military authorities...

IV.

The chiefs of the participating groups will report to me the following data continuously:

1. Number of Jews in their area...

2. Names of the cities which have been selected as concentration points.

3. The dates for Jewish migration into the cities.

4. Overview of all Jewish economic activity in their area important to the four year plan and industry.

V.

For the attainment of these goals, I expect complete participation of all of the security-police and the security service.

The neighboring chiefs of the participating groups must work together so that the goals will be quickly attained.

VI.

The general staff, the representative of the four year plan (Herr State Secretary Neumann), the Reich Interior Ministry (Herr State Secretary Stuckart), the minister for food and economy (Herr State Secretary Landfried) as well as the chiefs of the civilian administration of the occupied area have received this communication.

Early documentary evidence of the final solution: Letter from SS-Major Rolf-Heinz Höppner in German-occupied Poland to Adolf Eichmann, Reich Security Main Office, Berlin

(Biuletyn Glowney Komisji Badania
  Zbrodni Hitlerowskich W Polsce
[Warsaw, Wydawnictwo Prawnicze] XII, 1960, pp. 27F–29F.)
L Hö/S
[Higher SS and Police Leader in Warthegau/
  SS-Major Rolf-Heinz Höppner]
to
Reich Security Main Office
Office IV B 4
Attention SS-Lt. Col. Eichmann
Berlin
July 16, 1941

Dear Comrade Eichmann,

Enclosed is a memorandum on the results of various discussions held locally in the office of the Reich Governor. I would be grateful to have your reactions sometime. These things sound in part fantastic, but in my view are thoroughly feasible.

1 enclosure

L Hö/S Poznan July 16, 1941 Memorandum
Subject: Solution of the Jewish question

During discussions in the office of the Reich Governor various groups broached the solution of the Jewish question in Warthe province. The following solution is being proposed.

1. All the Jews of Warthe province will be taken to a camp for 300,000 Jews which will be erected in barracks form as close as possible to the coal precincts and which will contain barracks-like installations for economic enterprises, tailor shops, shoe manufacturing plants, etc.

2. All Jews of Warthe province will be brought into this camp. Jews capable of labor may be constituted into labor columns as needed and drawn from the camp.

3. In my view, a camp of this type may be guarded by SS-Brig. Gen. Albert with substantially fewer police forces than are required now. Furthermore, the danger of epidemics, which always exists in the Lodz and other ghettos for the surrounding population, will be minimized.

4. This winter there is a danger that not all of the Jews can be fed. One should weigh honestly whether the most humane solution might not be to finish off those of the Jews who are not employable by means of some quick-working device. At any rate, that would be more pleasant than to let them starve to death.

5. For the rest, the proposal was made that in this camp all the Jewish women, from whom one could still expect children, should be sterilized so that the Jewish problem may actually be solved completely with this generation.

6. The Reich Governor has not yet expressed an opinion in this matter. There is an impression that Government President Ubelhör does not wish to see the ghetto in Lodz disappear since he [his office] seems to profit quite well with it. As an example of how one can profit from the Jews, I was told that the Reich Labor Ministry pays 6 Reichsmark from a special fund for each employed Jew, but that the Jew costs only 80 Pfennige.

Letter from Reischsmarschall Hermann Göring to Reinhard Heydrich, Mandating a Final Solution of the Jewish Question

(Nuremberg document PS-710.)
REICH MARSHAL OF GREATER GERMAN REICH
GÖRING TO CHIEF OF SECURITY POLICE AND
SECURITY SERVICE HEYDRICH
BERLIN, JULY [31], 1941

Complementing the task already assigned to you in the decree of January 24, 1939, to undertake, by emigration or evacuation, a solution of the Jewish question as advantageous as possible under the conditions at the time, I hereby charge you with making all necessary organizational, functional, and material preparations for a complete solution of the Jewish question in the German sphere of influence in Europe.

In so far as the jurisdiction of other central agencies may be touched thereby, they are to be involved.

I charge you furthermore with submitting to me in the near future an overall plan of the organizational, functional, and material measures to be taken in preparing for the implementation of the projected final solution of the Jewish question.

Reinhard Heydrich's Letter to Under State Secretary Martin Luther, Foreign Office, November 29, 1941, Inviting Luther to a Discussion of the Jewish Question, to Be Held on December 9, 1941

(Bundesarchiv Koblenz, Allgemeine Prozesse 6/122, unpag.)

Dear Party Comrade Luther!

On July 31, 1941, Reichsmarschall Göring of the Great German Reich ordered me to make all organizational, factual, and material preparations for a collective solution of the Jewish question in Europe, in consultation with the other central authorities, and to send him a description of these preparations soon. I include a photocopy of the Reichsmarschall's order.

Given the extraordinary significance of the Jewish question, and to reach a consensus as to how a final solution may be achieved, I propose to hold a discussion. The matter is imperative because since October 15, 1941, Jews have been transported out of Reich territory, including the protectorate of Bohemia and Moravia, and evacuated to the east.

I invite you to a breakfast discussion to be held on December 9, 1941, in the offices of the International Criminal Police Commission, Berlin, am Kleinen Wannsee Nr. 16 [Luther crossed out the Kleiner Wannsee address and penciled in *am Großen Wannsee 56–58*].

I have sent similar invitations to Herr Generalgouverneur Dr. Frank, Herr Gauleiter Dr. Meyer, the Herr state secretaries Stuckart, Dr. Schlegelberger, Gutterer and Neumann, as well as Herr Reichs office director Dr. Leibbrandt, SS-Obergruppenführer Krüger, SS-Gruppenführer Hofmann, SS-Gruppenführer Greifelt, SS-Oberführer Klopfer and Herr Ministerial Director Kritzinger.

Reinhard Heydrich's Invitation Letter to the Director of the Race and Settlement Main Office, SS Gruppenführer (Lieutenant General) Otto Hofmann, Dated January 8, 1942, Regarding a Breakfast Discussion [The Wannsee Conference] on January 20, 1942

(Bundesarchiv, Koblenz, Potsdam division, Nuremberg trials, case XI, Nr. 372, Bl. 107)

On account of sudden events, I had to cancel the discussion planned for December 12, 1941, regarding the final solution of the Jewish question and related matters. I had to inform some of those invited at the last minute of the cancellation.

In order not to put off this matter too long, I invite you to a newly scheduled breakfast meeting on January 20, 1942, at 12 o'clock Berlin, Am Großen Wannsee 56–58.

The list of persons invited in my last letter is unchanged.

Reinhard Heydrich's Cover Letter for the Wannsee Protocol, Addressed to Under State Secretary Martin Luther, Foreign Office, January 26, 1942, with an Invitation to a Follow-up Discussion to Be Held on March 6, 1942

(Bundesarchiv, Koblenz, Allgemeine Prozesse 6/122, unpag.)

Enclosed is the protocol of the January 20, 1942, conference. Since only the baseline conditions of the final solution of the Jewish question were decided, and since there was unanimity, I invite you as a specialist to finish planning the matter, as per the order of the Reichsmarschall [Göring]. We still must deal with the technical and material demands, practical approaches, and other details.

I envision that the first discussion of these matters will be held on March 6, 1942, 10:30 A.M., in Berlin, Kurfürstenstraße 116. I ask you to please ask your specialists to get in touch with my representative, SS-Obersturmbannführer Eichmann.

Appendix C

The Wannsee Protocol

(Nuremberg document NG-2586)
Secret Reich Matter
Conference Protocol
30 copies
16th copy

I. The following participated in the conference of January 20, 1942, in Berlin, Am Grossen Wannsee 56–58, on the final solution of the Jewish question:

> Gauleiter Dr. Meyer and Reich Office Director Dr. Leibbrandt
> Reich Ministry for the Occupied Eastern Territories
> State Secretary Dr. Stuckart — Reich Ministry of the Interior
> State Secretary Dr. Neumann — [Office of the Plenipotentiary of the Four Year Plan]
> State Secretary Dr. Freisler — Reich Justice Ministry
> State Secretary Dr. Bühler — Office of Governor General [of Poland]
> Under State Secretary Luther — Foreign Office
> SS [Senior]-Colonel Klopfer — Party Chancellery
> Ministerial Director Kritzinger — Reich Chancellery
> SS-Major General Hofmann — Race and Resettlement Main Office
> SS-Major General Müller — Reich Security Main Office
> SS-Lt. Colonel Eichmann — Reich Security Main Office
> SS [Senior]-Colonel Dr. Schöngarth — Commanding Officer of Security Police and Security Service in General Government [Poland]
> SS-Major Dr. Lange — Commander of Security Police and Security Service for General Commissariat Latvia, as deputy of Commanding Officer of Security Police and Security Service for Reich Commissariat Ostland [Baltic states and White Russia]
> Security Police and Security Service

II. Chief of Security Police and Security Service, SS-Lieutenant General

146

Heydrich, opened the meeting by informing everyone that the Reich Marshal [Göring] had placed him in charge of preparations for the final solution of the Jewish question, and that the invitations to this conference had been issued to clarify fundamental questions. The Reich Marshal's wish to have a draft submitted to him on the organizational, functional, and material considerations of a final solution of the European Jewish question requires that all of the central agencies, which are directly concerned with these problems, first join together with a view to paralleling their lines of action.

The control of the treatment of the final solution of the Jewish question resides centrally with the Reichsführer-SS and chief of the German police (chief of the security-police and the security service), regardless of geographical borders.

The Chief of Security Police and Security Service then reviewed briefly the battle fought thus far against these opponents. The principal stages constituted

a) Forcing the Jews out of individual sectors of life [Lebensgebiete] of the German people

b) Forcing the Jews out of the living space [Lebensraum] of the German people

To carry out these measures, the accelerated emigration of the Jews from Reich territory is regarded as a temporary solution.

On instructions of the Reich Marshal, a Reich Central Office for Jewish Emigration was established in January 1939, and its direction was entrusted to the Chief of the Security Police and Security Service. In particular the office had the task of

a) taking every step to prepare for a larger volume of Jewish emigration,

b) steering the flow of emigration,

c) expediting emigration in individual cases.

The goal of the task was to cleanse the German living space of Jews in a legal manner.

Everyone was aware of the disadvantages that such a forced emigration entailed. Yet they must be accepted, in view of the absence, for the moment, of other solutions.

The migration work in the ensuing period was not only a German problem, but also one that concerned the offices of the countries of destination and immigration. Financial difficulties, such as increasingly demanding regulations on the part of various foreign governments regarding money the immigrant had to show or pay on landing, insufficient berths on ships, constantly increasing immigration restrictions and suspensions all placed extraordinary burdens on emigration efforts. In spite of these difficulties, some 537,000 Jews were moved out from the day of the seizure of power to October 31, 1941. Of this total

from January 30, 1933 out of the Old Reich..................ca. 360,000
from March 15, 1938 out of Austria..........................ca. 147,000
from March 15, 1939 out of the Protectorate
    Bohemia and Moravia.....................................ca. 30,000

The emigration was financed by the Jews (or Jewish political organizations) themselves. In order to avoid having a residue of proletarianized Jews, the Jews with means had to finance the departure of the Jews without means; an appropriate assessment and emigration tax were used to finance the payments of debts owed by the poor Jews in the course of their emigration.

In addition to this tax in Reichsmarks, possession or payment of foreign currencies was required on landing. In order to spare German foreign currency reserves, the Jewish financial institutions abroad were obligated by Jewish organizations at home to take care of collecting an appropriate amount of foreign currency. In this manner about $9,500,000 given by foreign Jews was made available up to October 30, 1941.

Meanwhile, in view of the dangers of emigration in time of war and in view of the possibilities in the east, the Reichsführer-SS and Chief of the German Police [Himmler] has forbidden the emigration of Jews.

III. In place of emigration, with the Führer's authorization, forced evacuation of the Jews to the east is another possible solution. Emigration and forced evacuation are only alternatives, however.

Other practical experiences have been gathered, and these will be of great importance in the coming final solution of the Jewish question.

Around 11 million Jews are involved in this final solution of the Jewish question. They are distributed as follows among individual countries:

	Country	Number
A.		
	Old Reich	131,800
	Austria	43,700
	Eastern Territories [Poland]	420,000
	General Government [Poland]	2,284,000
	Bialystok [Poland]	400,000
	Protectorate of Bohemia and Moravia	74,200
	Estonia free of Jews	
	Latvia	3,500
	Lithuania	34,000
	Belgium	43,000
	Denmark	5,600
	France/occupied territory	165,000
	unoccupied territory	700,000
	Greece	69,000
	Netherlands	160,000
	Norway	1,300

Country	Number

B.

Country	Number
Bulgaria	48,000
England	330,000
Finland	2,300
Ireland	4,000
Italy, including Sardinia	58,000
Albania	200
Croatia	40,000
Portugal	3,000
Rumania, including Bessarabia	342,000
Sweden	8,000
Switzerland	18,000
Serbia	10,000
Slovakia	88,000
Spain	6,000
Turkey (European portion)	55,500
Hungary	742,800
USSR	5,000,000
Ukraine	2,994,684
White Russia, excluding Bialystok	446,484

Total: over 11,000,000

With regard to Jews in various foreign countries, the numbers listed include only Jews by religion, since these countries still lack, to some extent, definitions of Jews according to racial principles. Given prevailing attitudes and conceptions, the treatment of the problem in individual countries will be difficult, especially in Hungary and Rumania. For example, even today a Jew in Rumania can buy for cash appropriate documents officially certifying him as a foreign national.

The pervasive influence of Jewry in the USSR is known. The European area contains some 5 million, the Asian barely a half million Jews.

The occupational distribution of Jewry in the European area of the USSR was approximately as follows:

agriculture	9.1%
urban workers	14.8%
trade	20.0%
state employees	23.4%
private professions —	
medical, press, theater, and so forth	32.7%

In the course of the final solution, the Jews should be brought under appropriate direction in a suitable manner to the east for labor utilization. Separated by sex, the Jews capable of work will be led into these areas in large labor columns to build roads whereby doubtless a large part will fall away.

The inevitable final remainder which doubtless constitutes the toughest element will have to be dealt with appropriately, since it represents a natural selection which upon liberation is to be regarded as a germ cell of a new Jewish development. (See the lesson of history.)

In the course of the practical implementation of the final solution, Europe will be combed from west to east. If only because of the apartment shortage and other socio-political necessities, the Reich area including the Protectorate of Bohemia and Moravia will have to be placed ahead of the line.

For the moment, the evacuated Jews will be brought bit by bit to so-called transit ghettos from where they will be transported farther to the east.

SS-Lieutenant General Heydrich pointed out further that an important prerequisite for the evacuation in general was the exact specification of the category of persons liable to be involved.

It is intended not to evacuate Jews over 65, but to transfer them to an old people's ghetto (the plan calls for Theresienstadt).

In addition to these age groups (some 30% of the 280,000 Jews who lived in the Old Reich and Austria on October 1, 1941, are over 65) the old people's ghetto will receive badly injured Jewish war veterans and Jews with war decorations (Iron Cross First Class). Many problems will be eliminated in one blow by means of this definitive solution.

The start of major individual evacuation operations will depend in large measure on military developments. With regard to the treatment of the final solution in European areas we occupy or influence, it was proposed that the appropriate specialists of the Foreign Office get together with the experts having jurisdiction in these matters within the Security Police and Security Service.

In Slovakia and Croatia the situation is no longer all that difficult, since the essential key questions there have already been resolved. Meanwhile, the Rumanian government has already appointed a plenipotentiary for Jewish affairs. To settle the matter in Hungary, it will be necessary before long to impose upon the Hungarian government an adviser on Jewish questions.

Regarding a start of preparations in Italy, SS-Lieutenant General Heydrich considers it appropriate to contact Police Chief [Himmler].

In occupied and unoccupied France, the seizure of Jews for evacuation should in all probability proceed without major difficulty.

Assistant Secretary Luther [Foreign Office] then pointed out that with a comprehensive treatment of these problems in some countries, such as the Nordic states, difficulties would emerge and that it would be best to hold off. In view of the insignificant number of Jews involved, the postponement would not amount to a substantial restriction. On the other hand, the Foreign Office sees no major difficulties in southeastern and western Europe.

SS-Major General Hofmann intends to dispatch a specialist of the Race and

Resettlement Office to Hungary as soon as the Chief of Security Police and Security Service is ready to tackle the situation over there. It was decided that temporarily the specialist of the Race and Resettlement Office who is not to become active should officially be an assistant to the Police Attaché.

IV. The Nuremberg laws should constitute the basis, so to speak, of the final solution, while a solution of the mixed marriage and mixed parentage questions is a prerequisite for the complete clearing up of the problem.

The Chief of the Security Police and Security Service addressed himself to a letter from the Chief of the Reich Chancellery, and speaking theoretically for the moment, dealt with the following points:

1. Treatment of Mischlinge of the 1st degree:

In view of the final solution of the Jewish question, Mischlinge of the first degree are placed into the same position as Jews. To be excepted from this treatment will be

a) Mischlinge of the 1st degree married to Germans, if this marriage produced offspring (Mischlinge of the 2nd degree). These Mischlinge of the 2nd degree are in the main placed into the same position as Germans.

b) Mischlinge of the 1st degree who in some (vital) area have been accorded exceptional treatment by the higher authorities of the party or state. Each individual case has to be examined anew, whereby one must not exclude an unfavorable decision for the Mischling.

Prerequisite for an exemption must always be basic merits of the Mischling himself (not merits of the German parent or marital partner).

To avoid any progeny and to clean up the Mischling problem once and for all, the Mischlinge of the 1st degree who are to be exempted from evacuation must be sterilized. Sterilization is voluntary, but it is a prerequisite for remaining in the Reich. The sterilized "Mischling" is then liberated from all the constricting ordinances to which he has heretofore been subjected.

2. Treatment of Mischlinge of the 2nd degree:

In principle, the Mischlinge of the 2nd degree will be treated as Germans, with the exception of the following cases in which Mischlinge of the 2nd degree will be placed into the same position as Jews:

a) The descent of the Mischling of the 2nd degree from a bastard marriage (both parts Mischlinge).

b) Racially exceptionally poor appearance of the Mischling of the 2nd degree, so that for external reasons alone he has to be considered a Jew.

c) A particularly unfavorable appraisal from a police and political viewpoint which indicates that the Mischling of the 2nd degree feels and behaves like a Jew.

Even these considerations, however, should not apply if the Mischling of the 2nd degree is married to a German.

3. Marriages between full Jews and Germans:

In individual cases, it must be decided whether the Jewish partner is to be evacuated or whether, considering the effect of such a measure on the German relatives, he is to be transferred to an old people's ghetto.

4. Marriages between Mischlinge of the 1st degree and Germans:

a) Without children:

If there are no children, the Mischling of the 1st degree is to be evacuated, or transferred to an old people's ghetto (same treatment as in the case of marriages between full Jews and Germans, point 3).

b) With children:

If there are children (Mischlinge of the 2nd degree) and they are placed into the same position as Jews, they will be evacuated along with the [parent who is a] Mischling of the 1st degree, or transferred to a ghetto. Insofar as these children are placed into the same position as Germans (the regular case) they are to be exempted from evacuation, and so will [the parent who is a] Mischling of the 1st degree.

5. Marriages between Mischlinge of the 1st degree and Mischlinge of the 2nd degree or Jews:

In the case of these marriages, all the elements (including the children) are to be treated as Jews and hence evacuated, or transferred to an old people's ghetto.

6. Marriages between Mischlinge of the 1st degree and Mischlinge of the 2nd degree:

Both partners, without regard to children, are to be evacuated, or placed into an old people's ghetto, since racially the children, if any, regularly reveal a stronger Jewish blood component than do Mischlinge of the 2nd degree.

SS-Major General Hofmann is of the view that one will have to make widespread use of sterilization, especially since the Mischlinge, faced with the choice of being evacuated or sterilized, would rather submit to sterilization.

State Secretary Dr. Stuckart [Interior Ministry] stated that in this form the practical implementation of the possibilities just mentioned for clearing up the mixed marriage and mixed parentage problem would entail an endless administrative task. In order to be sure, however, of also taking into account the biological facts, State Secretary Dr. Stuckart proposed to proceed with compulsory sterilization.

To simplify the Mischling problem, one should further think about the possibility of enabling the lawmaker to say in so many words: "These marriages are dissolved."

As for the effect of the evacuation of the Jews on economic life, State Secretary Neumann [Four Year Plan] declared that at the moment Jews employed in important war work could not be evacuated until replacements became available.

SS-Lieutenant General Heydrich pointed to the fact that in accordance with directives authorized by him for current evacuations, these Jews were not being evacuated anyhow.

State Secretary Dr. Bühler stated that the General Government [of Poland] would welcome the start of the final solution in its territory, since the transport problem was no overriding factor there and the course of the action would not be hindered by considerations of work utilization. Jews should be removed from the domain of the General Government as fast as possible, because it is precisely here that the Jew constitutes a substantial danger as carrier of epidemics and also because his continued black market activities create constant disorder in the economic structure of the country. Moreover, the majority of the 2½ million Jews involved are not capable of work.

State Secretary Dr. Bühler stated further that the Chief of the Security Police and Security Service was in charge of the final solution of the Jewish question in the General Government and that his work was being supported by the offices of the General Government. He only had one favor to ask: that the Jewish question in this territory be solved as rapidly as possible.

Finally there was a discussion of the various possible solutions, with both Gauleiter Dr. Meyer and State Secretary Dr. Bühler expressing the view that they could carry out certain preparatory measures in their territories on their own, provided, however, that any disturbance of the [non-Jewish] population had to be avoided.

The conference was closed with a plea of the Chief of Security Police and Security Service for the cooperation of all the participants in the implementation of the final solution.

Appendix D

Biographies of Wannsee Conference Participants

MARTIN LUTHER

Martin Luther was born in Berlin on December 16, 1895. His father was a civic counselor, and his mother, née von Schönberg, was of noble birth. He joined the German army in August 1914, serving in railway units throughout the war. A furniture remover by profession, Luther joined the SA and the Nazi party as member number 1,010,333 on March 1, 1932.

In 1936 Luther entered the Bureau Ribbentrop, a Nazi party agency for advising Hitler on foreign policy, in the modest role of forwarding agent in charge of office equipment. The industrious Luther rose rapidly — in spite of an indictment against him for embezzling party funds which was eventually dropped — and on May 7, 1940, he was appointed head of the new *Germany* division (Abteiling Deutschland) within the Foreign Office, a position he held until his fall in April 1943. Luther was responsible for propaganda and liaison with all Party organizations, the SS, and the police. He soon became one of Himmler's and Heydrich's most powerful agents and gradually undermined the position of his boss, Foreign Minister Joachim von Ribbentrop, a former champagne salesman with a rich wife.

Luther's talent for organization, his efficiency and skill in bureaucratic infighting, and his cold, calculating, and unscrupulous methods made him a formidable adversary in the internal power struggles of the Third Reich. Promoted to Unterstaatssekretär in July 1941, he worked with Eichmann and learned that mass murder of the Jews had begun. At the Wannsee Conference, Luther agreed with Heydrich to promote cooperation between the Foreign Office and the Reich Security Main Office in the murder of European Jews.

Luther was deeply involved in the deportation of Jews from western and southeastern Europe (Russia and Poland were excluded from Foreign Office concern). His letter to the German legation in Preßburg, February 16, 1942, docu-

Martin Luther. An *Unterstaatssekretär* in the Foreigh Office, Luther had worked with Eichmann. At the Wannsee Conference, Luther agreed with Heydrich to promote cooperation between the Foreigh Office and the Reich Security Main Office in the murder of European Jews. (Ullstein Bilderdienst)

ments this activity: "In carrying out the measures for the final solution of the European Jewish question, the German government is ready immediately to seize and transport 20,000 young, strong Slovak Jews to the East, where there is work for them. Please notify the local government. As soon as an understanding is reached with the Slovak government, details will be discussed orally with the advisor for Jewish questions."

Luther also ceaselessly prodded hesitant governments to undertake more aggressive deportation measures. An extensive investigation into Luther's activities is contained in *The Final Solution and the German Foreign Office* by Christopher R. Browning.

Luther's career ended abruptly in April 1943 with his unsuccessful coup against von Ribbentrop. Luther was sent to the Sachsenhausen concentration camp, just north of Berlin. After a botched suicide attempt, he was released as the Russians were closing in on Berlin; he died of heart failure in a local hospital, May 13, 1945. The Allies executed his nemesis, von Ribbentrop, at Nuremberg a year later.

DR. JOSEF BÜHLER

Bühler was born February 16, 1904 in Waldsee/Würtemberg, the son of a baker. The Catholic Bühler family had twelve children. Josef Bühler studied law and later worked in the Munich offices of Hans Frank, Hitler's lawyer. Bühler helped Frank defend the Nazis against various accusations during the Weimar period.

On April 1, 1933, Bühler joined the Nazi party as member number 1,663,751.

Josef Bühler (left) confers with Hans Frank (center) and Dienstleiter Schalk (Right) of the Reich Labor Office. When Hitler named Frank, a lawyer, governor general of the German occupied section of Poland, Frank appointed Bühler chief of the governor general's bureau. On January 20, 1942, Bühler represented Frank at the Wannsee Conference. Bühler recommended that the Polish Jews be annihilated first. Thus in March 1942, the destruction of the Jews began around Lublin and continued until stationary gas chambers were built at Belzec. (Bundesarchiv)

When he was in the dock at Nuremberg, he said he had joined to get a civil service job. In fact, he did become a public prosecutor in Munich, but he had held the same post, without the support of the Nazis, before he went to work for Frank.

Bühler's ascent was rapid. On February 1, 1935, he became a senior public prosecutor. His patron, Frank, became a Reichsminister and, shortly before the war began, he appointed Bühler a ministerial counselor.

The decisive moment in Bühler's career occurred in 1939, just after Poland had been overrun. When Hitler named Frank governor general of the German occupied section, Frank appointed Bühler chief of the governor general's bureau. Frank's and Bühler's elegant offices were situated in Krakow, in Wawel Castle, ancient seat of the rulers of Poland. In the meantime, all official references to the state of Poland disappeared.

In March 1941, Bühler acquired the title of acting state secretary. Two months later he became permanent state secretary, and in June 1941 he was named Frank's permanent representative. In this capacity, Bühler was involved in all crimes committed against the Poles, as well as the mass murder of Jews, until he fled the advancing Red Army in January 1945.

On January 20, 1942, Bühler represented Frank at the Wannsee Conference. Bühler recommended that the Polish Jews be annihilated first. Thus in

March 1942, the destruction of the Jews began around Lublin and continued until stationary gas chambers were built at Belzec.

Bühler was arrested on May 30, 1945. During the first Nuremberg trials in 1946, he was a called as a witness against Frank. Bühler tried to trivialize Frank's murderous threats against Poland and the Jews, calling them a product of Frank's luxuriant rhetoric and imagination.

Bühler mentioned the Wannsee Conference incidentally when the Polish state prosecutor, Jerzy Sawicki, interrogated him in February 1946. Since the Wannsee Protocol had not been found, Bühler was able to give a totally untrue account of his conversations with Heydrich at the conference. He was convinced, he told Sawicki, that "the Jews would be resettled in a humane manner."

To distance himself from the Nazis and save his own skin, Bühler maintained that he was an opponent of the high SS and Gestapo officers' anti-Polish measures. But all his lies did him no good. In accord with previous agreements, the Allies turned Bühler over to the Poles, since his criminal activities were so clearly carried out on Polish territory. The Polish Supreme Court tried him and sentenced him to death on July 5, 1948.

DR. ROLAND FREISLER

Freisler came from a family of peripatetic reformed Protestants. Shortly before his birth on October 30, 1893, the family moved from Moravia to Celle. In the same year, the Freislers moved to Hannover, in 1895 to Hameln, and in 1896 to Duisberg, where Freisler's father worked as an engineer for the local harbor-planning authorities. In 1900 the family moved to Aachen, where Freisler père was employed as an engineering teacher in the Imperial School of Architecture.

Roland Freisler went to high school in Aachen, but he did not finish college until the family had moved, once more, to the city of Kassel. He then matriculated at the University of Kiel, where he began the study of law.

The outbreak of war in 1914 interrupted Freisler's law studies. On August 4 he joined the 167th infantry regiment, was wounded at the bat-

Dr. Roland Freisler. Representing the Ministry of Justice, Freisler attended the Wannsee Conference. This ministry had codified all measures for the persecution of German Jews since the advent of the Nuremberg laws in 1935. On August 23, 1942, Freisler was named president of the people's court. In his red robe, he became a living terror. His fiendish, raucous judicial temperament is well preserved on newsreel film, showing him as he presided at the trial of the July 20, 1944, conspirators who tried to assassinate Hitler. (Ullstein Bilderdienst)

tle of Langemarck, and was sent to the eastern front after his recovery. The Russians captured him on October 18, 1915, and he spent the rest of the war in a prison camp. By the armistice, he had won the Iron Cross, both second and first class.

Freisler began his law studies again in 1920 at Jena. In early 1922, he submitted to the legal faculty his dissertation, "Fundamentals of Business Organization," and graduated with the degree, Doctor of Law (Dr. jur.). The dissertation was well received and published in the University's *Proceedings of the Institute for Economic Law.* His preceptors, Professors Justus Wilhelm Hedemann and Otto Koellreuter, later wrote many fascist legal articles.

Freisler went to work as an assistant prosecutor for the district court in Celle; he took his state examination in Berlin, October 2, 1923. He began working as a lawyer in Kassel on February 13, 1924, and his younger brother soon entered his firm.

In 1924 Freisler joined a local far-right-wing political organization, the People's Social Party, and on July 9, 1925, he joined the Nazi party as member number 9,679. Because he had become a member so early, he was one of the Alte Kämpfer (old fighters), and in 1934 the Nazis honored him with a golden party insignia.

An eager, ambitious Nazi, Freisler frequently defended party members. He was named acting Gauleiter of Hessen-Nassau-North but failed to become permanent Gauleiter. He made another grab for power in Kassel, when he and other party members occupied the city hall and raised the Nazi flag over the courthouse.

When Hitler came to power, Freisler's many years of service to the party assured him a plum job. In February 1933, he became ministerial director in the Prussian Ministry of Justice, which was headed by Dr. Hans Kerl, another old party member. On June 1, 1933, Freisler was appointed under state secretary. His first act was to submit a memorandum on Nazi criminal justice recommending a complete dehumanization. For example, should someone have the intention to commit a crime and be apprehended, this person should immediately be classed as subhuman and an enemy of the state. Anyone considered a terrorist should have no legal protection. When the Reich and Prussian Justice Ministries were combined, Freisler became a state secretary of the new entity. Among his responsibilities was the so-called people's court, which punished citizens according to the terrible new laws.

Shortly after the attack on Poland in September 1939, Freisler went to Bromberg (Bydgoszcz) to organize military courts and special courts. But the persecutions and murders already taking place were not generally under the jurisdiction of these courts. Freisler formulated a harsh German-Polish criminal code, which took effect January 1, 1942, and was justified by the "antisocial nature of the Poles."

Representing the Ministry of Justice, Freisler attended the Wannsee Conference. This ministry had codified all measures for the persecution of German Jews since the advent of the Nuremberg Laws in 1935.

On August 23, 1942, Freisler was named president of the people's court. In his red robe, he became a living terror. His fiendish, raucous judicial temperament is well preserved on newsreel film, showing him as he presided at the trial of the July 20, 1944 conspirators, who tried to assassinate Hitler.

The first eight officers were brought before the court on August 7. The defendants entered the courtroom of the Kammergericht in Berlin wearing old clothes. Field Marshal Erwin von Witzleben, without his false teeth, looked like a tramp in a comedy as he kept hitching up his oversize, beltless pants. Freisler, an expert on Soviet law, screamed like the Soviet judges he so admired: "You dirty old man, why do you keep fiddling with your trousers?"

"Never before in the history of German justice," wrote one shorthand secretary, "have defendants been treated with such brutality, such fanatic ruthlessness, as at these proceedings." In a stentorian voice, Freisler pronounced all eight men guilty of treason against the Führer, which they were, and against German history, which they were not.

According to Hitler's instructions, the condemned men were taken to a small room in Plötzensee Prison, stripped to the waist, hung by piano wire from meat hooks, and slowly strangled. The death chamber is preserved to this day as a memorial to the anti–Hitler resistance. A motion picture cameraman was present to film the gruesome executions.

An SS officer invited Albert Speer, as Hitler's armaments minister, to a showing of the film. Speer declined the invitation. "The very thought made me sick," he told journalist Gitta Sereny three decades later.

Historian John Toland quoted (from a 1971 *Playboy* interview) Speer's saying that "Hitler and his guests attended a screening," and that "Hitler loved the film and had it shown over and over again: it became one of his favorite entertainments."

"I didn't say that," Speer told Sereny. "As far as I knew Hitler never saw the film, and I have always said so. It was not his nature to want to see a thing like that. I doubt, too, that he looked at the photographs any more than I did." He added mildly, "I think a number of misquotes were probably due to linguistic misunderstandings, no doubt my fault; my English was not that good." He shrugged. "It happens often."

Colonel Nikolaus von Below, Hitler's adjutant, who was at headquarters throughout, in his memoirs agrees with Speer. "I declined to look at these photographs. And Hitler would have found no more pleasure in looking at them than in seeing photographs of destroyed cities. He literally closed his eyes if forced to see the consequences of his orders...."

In any case, Roland Freisler's Ministry of Justice indicted 10,289 people and put 8,909 to death for the conspiracy. Some defendants screamed at Freisler that the Allies would hang him after the war. But he died during an Allied bombing raid on Berlin, February 3, 1945, while conducting another treason trial. On the site of Freisler's People's Court in Berlin is SONY's corporate headquarters.

OTTO HOFMANN

Otto Hofmann, the son of a merchant, was born March 16, 1896, in the Austrian city of Innsbruck. From the age of eight, he grew up in the house of his step-grandfather, an army major educated in Germany. Hofmann attended elementary school and high school in Munich.

At the outbreak of World War I, Hofmann volunteered for service in the 9th Bavarian field artillery regiment. He was stationed in Landsberg am Lech, in France, and on the eastern front. In March 1917, he joined an air regiment. In June a Russian flier shot him down near the Polish town of Cernowitz. After five weeks of captivity he escaped. Hofmann had begun pilot training as the war ended, and he won the Iron Cross first and second class as well as the Bavarian War Service Cross and other medals.

Released from the army in March 1919, Hofmann joined the Bavarian border patrol; later he worked as a salesman for his father-in-law, a Nuremberg wine wholesaler. After his divorce, he became an independent representative for local and foreign wine producers.

Hofmann was a Nazi party member until the party was outlawed after the putsch of November 1923. On August 1, 1929, he rejoined as member number 145,729 and on April 1, 1933 joined the SS as member number 7,646. At first he assumed only honorary SS ranks: on December 17, 1931 Untersturmführer (2nd Lieutenant); on September 9, 1932 Hauptsturmführer (Captain); and on January 30, 1933 Sturmbannführer (Major). In April 1933 Hofmann became a regular SS member and an adjutant to the leader of the "political help police," responsible for finding and arresting antifascists. Thereafter he rose rapidly through the ranks and by 1935 was an Oberführer (Brigadier General).

Otto Hofmann. In 1937 Hofmann, an SS officer, was transferred to the Race and Settlement main office in Berlin. On September 7, 1940 he became a chief of this office. On April 20, 1941, he was promoted to SS-Gruppenführer (lieutenant general). In this capacity Hofmann attended the Wannsee Conference, and played a large part in the criminal acts which took place in Poland, the Soviet Union, and the rest of eastern Europe. (Bundesarchiv)

In 1937 Hofmann was transferred to the Race and Settlement main office in Berlin. On September 7, 1940, he became a chief of this office. On April 20, 1941, he was promoted to SS Gruppenführer (Lieutenant General). In this capacity Hofmann played a large part in the criminal acts which took place in Poland, the Soviet Union, and the rest of eastern Europe.

Hofmann spent a great deal of time in these areas, thereby incurring Himmler's criticism. The SS boss felt that Hofmann should concern himself with overall policies and confine himself to the main office.

On March 13, 1943, Himmler accepted Hofmann's "voluntary withdrawal" from his posting and sent him to Stuttgart. But as the Allies approached the western border of the Reich, Himmler bombarded Hofmann with criticism. The SS boss was especially furious that SS and security police had fled Alsace in panic as the Allied soldiers drew near. Reminding Hofmann that he had already ordered the shooting of an SS chief in Paris, Himmler advised his subordinate to spend more time on the west bank of the Rhine.

The end of the war found Hofmann an Allied prisoner. He was tried at Nuremberg and on March 10, 1948 was sentenced to twenty-five years imprisonment for war crimes and crimes against humanity. He received amnesty in 1954 and was released from Landsberg Prison, the same jail in which Hitler had been incarcerated after the 1923 putsch. Hofmann went to work as a business clerk in Württemberg. He died in 1982.

DR. GERHARD KLOPFER

Gerhard Klopfer was born in the Silesian (east Prussian) town of Schreibersdorf on February 18, 1905. His father was a farmer and provincial official who sent his son to the local high school. After graduation, Klopfer attended the universities of Breslau and Jena, where he studied law. His doctoral thesis was entitled "The True Duty of the Employee in the Employment Relationship" and led to a judgeship.

Klopfer joined the Nazi party on April 1, 1933, as member number 1,706,842. A few weeks later, he joined the SA (Sturmabteilung), the private Nazi army, and also the SS as member 272,227. On November 1, 1933, Klopfer became a state prosecutor in Düsseldorf. Many such positions had

Dr. Gerhard Klopfer. In 1941, Klopfer, a lawyer, was named to the party chancellery, as assistant to Martin Bormann, and he also became a state secretary. In this capacity he attended the Wannsee Conference. Although Klopfer was unknown to the German public, he was one of the most influential and best informed Nazi bureaucrats. (Bundesarchiv)

become available because right-wing officials had forced out large numbers of civil servants, especially Jews.

The prosecutor position was only temporary. On December 1, 1933, Klopfer became an official in the Prussian State Ministry for Agriculture, Land, and Forests under Walther Darré. Hitler had appointed Darré, a fanatical Nazi and SS Gruppenführer (Lieutenant General), as Reich Agriculture Leader and Reich Food Minister.

On August 1, 1934, Klopfer was promoted to government counselor, and on December 8 he was given a position in the Gestapo. The SS made it a practice to elevate their most reliable people to key positions of power and did so for Klopfer. On April 18, 1935, he joined the staff of the "Representatives of the Führer," headed by Rudolf Hess and Martin Bormann, Hess's former deputy. When Hess made his famous unauthorized flight to England in 1941, Klopfer was named to the party chancellery, as assistant to Bormann, and he also became a state secretary. In this capacity he attended the Wannsee Conference.

Although Klopfer was unknown to the German public, he was one of the most influential and best informed Nazi bureaucrats. When he was imprisoned after the war, he tried to minimize his importance and maximize his ignorance, as did most of his confrères. He was a witness during the Wilhelmstraße trials of many of the former Nazi state secretaries at Nuremberg in 1948. Under questioning, Klopfer strenuously denied having had anything to do with the destruction of the Jews, admitting only to hearing "rumors" about it.

American investigators were very suspicious of Klopfer and wanted to include him in another group of Nazis to be tried. According to one of the American prosecutors, Robert M. W. Kempner, the indictments had already been completed when pressure from Washington led to cancellation of the trials. The cold war had begun, and unity became more important than the pursuit of criminal justice.

The material incriminating Klopfer was given to German authorities investigating Nazi crimes, and German prosecutors tried to indict him. But on January 29, 1962, they dropped the matter. Klopfer died in Ulm, Germany in 1987, having outlived all other participants at the Wannsee Conference.

FRIEDRICH WILHELM KRITZINGER

Friedrich Wilhelm Kritzinger was born April 14, 1890, in Grünfier, the son of a Lutheran pastor. He attended high school in the towns of Posen and Gnesen, graduating in 1908. After finishing law studies, he served legal apprenticeships in Mogilno, Gnesen, Berlin, and Hirschberg (Silesia — east Prussia). He passed a bar examination in 1913 and joined a law practice in Berlin.

In 1913 Kritzinger entered military service in Infantry Battalion number 5 and served throughout World War I. He was awarded the Iron Cross first and second classes and the Order of the House of Hohenzollern, a medal named after the rulers of Prussia. At the end of the war, he again practiced law.

Kritzinger was employed by the district court in the town of Striegau when he married Countess Schwerin-Krosigk, the daughter of a large land owner. Now having considerable money, Kritzinger went to work in the Reich Justice Ministry as an assistant in the department of international law, and he climbed the civil service ladder. Later, he was to insist that his job as a bureaucrat was his true life's vocation and that he was loyal to the prevailing government, be it Weimar or Nazi. Kritzinger moved in 1924 to the Prussian department of commerce, where he served as court adviser for savings banks. A year later, he was with the Reich Justice Ministry as senior executive officer for international and constitutional law. He joined the Nazi party on December 1,1935 as member number 4,814,517 and received a Wehrmacht appointment as Oberleutnant (First Lieutenant).

In 1938 Kritzinger made a consequential career move, joining the Reich Chancellery after receiving a job offer from the chief, Hans Heinrich Lammers. Soon Kritzinger was the number two man, responsible for the economy, finance, labor, state railroads, and postal service. As an under state secretary he represented his ministry at the Wannsee Conference.

Kritzinger was arrested in 1946 and interrogated by Robert M. W. Kempner. Insisting that his behavior was comparable to that of a sailor who would not abandon his ship in time of danger, Kritzinger said that during the war he had three times asked to be sent to the front and was ashamed to have had a desk job. He was the only Wannsee Conference participant, beside Eichmann, to describe in detail everything that had occurred and to acknowledge the criminal nature of the gathering. Kempner demanded an affidavit from Kritzinger and informed him that he would be prosecuted. But the former under state secretary became so ill in prison that he was released, and he died October 1947 in a Nuremberg hospital.

DR. RUDOLF ERWIN LANGE

Rudolf Lange was born April 18, 1910, in Weißwasser, Kreis Rothenburg, into a Lutheran family. He graduated from high school in Staßfurt in 1928, went on to study law, and received a Doctor of Jurisprudence degree from the University of Jena on December 12, 1932. He joined the SA in November 1933. However, he felt he had made a bad career move, and three years later he joined the SS as member number 290,308 with the rank of Sturmmann (Private First Class). By 1943 he had risen to Obersturmbannführer (Lieutenant Colonel).

Stationed in Berlin, Vienna, Weimar, Erfurt, and Kassel, Lange was one of hundreds of Gestapo officials who maintained the terror apparatus of the Nazi state. Later, as commander of Einsatz-group A, he was responsible for the murder of Jews in eastern Europe. Appointed December 3, 1941, as commander of the Reich security police and Reich security service in Latvia, he ordered the massacre of Latvian and German Jews near Riga.

Lange remained in Riga and was decorated for his service with the Iron

Dr. Rudolf Erwin Lange. Stationed in Berlin, Vienna, Weimar, Erfurt, and Kassel, Lange was one of hundreds of Gestapo officials who maintained the terror apparatus of the Nazi state. Later, as commander of *Einsatz*-group A, Lange was responsible for the murder of Jews in eastern Europe. Appointed December 3, 1941 as commander of the Reich security police and Reich security service in Latvia, Lange ordered the massacre of Latvian and German Jews near Riga. Heydrich did not initially ask a representative of the security police from the occupied Baltic to the Wannsee Conference, probably because the mass shootings in Riga had already created a sensation. As head of the security police in Riga, Lange was one of the last officials invited to the conference. (Bundesarchiv)

Cross first class. In early 1945, he was ordered to Posen (in Poland) to command the security police. Just as he reached his new post, the Red Army surrounded and bombarded the city. Lange commanded the defense with a fanaticism born of the knowledge that the Allies would punish him severely for his heinous crimes. He was wounded in battle, and promoted to SS Standartenführer (Colonel) on January 30, 1945. Hitler also awarded him the seldom-given German Cross in Gold. Lange died fighting at Posen.

DR. ALFRED MEYER

Alfred Meyer was born in Göttingen on October 5, 1891, to a Lutheran family, son of a civic counselor. He graduated from high school in 1911 and began the study of law in Lausanne in 1912.

A year later he left school and enlisted in Infantry Regiment 68 in Koblenz. Intending to become a career officer, Meyer enrolled in the war college in Metz. During World War I he fought in France, won the Iron Cross first and second class, and was promoted to battalion leader. In April 1917 he was wounded, captured by the French, and did not return to Germany until 1920.

Discharged from the army as Hauptmann (Captain), Meyer worked as a salesman for Deutscher Erdöl AG, a German oil company in Gelsenkirchen. He subsequently matriculated at the Universities of Bonn and Würzburg, where he studied economics and international law, and received a doctorate from Würzburg. He then returned to his job at Deutscher Erdöl.

On April 1, 1928, Meyer joined the Nazi party as member number 28,738, and he rose rapidly. He was district group leader in Gelsenkirchen and, in 1930, the single deputy of his party to the city government. He advanced to district leader in Emscher-Lippe and on January 1, 1931, to Gauleiter in the district of Westphalia North.

Meyer now decided on a full-time political career and gave up his position

Alfred Meyer. Appointed state secretary for the occupied eastern territories in 1941, Meyer was involved in exploiting and plundering the conquered Soviet Union, as well as impoverishing, terrorizing and liquidating its inhabitants. Meyer was invited to the Wannsee Conference because the annihilation of Jews had been his prime responsibility. (Ullstein Bilder-dienst)

as an oil company official. He was elected to the Prussian state parliament and, in March 1933, became a member of the Reichstag. Since 1932 he had been an editor of the Nazi newspaper *Red Earth,* published in Bochum.

After Hitler came to power in 1933, Meyer remained at his regional post and continued to advance. He became a member of the state parliament of the province of Westphalia and representative to the provincial Reich council. More important was his May 1, 1933, nomination to be a Reich-governor. To his Gauleiter post, he added a more important one on November 17, 1938, when he became president of the province of Westphalia. In the same month, he was named an SA Obergruppenführer (General).

After his many jobs and sinecures, Meyer was appointed as state secretary for the occupied eastern territories in 1941. In this capacity, he was involved in exploiting and plundering the conquered Soviet Union, as well as impoverishing, terrorizing, and liquidating its inhabitants.

Meyer was invited to the Wannsee Conference because the annihilation of Jews had been his prime responsibility. At the conference, he suggested that "certain preparatory work" be carried out "on the spot at the places in question, yet without creating unrest among the civilian population." In July 1942 he urged that persons of "mixed blood" in the Soviet Union be subjected to the same measures as Jews. But as increasing numbers of western European Jews were shipped to his area, Meyer saw mounting chaos erupt. In May 1945 he committed suicide.

DR. GEORG LEIBBRANDT

The son of a German expatriate, Georg Leibbrandt was born September 5, 1899, in Hoffnungsthal, near Odessa, and went to school in the area. When German troops advanced into the Ukraine in 1918, Leibbrandt served as interpreter and also belonged to a local "self-defense" group.

Because of the Russian Revolution, Leibbrandt moved to Berlin. He studied theology, philosophy, and history and graduated with a degree in political economy in 1927, after which he studied in Paris, London, and the Soviet Union. He published on the emigration of Swabian Germans to Russia, on German

Dr. Georg Leibbrandt, head of the main division of the Reichsministry for the eastern territories. At the Wannsee Conference, Leibbrandt did not wholeheartedly endorse Heydrich's ruthless plans for the elimination of the Jews. Thereupon Heydrich decided to create a special Jewish office in the Ministry for the Eastern Territories, which would also have ties to the Reich Security Main Office. (Ullstein Bilderdienst)

colonies in Bessarabia (Rumania), and on the "true face of Bolshevism."

In 1930 Leibbrandt received a Rockefeller grant to study in the United States. While in America, he was in contact with a Nazi party group, and he continued the interaction when he moved to Geneva, where he remained until 1933. During this period he began working with the Nazi Foreign Affairs Department (APA), headed by Alfred Rosenberg. One of Hitler's earliest mentors, who became the semi-official philosopher of nazism, Rosenberg was executed at Nuremberg for war crimes in 1946.

On July 1, 1933, Leibbrandt became Nazi party member number 1,976,826, and on October 15 he was rewarded for his loyalty with a permanent job in the Foreign Affairs Department. By 1935 the sophisticated Leibbrandt, who spoke Russian, Ukrainian, French, and English, had been promoted to a high managerial post.

Alfred Rosenberg's appointment as Reichsminister for the eastern territories was announced on November 13, 1941. The ministry was established in Berlin, in the building formerly housing the Yugoslav and Soviet Embassies. Rosenberg appointed Leibbrandt to head the important main political division, with authority for the Ukraine, Estonia, the Caucasus, and Russia, as well as for culture and the press. Because of this appointment, Leibbrandt was implicated in the criminal activity of the occupation authorities in the Soviet Union. Yet he got into arguments over the short-term usefulness and long-term durability of the brutal fascist colonial politics. Like some of his colleagues, he leaned toward a more flexible policy in the eastern territories, and he felt the atrocities being committed would only foster permanent unrest.

Historians are not certain why Alfred Meyer, a state secretary of Rosenberg's ministry, brought Leibbrandt with him to the Wannsee Conference. Their best guess is that the matter might have been decided at a meeting between Meyer and Heydrich on October 4, 1941, at which Leibbrandt was also present. At the conference, Leibbrandt would not wholeheartedly endorse Heydrich's ruthless plans for the elimination of the Jews. Heydrich then decided to create a special Jewish office in the Ministry for the Eastern Territories, which would also have ties to the Reich Security Main Office.

Leibbrandt's moderate views were probably the reason he was forced out of his ministry job in 1943. SS Obergruppenführer (General) Gottlob Berger, Himmler's close associate, replaced him. Leibbrandt joined the navy as a sailor and survived the war. He was interned in 1945 but escaped punishment. After his release from detention in 1949, he worked in an American cultural institute in Munich. The district court of Nuremberg began a preliminary investigation against him in January 1950 but dropped it in August. He died in 1982.

HEINRICH MÜLLER

Heinrich Müller was born in Munich on April 28,1901, of Catholic parents. During World War I he served as a flight leader on the eastern front and was awarded the Iron Cross first class. After the war, the enterprising Müller made his career in the Bavarian police, specializing in the surveillance of Communist Party functionaries and making a special study of Soviet Russian police methods. Partly because of his expertise in this field, Reinahrd Heydrich picked him to be his closest associate and second-in-command of the Gestapo.

From 1935 the short, stocky Müller, with his square peasant's head and hard, dry, expressionless face, was virtual head of the Gestapo. The man Adolf Eichmann described as a "sphinx" was cold, dispassionate, and a bureaucratic fanatic.

Müller was politically suspect to influential members of the party, who resented his past record in the Munich State Police, when he had worked against the Nazis. Not until the end of 1938 was he officially admitted to the party, as member number 4,583,189. Yet the obdurate, bigoted Müller was highly regarded by both Himmler and Heydrich, who admired his professional competence, blind obedience, and willingness to execute "delicate missions," spying on colleagues, and unscrupulously disposing of political adversaries. Müller combined excessive zeal in his duties with docility towards his masters. Heydrich rapidly promoted Müller to SS Standartenführer (Colonel) in 1937; SS Oberführer (Brigadier General) on April 20, 1939; SS Brigadeführer (Major General) on December 14, 1940; and SS Gruppenführer (Lieutenant-General) and Police Chief on November 9, 1941.

As head of Amt IV (Gestapo) in the Reich Security Main Office from 1939 to 1945, Müller was more directly involved in murdering Jews than even his superiors, Heydrich and Himmler.

Heinrich Müller. As head of *Amt IV* (Gestapo) in the Reich Security Main Office from 1939 to 1945, Müller was more directly involved in murdering Jews than even his superiors, Heydrich and Himmler. No doubt this qualification was responsible for his presence at the Wannsee Conference. (Ullstein Bilderdienst)

No doubt this qualification was responsible for his presence at the Wannsee Conference. His cruelty and callousness toward the fate of the Jews are demonstrated in a letter he sent February 28, 1942, to Martin Luther at the Foreign Office: "I am writing with regard to the anonymous letter sent to the Foreign Office about the solution of the Jewish question in the Warthegau [German occupied western Poland]. You included this letter in your communication of February 6, 1942, and I have referred it for investigation. The results should be available soon.

Such protests are unavoidable. We must let the chips fall where they may. The opponent will always try to use any and all measures to arouse pity and engender hope. Since we began working to crush him, the Jew tries to escape his fate by sending anonymous letters everywhere in the Reich." Müller subsequently signed an order and many similar mandates, requiring the immediate delivery to Auschwitz by January 31, 1943, of forty-five thousand Jews for liquidation. In the summer of 1943 he was sent to Rome to pressure the Italians, who were proving singularly inefficient and unenthusiastic in arresting Jews. Until the end of the war, Heinrich Müller continued his remorseless prodding of subordinates to greater efforts in sending Jews to Auschwitz. In his hands, mass murder was just another administrative procedure. Müller ordered the murder of Russian prisoners of war and gave the order to shoot British officers who had escaped from detention, near Breslau, at the end of March 1944.

Müller's whereabouts at the end of the war are still a mystery. He was last seen in the Führerbunker on April 28, 1945, after which he disappeared. Though his burial was recorded on May 17, 1945, when the body was later exhumed it could not be identified. There were persistent rumors that he had defected to the east (he had established contact with Soviet agents before the end of the war), either to Moscow, Albania, or East Germany. Other uncorroborated reports placed him in Latin America.

ERICH NEUMANN

The son of a factory owner, Erich Neumann was born into a Lutheran family on May 31, 1892, in the town of Forst-Lausitz. After high school, he studied law and political economy at the Uni-

Erich Neumann. Reichsmarschall Hermann Göring had appointed Neumann to the Office of the Four Year Plan. This organization was the economic center for war preparations, responsible for management of the currency, one of the most important government tasks. Neumann was soon named State Secretary for the Four Year Plan and in this capacity attended the Wannsee Conference. (Ullstein Bilderdienst)

versity of Freiburg. He joined an infantry regiment in August 1914. He fought until October 1917, when he received a severe hand wound and was discharged as a reserve lieutenant with an Iron Cross second class. On January 25, 1918, he became a civil service trainee in the Baltic town of Stettin.

In October 1920, he became a government official and was assigned to a temporary position in the Prussian Interior Ministry. He became a government counselor in October 1923; he went to Berlin in December 1924 as a temporary employee in the Prussian Ministry for Trade and Industry. In November 1926 he was a municipal counselor in Freystadt, a Silesian (east Prussian) town, and on November 1, 1928, he rejoined the Ministry for Trade and Industry as a ministerial counselor.

In September 1932, when the Social Democratic government was on the verge of collapse, Neumann received a special appointment to the Prussian State Ministry. There he ascended to the post of ministerial director, and on May 1, 1933, he joined the Nazi party as member number 2,645,024 and shortly thereafter the SS as member number 222,014.

His old war wound unnoticed, Neumann received some basic military training and joined the Wehrmacht reserves as Oberleutnant (First Lieutenant). By the beginning of the war in 1939, Neumann had risen to Oberführer (Brigadier General) in the SS.

Reichsmarschall Hermann Göring noticed the highly experienced, well-versed Neumann and appointed him to the Office of the Four Year Plan. This organization was the economic center for war preparations, responsible for management of the currency, one of the most important government tasks. Neumann was named State Secretary for the Four Year Plan and in this capacity attended the Wannsee Conference.

At the conference, when Neumann asked that Jews essential to war production be retained, rather than deported, Heydrich promised that these Jews would not be deported under the guidelines he had established. Neumann's influence on Göring soon diminished rapidly, and he lost his post as state secretary. Until the collapse of Nazi Germany, he was general manager of the German Potash Syndicate.

A few days after the discovery of the Wannsee Protocol, American prosecutor Robert M. W. Kempner met Neumann, the first participant in the Wannsee Conference he could interrogate. Although Neumann's request at the conference to spare the Jews could not be taken as a criticism of the final solution, Kempner did note it when Neumann was interned after the war. Released for health reasons, Neumann died in 1948.

DR. EBERHARD SCHÖNGARTH

Karl Georg Eberhard Schöngarth was born April 22, 1903, in Leipzig. In 1914 he began high school but did not finish, instead going to work in a garden center. Because this employment was considered important to the war effort, he was awarded a Young Men's Iron Medal on March 7, 1918. At war's end he went back to school. In 1921 he joined a Freikorps paramilitary group in Thuringia. In November 1923, when the Hitler putsch occurred, Schöngarth was a member of a local Nazi group in Erfurt. He fled to Coburg, returned to Erfurt, was arrested and tried for treason, but was given amnesty. He finished high school and in 1924 went to work in the Erfurt branch of the Deutsche Bank, at the same time joining Army Infantry Regiment I/15 in Gießen.

After the prohibition of the Nazi party in Prussia, Schöngarth joined the SA as member number 43,870, claiming he was expelled from the army. This statement is dubious and probably was prompted by his intent to pretend he was an Alter Kämpfer, an old Nazi party stalwart.

What is not dubious is the fact that by 1924 Schöngarth had little more to do with the beaten, post-putsch Nazi party. He enrolled in the University of Leipzig, majored in economics and law, took his first bar exam in 1928, and went to work for the superior court in Naumburg. He studied at the Institute for Labor Law and earned a doctorate from the Leipzig law faculty on June 28, 1929. He took a second bar examination and in December 1933 became a court official for Magdeburg, Erfurt, and Torgau.

With the Nazis in power, Schöngarth began to ingratiate himself with the organization he had spurned a few years before. On February 1, 1933, he joined the SS as member number 67,174 and on May 1, 1993, he became Nazi number 2,848,857. Party membership was necessary for any important government job, and after joining, Schögarth became a postmaster in Erfurt.

On November 1, 1935, Schöngarth changed the course of his life by leaving the post office for the Gestapo. He worked in the main press office, the political-church council, and the Arnsberg district office in Dortmund. In Bielefeld and Münster he served as police chief and was named a government counselor. He was also rising in the SS: Obersturmführer (First Lieutenant), Hauptsturmführer (Captain), and Sturmbannführer (Major), Obersturmbannführer (Lieutenant Colonel) in 1939, Standartenführer (Colonel) to Oberführer (Brigadier General) in 1940.

At the outbreak of war in September 1939, Schöngarth was an executive government counselor and security police inspector for Dresden and the Sudetenland (Czechoslovakia). In order to remove the blemish on his record that lack of military service had created, he volunteered for an air defense battalion in France and became an army lieutenant. On January 30, 1941, he was promoted to colonel and given command of the security police and security service in Krakow. In this post, he was involved in the repression, robbery, and murder of Poles and Jews. During the invasion of the Soviet Union, he commanded an Einsatz group that killed local Soviet officials and Jews. On January 30, 1943, Schöngarth was promoted to army Brigadeführer (Major General) but lost his job in Krakow because of infighting, which also threatened the Polish governor general, Hans Frank. Nevertheless, in late 1943 Schöngarth was promoted successively to Waffen-SS Untersturmführer (Second Lieutenant) and Obersturmführer (First Lieutenant) and sent to the front as commander of an SS police grenadier division.

The increasingly precarious military situation led to intensified local resistance and a demand for experienced officers. After Hitler had given his express permission, Reich Security Main Office chief Ernst Kaltenbrunner arranged Schöngarth's release from the Waffen-SS and sent him to command the security police in the occupied Netherlands. Just after his arrival on June 1, 1944, partisans attacked a truck carrying a Nazi official, Hanns Albin Rauter. Although Rauter was not killed, Schöngarth had 263 people shot. On November 21, 1944, near the town of Enschede, Schöngarth ordered the shooting of a captured allied pilot. For his army service, Schöngarth was awarded the Iron Cross first and second class.

The British, who captured Schöngarth, were not as appreciative. He was hauled before a military tribunal at Burgsteinfurt, convicted, and executed on May 16, 1946. Shortly thereafter, an executioner also dispatched Kaltenbrunner and Rauter.

DR. WILHELM STUCKART

Wilhelm Stuckart was born November 16, 1902, the son of a railroad worker in Wiesbaden. Even before his high school graduation in 1922, he had joined a right wing group, the German National People's Party. In 1922, while studying law and political economy in Munich, he joined the Nazi party, and remained a member until the Party was outlawed after the 1923 putsch. As a member of the Freikorps Epp, he passively resisted the occupation of the Ruhr and was twice arrested by the French.

To support his parents, Stuckart had to abandon his studies temporarily. He worked in the Nassau Regional Bank in Frankfurt until returning to school in

Dr. Wilhelm Stuckart. On March 7, 1935, Stuckart, a lawyer, joined the Reich Ministry of the Interior, Division I, with responsibility for constitutional law, citizenship and racial regulations. In this position, he was one of the officials responsible for drafting the *Laws for the protection of German blood and German honor*, the notorious Nuremberg Laws, which, among other things, withdrew German citizenship from German Jews. Stuckart himself called these laws "a preliminary solution of the Jewish question." Further laws he and his colleagues drafted in 1938, in Stuckart's words, were "material preparation for the final solution," which he later insisted he took to mean expulsion of the Jews from Germany. As state secretary of the Reich Ministry of the Interior, Stuckart attended the Wannsee Conference. (Ullstein Bilderdienst)

1924. In 1928 he received his doctorate with a thesis entitled "Explanations to the Public" and in 1930 passed his bar examination.

In Wiesbaden, Stuckart revived his association with the Nazi party and provided members with legal counsel. But he did not renew his own membership immediately, because he was working as a judge for the district court, which prohibited political activity. To get around this restriction, his mother joined the party for him, as member number 378,144.

In 1932 Stuckart moved to Stettin, where he worked as a lawyer, occupied various Nazi party positions, and joined the SA. When Himmler told him that membership in the SS provided a fast track to the top, he joined on December 16, 1933.

Stuckart's rise was swift. On April 4, 1933, he became mayor and state-commissioner in Stettin. After one of the last elections, he became a member of the state parliament and the Prussian council of state. On May 15, 1933, he was appointed Ministerial Director of the Prussian Ministry of Education and the Arts in Berlin. On June 30, 1933, he was made a state secretary. In 1934 he wrote *A History of History Teaching*. Conflicts with his boss led Stuckart to move to Darmstadt, where he was named president of the superior district court. This job lasted only a few weeks.

On March 7, 1935, Stuckart joined the Reich Ministry of the Interior, Division I, with responsibility for constitutional law, citizenship, and racial regulations. In this position, he was one of the officials responsible for drafting the *Laws for the Protection of German Blood and German Honor*, the notorious Nuremberg Laws, which, among other things, withdrew German citizenship from German Jews. Stuckart himself called these laws "a preliminary solution of the Jewish question." Further laws he and his colleagues drafted in 1938, in Stuckart's words, were "material preparation for the final solution," which he later insisted he took to mean expulsion of the Jews from Germany. As chairman of the Reich Committee for the Protection of German Blood, Stuckart and Hans Globke published commentaries on the interpretation of the Nuremberg Laws. As state secretary of the Reich Ministry of the Interior, Stuckart attended the Wannsee Conference.

Stuckart's career in the SS, as member number 280,042, prospered as luxuriantly as his civil service career. From Standartenführer (Colonel), he rose to Oberführer (Brigadier General) on January 30, 1937; Brigadeführer (Major General) on January 30, 1938; Gruppenführer (Lieutenant General) on January 30, 1942; and Obergruppenführer (General) on January 30, 1944.

Having never served a day in the Wehrmacht, Stuckart applied for military service in 1940, but Hitler personally scotched the application. Yet his labors did benefit the military. After the German debacle at Stalingrad in November 1942, older and older men were conscripted, and Stuckart helped "comb out" this cannon fodder, in the form of superfluous employees, from the government ministries.

At the end of the war, the Allies imprisoned Stuckart. His role in formulating and carrying out anti-Jewish laws emerged during testimony at the Nuremberg trials in 1946. In the Wilhelmstraße trials of the state secretaries, an American court in Nuremberg tried Stuckart. He was characterized as a "bitter enemy of the Jews," one of many men who "in the peaceful stillness of their ministry offices" took part in the anti-Semitic campaign. The charges were supported by numerous documents, one an affidavit from Bernhard Lösener, a former co-worker in the Reich Interior Ministry, who dealt until 1943 with Jewish issues. Lösener attested to Stuckart's knowledge of the murder of German Jews even before the Wannsee Conference.

The court considered whether Stuckart repeatedly suggested the sterilization of mixed breeds in order to delay or prevent more extreme measures. Unable to resolve the question, the judges gave him the benefit of the doubt. They sentenced him to the three years, ten months, and twenty days he had already served during internment and detention. Freed at the end of his trial, Stuckart went to work as city treasurer in Helmstedt, then as manager of the Institute for the Promotion of the Economy in lower Saxony. A de-Nazification court classified him as a "fellow traveler" in 1951 and fined him five hundred marks. He died November 15, 1953, in a car accident near Hanover.

Appendix E

Adolf Eichmann's Testimony in Jerusalem About the Wannsee Conference

(English transcript of the Eichmann trial [mimeographed], June 23, 1961, session 78, pp. Zl, Aal, Bbl; June 26, 1961, session 79, p. Bl; July 24, 1961, session 107, pp. El, Fl, Gl. Dr. Robert Servatius was Eichmann's German attorney.)

Dr. Servatius: ... Will the Witness explain what do you know in connection to the initiative to call this conference?

Accused: Without any doubt, the main reason for the convening of the conference was Heydrich's intention to extend the scope of his influence.

Dr. Servatius: Was he afraid of any difficulties? Did he have reason to be afraid?

Accused: Experience up to then showed that all those questions were usually dealt with by various authorities and if it were, there was no coordinated activity and, therefore, actions were delayed considerably as there were all sorts of activities carried out within various offices. And, in a nutshell, one may point out that in the deliberations which were held so far they wouldn't see the wood for the trees, and they wouldn't arrive at any definite solution or any coordinated solution. This is one of the reasons why Heydrich convened the Wannsee Conference, why he actually convened it on his own initiative in order to imprint his own will and that of the Reichsführer SS.

Dr. Servatius: The witness I believe already declared here in Court that you prepared Heydrich's speech. Or this may be collected from the appendix to the Sassen report.

Presiding Judge: Yes.

Dr. Servatius: Are you ready to repeat once again your explanation how it came about that you were asked to prepare this speech?

Accused: Yes. I was instructed to collect material which Heydrich thought relevant for his speech which he was about to hold. That means to say that it should have been a general survey of all the operations that had been carried out in the course of the last years in the realm of the emigration of Jews. It had to be a survey of the results and the difficulties of the operations in question. These prepared remarks that I drew for Heydrich's speech can be seen on the seven pages of the document in front of us, but it struck me that certain points which I prepared were [not] prepared by me. They are not the fruit of my pencil, so to speak, but simply expressed by Heydrich without taking heed of what I had prepared. Because very often as I had seen from experience he would speak very freely, without always taking care of the prepared points. And here on page 6 the last passage, according to which Jews were earmarked for special labor effort and they were to be sent, within the framework of the final solution, to the eastern territories and, as I said, this was to conform with the framework set for the labor effort in the east. The labor columns were to be formed and a separation was to be carried out between the sexes so that the Jews fit for work would be brought within the framework of this plan and would be employed in the construction of the roads. This particular passage could not have possibly stemmed from me and the remarks couldn't possibly been ascribed to what I wrote because this particular passage actually constituted a turning point in the policy towards the Jews and this policy appears for the first time in the Wannsee conference.

Presiding Judge: I believe there is a written translation into the Hebrew of this document.

Court Interpreter: I do not have it before me.

Accused: May I further point out, your Honors, to complete the picture, that the second function which was bestowed upon me was the function of keeping minutes of the meeting together with a secretary.

Dr. Servatius: Do the minutes describe the contents of the deliberations correctly?

Accused: These minutes to which I was referring were rendering the salient points quite clearly. But so far as the particulars were concerned, I have to point out that this was not a verbatim report because certain colloquialisms were then couched by me in official language and certain official terms had to be introduced. Later on it had been revised three or four times by Heydrich. It came back through official channels to us through the channel of Mueller and then again we had to elaborate on it until it assumed its final form.

Dr. Servatius: What is not reflected in the protocol is the spirit which reigned at this conference. Can you report or comment regarding the spirit and attitude at this conference?

Accused: Yes, the climate of this conference was characterized as it were by a relaxed attitude of Heydrich who had actually more than anybody else expected considerable stumbling blocks and difficulties.

Q. It is important how these things found expression on the part of the other participants.

A. It was an atmosphere not only of agreement on the part of the participants, but more than that, one could feel an agreement which had assumed a form which had not been expected. Unflinching in his determination to participate fully in the functions with regard to the final solution of the Jewish problem and particularly outstanding in the enthusiastic and unexpected form of agreement was the State secretary, Buhler [Bühler], and even more than Buhler, Stuckart had evinced boundless enthusiasm. He was usually hesitating, and reserved, reticent and furtive, but all of a sudden he gave expression to boundless enthusiasm, with which he joined the others with regard to the final solution of the Jewish question.

Q. The witness saw before the calling of this conference the preparations in the East for the extermination? He saw the steps taken there?

A. Yes, sir.

Q. Did the participants at this conference know anything about the way for the final solution?

A. I have to assume that the things were known to the participants of the Wannsee Conference because after all the war against Russia had been going on already about six months. As we saw in some various relevant documents, the operational groups were already acting in the Russian war theater and all those key personalities in the Reich Government must have known about the state of affairs at that time.

Q. How long did this conference go on and what happened after the conference was over?

A. The conference itself took only a very short period of time. I can't recall exactly how long it lasted, but it seems to me that I would not be mistaken in saying that it didn't take longer than an hour or an hour and a half. Of course, the gentlemen who participated in it would later on be standing in small groups to discuss the ins and outs of the agenda and also of certain work to be undertaken afterwards. After the conference had been a[d]journed, Heydrich and Mueller still remained and I was also permitted to remain and then in this restricted get-together, Heydrich gave expression to his great satisfaction I already referred to before....

Presiding Judge: ... Now in connection with the Wannsee conference, you answered my colleague Dr. Raveh that this part of the meeting, which is not mentioned in the protocol, the discussion was about means of extermination. Systems of killing.

A. Yes.

Q. Who discussed this subject?

A: I do not remember it in detail, Your Honor. I do not remember the circumstances of this conversation. But I do know that these gentlemen were standing together, or sitting together, and were discussing the subject quite bluntly, quite differently from the language which I had to use later in the record. During the conversation they minced no words about it at all. I might say furthermore, Your Honor, that I would not have remembered this unless I had later remembered that I told myself, Look here, I told myself, even this guy Stuckart, who was known as one of these uncles who was a great stickler for legalities, he too uses language which is not at all in accordance with paragraphs of the law. This incident remained engraved in my memory and recalled the entire subject to my mind.

Q: What did he say about this subject?

A: In detail I do not —

Q: Not details in general, what did he say about this theme?

A: I cannot remember it in detail, Your Honor, but they spoke about methods for killing, about liquidation, about extermination. I was busy with my records. I had to make the preparations for taking down the minutes; I could not perk up my ears and listen to everything that was said. But it filtered through the small room and I caught fragments of this conversation. It was a small room so from time to time I heard a word or two.

Q: I believed that this was the official part of the meeting, of the conference.

A: The official part did not take too long.

Q: Was this in the official part of the conference, or not? It was my belief that this was in the official conference because this should have been included in the protocol of the meeting, although nothing is mentioned.

A: Well of course, it was in the official part, Your Honor. But again this official part had two subdivisions. The first part where everyone was quiet and listened to the various lectures, and then in the second part, everyone spoke out of turn and people would go around, butlers, adjutants, and would give out liquor. Well, I don't want to say that there was an atmosphere of drunkenness there. It was an official atmosphere, but nevertheless it was not one of these stiff, formal, official affairs where everyone spoke in turn. But people just talked at cross vertices.

Q: And were these also recorded by the short-hand typists?

Accused: Yes, yes they were taken down.

Presiding Judge: And you were ordered by someone not to include it in the memorandum of the meeting in the official Protocol of this meeting, weren't you?

Accused: Yes, that's how it was. The stenographer was sitting next to me and I was to see to it that everything would be taken down; then she deciphered this and then Heydrich gave me his instructions as to what should be included in the record and what should be excluded. Then I showed it to Heydrich and he polished it up and proof-read it and that's how it was kept.

Q. And that which was said about this very important theme, you cannot remember at all is this what you say?

A. Well, the most important thing here was...

Q. I did not say, the most important I said it was an important theme, and important enough to be excluded from the record.

A. Well, no. The significant part, from Heydrich's point-of-view, was to nail down the Secretaries of State, to commit them most bindingly, to catch them by their words; and therefore, it was quite the contrary the important part did go into the record and the less significant ones were excluded. It was, I would say, that Heydrich wanted to cover himself, wanted to be sure that each and every one of these Secretaries of State would be nailed-down and these matters, therefore, were put down.

Q. That means to say that the methods of killing the systems of extermination was not an important theme?

A. Ah! the means of killing....

Q. That is what we are speaking about the means of killing.

A. No, no this of course was not put into the record no, no!

Q. Did they discuss killing by poison gas?

A. No, with gas no.

Q. But, how then?

A. It was...this business with the engine, they spoke about this; they spoke about shooting, but not about gas.

Q. Later, the Protocol goes on to say, in the same passage, that Gauleiter Mayer and Secretary of State Dr. Bühler (?) believed and were of the opinion, that certain preparations, for implementation in various districts, be made at the same time; certain preparatory work in connection with the "final solution" should be made immediately, in the discussed areas, but unrest amongst the population should be avoided. Can you remember this?

A. What did you mean, Your Honor; I did not understand it.

Q. You did not understand? All right I will read it out to you once again: Dr. Mayer and Dr. Bühler that their opinion was that preparatory work should begin immediately for the "final solution" in the various areas, but at the same time to avoid unrest and anxiety on the part of the population.

A. Ah, yes...

Q. To which preparatory work does this refer?

A. I cannot imagine anything, but...

Q. Don't imagine! My question is and I put it to you, as the Attorney-General put it to you before and all the time what can you remember? This was a turning point, in fact.

A. I was there and I witnessed the preparatory work, with these two little houses in the Lublin area.

Q. Which two little huts in the Lublin area? I'm asking you this question about the Conference.

A. Well, I had seen the preparatory work before in fact, but I don't really know. They spoke about the matter, at the meeting, of not creating any anxiety and perplexity amongst the local population, so all I thought was being discussed, was this same kind of business.

Q. And did you report what you saw to this Conference?

A. At the Wannsee Conference? No, I never uttered a syllable; I was not authorized to open my mouth. No, I had no permission.

Q. So, who was it, who brought the technical details to the Conference?

A: Well, no one discussed the technical details. That is to say, Heydrich opened the meeting and then everyone spoke about it. Well, I mean maybe Büller [Bühler] spoke about it or possible Krueger. I suppose he would have; he was the senior SS and Police Commander in the Government General. In a way he was the head of the entire business, in charge of it. Globocnik was subordinated to this man Krueger. Krueger, as the boss, must have known it in detail.

Presiding Judge: But Krueger did not take part at the Wannsee Conference, according to the list of participants.

A. Yes, but earlier he visited Heydrich and extracted from him an invitation for Büller [Bühler] to take part at the meeting. And then, one spoke about it in detail. Heydrich and Krueger discussed it and for that reason I had to issue special invitations for Krueger and Büller [Bühler].

Q. You told the Court that you do not consider yourself an anti-Semite and that you never were an anti-Semite.

A. An anti-Semite I never was no.

Appendix F

Notes on the Film "The Wannsee Conference"

The Wannsee Conference
Austria-Germany (1984): Historical/War
The Leonard Maltin review gives the film 3.5 stars out of 4
The film is 87 min., in color and available on videocassette and laserdisc.
Director
Heinz Schirk
Cast Includes
Dietrich Mattausch Gerd Bockmann
Friedrich Beckhaus Günter Spoerrie
Martin Luttge Peter Fritz

According to Maltin, the film presents a fascinating, chilling recreation of the conference. Nazi officials discuss implementation of the Final Solution. Participants plot the destruction of millions with a casual air, which only adds to the terror. The film is based on the Wannsee Protocol, and the film's length matches the event's actual running time.

Chapter Notes

I. The Wannsee Villa and Fritz Haber

"Wannsee signifies two things": *Baedeker's Berlin*. 3rd ed. (New York: Macmillan, 1994), 231.

"The land under the Wannsee Villa had been incorporated": Johannes Tuchel, *Am Großen Wannsee 56–58. Von der Villa Minoux zum Haus der Wannsee-Konferenz*, Edition Hentrich (Berlin: Gedenkstätte Haus der Wannsee-Konferenz, 1992), 12.

"The court painter of the Kaisers, Anton von Werner, built a summer home": Anton von Werner (Munich: Hirmer Verlag, 1997), *Geschichte in Bildern. Herausgegeben von Dominik Bartmann.*

"A prosperous Berlin merchant and factory owner, Ernst Marlier": Tuchel, *Am Großen Wannsee 56–58*, 12.

"Fritz Haber was born in Breslau": Max F. Perutz, Le cabinet du Docteur Fritz Haber. Comment un égal acharnement produit des engrais, des gaz de combat et le Zyklon B, *La Recherche* 297:78–84, 1997.

"What Fritz has gained during the past eight years, I have lost": Max Perutz, The cabinet of Dr. Haber, *New York Review of Books*, June 20, 1996, 43:31–36.

"Haber discovered that the synthesis of ammonia required extreme conditions never before achieved in a laboratory: a temperature of 600°C": S. Tekeli, "Fritz Haber," *in Dictionary of Scientific Biography*, ed. in chief C. C. Gillespie (New York: Charles Scribner's Sons, 1972).

"I must admit that the task of poisoning the enemy like rats was repugnant to me": Janusz Piekalkiewicz. *Der Erste Weltkrieg* (Dusseldorf: ECON Verlag, 1988), 193.

"The first test of Zyklon B…": Reinhard Krumm, Luftdicht in blechdosen, *Der Spiegel* 11:63, 1999.

II. Friedrich Minoux Buys the Wannsee Villa and Enters Politics

"Friedrich Minoux, the second owner of the Wannsee Villa, was born March 21, 1877": Tuchel, *Am Großen Wannsee 56–58*, 17.

"The German hyperinflation of 1923 was caused, to a great extent": Otto Friedrich, *Before the Deluge* (New York: Harper and Row, 1972), 121.

"Minoux's efforts to stabilize the Mark caused some conflict with Hugo Stinnes": Tuchel, *Am Großen Wannsee 56–58*, 23.

Friedrich, *Before the Deluge*, 79.

"Minoux's program for Seeckt had subordinated Stinnes' single interest": Tuchel, *Am Großen Wannsee 56–58*, 27.

"Ludendorff, a man with a gluttony for work and a granite character": Barbara Tuchman, *The Guns of August* (New York: Macmillan, 1962), 168.

"When the First World War ended, Ludendorff had hidden in a Berlin boarding house": Friedrich, *Before the Deluge*, 18.

"According to Ludendorff's memoirs, Hugo Stinnes had arranged the meeting with Minoux and Seeckt": Tuchel, *Am Großen Wannsee 56–58*, 27.

"Warburg had met Ludendorff in 1918": Ron Chernow, *The Warburgs* (New York: Random House, 1993), 199.

"Minoux's talents impressed Ludendorff": Konrad Heiden quoted in Tuchel, *Am Großen Wannsee 56–58*, 32.

"These words pronounced by a Stinnes created the most incredible confusion": *Adolf Hitler. Mein Kampf,* trans. Ralph Mannheim (Boston: Houghton Mifflin, 1943), 236.

"After Minoux and Stinnes parted ways in 1923": Tuchel, *Am Großen Wannsee 56–58*, 39.

"Within a few months of the Wall Street crash of 1929": Friedrich, *Before the Deluge*, 300.

"In November 1930, Friedrich Minoux met with Brüning": Tuchel, *Am Großen Wannsee 56–58*, 43.

III. Aryanization, Friedrich Minoux, and the Plundering of the German Jews

"As Gordon A. Craig has written, antipathy toward the Jews was quite ancient": Gordon A. Craig, *The Germans* (New York: New American Library, 1983), 127 ff.

"Aryanizations rose exponentially": Schnäppchen aus Judenkisten, *Der Spiegel* 5:66–68, 1998.

"A Frankfurt businessman, Philipp Offenheimer, had founded Okriftel": Tuchel, *Am Großen Wannsee 56–58*, 55.

"Most of the Aryanizations involved small to medium-sized businesses": Saul Friedländer, *Nazi Germany and the Jews.* Volume I, *The Years of Persecution, 1933–1939* (New York: Harper Collins, 1997), 260.

"The history of CF Peters began in 1800": *Daten zur Geschichte des Musikverlages Peters,* Leipzig: Ministerium für Kultur der DDR und der Hauptverwaltung Verlage und Buchhandel.

IV. Friedrich Minoux Defrauds the Berlin Gas Company

"Friedrich Minoux, one of the largest Berlin coal dealers": Tuchel, *Am Großen Wannsee 56–58*, 59 ff.

V. Reinhard Heydrich and the Nordhav Foundation

"Reinhard Heydrich was the son of Bruno Heydrich": Callum MacDonald, *The Killing of Reinhard Heydrich* (New York: Da Capo Press, 1998), 5.

"On July 30, 1939, Heydrich organized the Nordhav Foundation": Tuchel, *Am Großen Wannsee 56–58*, 76.

"The son of a Catholic secondary schoolmaster, Himmler received a diploma in agriculture": Robert S. Wistrich, *Who's Who in Nazi Germany* (London: Routledge, 1982).

"For the Heydrich house on Fehmarn": Tuchel, *Am Großen Wannsee 56–58*, 91.

"Why do we call the whole world's attention to the fact that we have no past?": Albert Speer, *Inside the Third Reich,* trans. Richard and Clara Winston (New York: Avon Books, 1971), 141.

"Undeterred by Hitler's sarcasm": Tuchel, *Am Großen Wannsee 56–58,* 94.

VI. Planning to Murder the Jews of Europe

"But now a German scholar, Christian Gerlach": Alan Cowell, Hitler's genocide order: 5 days after Pearl Harbor?, *New York Times,* January 21, 1998, Foreign Desk, Section A, 4.

"And one more thing I would like now to state": Hitler quoted in Lucy S. Dawidowicz. *The War Against the Jews: 1933–1945* (New York: Bantam Books, 1975), 142.

"From the rostrum of the Reichstag": Henry Picker, *Hitler's Tischgespräche, Bibliothek der Zeitgeschichte* (Frankfurt: Verlag Ullstein, 1989), 305.

"One report, for example, from *Einsatz*-group 1": Peter Klein, *Die Wannsee Konferenz vom 20. January 1942: Analyse und Dokumentation,* Edition Hentrich (Berlin: Gedenkstätte Haus der Wannsee-Konferenz, 1997), 5.

"The *Einsatz*-groups were not the only murderers": Alan Cowell, The Past Erupts in Munich as War Guilt Is Put on Display, *New York Times,* Late Edition (East Coast), March 3, 1997, Foreign Desk, Section A, 3.

"The Wannsee Conference facilitated the killing": Klein, *Die Wannsee Konferenz,* 7.

"On November 29, 1941, Adolf Eichmann sent Reinhard Heydrich's letter": Klein *ibid.,* 8.

"It was 1938 in Berlin, and 19-year-old Hannah was shocked to hear": Warren Hoge, Rare look uncovers wartime anguish of many part-Jewish Germans. *New York Times,* Late Edition (East Coast), April 6, 1997 *Foreign Desk* Section 1, 16.

"But the number of such declarations was small": Selten Gnade, *Der Spiegel* 20:20, 1998.

"The Wannsee Protocol is a fifteen page typewritten document which does not carry the name of an individual author": Klein, *Die Wannsee Konferenz,* 15.

"The Nazis had devised this plan": Louis L. Snyder, *Encyclopedia of the Third Reich* (New York: McGraw Hill, 1978).

"On February 10, 1942, Rademacher had informed colleagues" Klein, *Die Wannsee Konferenz,* 16.

"Many guilt-burdened Germans, among others": Klein, *Die Wannsee Konferenz,* 19.

"In his March 2, 1942, cover letter sent with the Foreign Office copy": Klein *ibid.,* 17.

"Yet mixed marriages remained a thorny problem for the Nazis": Anthony Read and David Fisher, *Berlin Rising* (New York: W.W. Norton, 1994), 235.

"Needless to say, the conference raised more issues than it settled": Klein, *Die Wannsee Konferenz,* 57.

"Heydrich did not have long to live after the Wannsee conference": Gitta Sereny, *Albert Speer: His Battle with Truth* (New York: Alfred A. Knopf, 1995), 326 ff.

"He highlighted his rising status by an act of homage to his father": MacDonald, *Killing of Heydrich,* 166.

"But this atrocity was not Heydrich's most terrible legacy": Sereny, *Albert Speer,* 326.

"Eichmann was born in Solingen on March 19, 1906": *Eichmann Interrogated, Transcripts from the Archives of the Israeli Police,* ed. Jochen von Lang in collaboration with Claus Sibyll, trans. from the German by Ralph Mannheim (New York: Farrar, Straus, & Giroux, 1983), 5.

"On April 1, 1932, Eichmann joined the Austrian Nazi Party": Kurt Pätzold, and

Erika Schwarz. *Tagesordnung: Judenmord, Die Wannsee-Konferenz am 20.* January (Berlin: Metropol Verlag, 1992), 206.

"The 82 year old Sigmund Freud received the attentions": Ernest Jones, *The Life and Work of Sigmund Freud,* edited and abridged in one volume by Lionel Trilling and Steven Marcus (New York: Basic Books, 1961), 513.

"In April 1939, Franz Walter Stahlecker, a former superior, summoned Eichmann to Prague": Pätzold and Schwarz, *Tagesordnung: Judenmord,* 207.

"In 1950, Eichmann decided to leave Germany": Michel Faure, Argentine: Sur le piste des derniers Nazis, *L'Express,* April 9, 1998, 44–51.

"Israeli Mossad agents kidnapped Eichmann on May 11, 1960": Calvin Sims, Film stirs Argentines' memories of a Nazi, *New York Times,* March 5, 1996, Section C, 11. Also, see Peter Z. Malkin and Harry Stein, *Eichmann in My Hands* (New York: Warner Books, 1990).

"An Israeli captain, Avner Less, interrogated Eichmann, and recorded the proceedings on tape": *Eichmann Interrogated,* 4.

"Seated in a bulletproof glass booth": Walter Goodman, Crime and punishment: the trial of Eichmann, *New York Times,* Late Edition (East Coast), April 30, 1997, Section C, 14.

"On January 30, 1942, ten days after the Wannsee Conference": Klein, *Die Wannsee Konferenz,* 57.

"The deportations proceeded with clockwork efficiency": Permanent Exhibit. House of the Wannsee Conference. Guide and Reader. Edition Hentrich. Berlin, 31

"Especially controversial were the Dachau studies of hypothermia": Marcia Angell, The Nazi hypothermia experiments and unethical research today, *New England Journal of Medicine* 322 (20): 1462–64, 1990.

"Behind the barbed wire and the electric fence": Rick Lyman, Martha Gellhorn, daring writer, dies at 89. *New York Times,* February 17, 1998, Section B, 11.

"A recent survey of German women": Marianne Brentzel, *Nesthäkchen kommt ins KZ: Eine Annäherung an Else Ury 1877–1943* (Frankfurt am Main: Fischer Taschenbuch Verlag, 1992).

"Sam Cohen, doyen of the Zabar's appetizing department": Vic Ziegel, Taste of 45 yrs. at Zabar's, *Daily News,* February 14, 1998, 22.

War and Holocaust: the view from the Berlin Morgue. Marco Evers, Annalen des Todes, *Der Spiegel* 13:268, 1999.

VII. Ordinary Germans, the Catholic Church, and the Holocaust

"Arendt maintained that she was simply trying to make a calm assessment": David Bird, Hannah Arendt, political scientist, dead, *New York Times,* December 6, 1975, 32.

"Goldhagen's book is a huge best seller in Germany": Amos Elon, The Antagonist as Liberator, *New York Times Magazine,* January 26, 1997, Section 6, 40.

"More criticism is contained in a book, *A Nation on Trial: the Goldhagen Thesis and Historical Truth*": Ralph Blumenthal, Cries to halt publication of Holocaust book, *New York Times,* January 10, 1998, Section 2, B, 7.

"Finkelstein found that Goldhagen had taken quotations out of context": Goldhagen — ein Quellentrickser? *Der Spiegel* 33:156–58, 1997.

"Reviewing the Finkelstein-Birn book for the New York Times": Max Frankel, Willing Executioners? Essays by two scholars dissect the work of Daniel Jonah Goldhagen, *The New York Times Book Review,* June 28, 1998, 7.

"Efraim Zuroff, director of the Simon Wiesenthal Center in Israel": Rudolf Augstein, Todbringende "Humanisten," *Der Spiegel* 33:40–55, 1996.

"Researching the book, reporters from *Der Spiegel*": Getuschel im Treppenhaus. *Der Spiegel* 41:148–49, 1997.

"Lehmann Katzenberger was the owner of a Nuremberg shoe wholesale business": Christiane Kohl, *Der Jude und das Mädchen: Eine verbotene Freundschaft in Nazi Deutschland* (Hamburg: Spiegel Buchverlag Hoffman und Campe, 1997).

"As Celestine Bohlen reported in the New York Times": Celestine Bohlen, Pope ties "unjust teachings" to anti-Semitism, *New York Times,* November 1, 1997, Foreign Desk, Section A, 6.

"It is regrettable that the Vatican has not yet found the courage": The Vatican's Holocaust report, Editorial, *New York Times,* March 18, 1998, Section A, 20.

"In September 1997, the American professor and rabbi David Blumenthal lectured": Rudolf Augstein, "Das ist eine Schande," *Der Spiegel* 43:92–107, 1997.

"Pacelli was an extremely intelligent man, dry, skeptical, and realistic": Rolf Hochhuth, *The Deputy,* trans. Richard and Clara Winston (New York: Grove Press, 1964). At the end of the book, Hochhuth has written an essay, "Sidelights on History," describing the factual background material and references he used in his play.

VIII. The Wannsee Villa After the Wannsee Conference

"One noteworthy wartime guest at the Wannsee Villa": Tuchel, *Am Großen Wannsee 56–58,* 143.

"Joseph Wulf was born in Chemnitz": Gerhard Schoenberner, "Ein Blatt für Joseph Wulf," in Nicht Vergessen Sachor, *Erinnerung an Joseph Wulf* (Berlin: Aktion Sühnezeichen/Friedensdienste, 1989), 16.

"In this house, on January 20, 1942, a barrier of civilization was broken": Stephen Kinzer, Germany marks place where horror began, *New York Times,* January 20, 1992, Section A, 1.

Appendix D: Biographies of Wannsee Conference Participants

Pätzold and Schwarz, *Tagesordnung: Judenmord.*

Permanent Exhibit. House of the Wannsee Conference. Guide and Reader. Edition Hentrich. Berlin.

"On the site of Freisler's People's Court in Berlin": Braune Suppe im Boden, *Der Spiegel* 8:28–29, 1998.

Bibliography

Angell, Marcia. The Nazi hypothermia experiments and unethical research today. *New England Journal of Medicine* 322 (20): 1462–64, 1990.

Arendt, Hannah. *Eichmann in Jerusalem: A Report on the Banality of Evil.* New York: Viking Press, 1965.

Augstein, Rudolf. Todbringende "Humanisten." *Der Spiegel* 33:40–55, 1996.

_____. "Das ist eine Schande." *Der Spiegel* 43:92–107, 1997.

Baedeker's Berlin. 3rd Edition. New York: Macmillan, 1994.

Bajohr, Frank. *"Arisierung" in Hamburg.* Hamburg: Christians Verlag, 1997.

Beevor, Antony. *Stalingrad.* New York: Viking, 1988.

Berger, Marilyn. P. Kissinger, 97, the mother of a statesman. *New York Times,* November 16, 1998. Section B, 10.

Berger, Robert L. Nazi science — the Dachau hypothermia experiments. *New England Journal of Medicine* 322 (20):1435–40, 1990.

Bird, David. Hannah Arendt, political scientist, dead. *New York Times.* December 6, 1975, 32.

Blumenthal, Ralph. Cries to halt publication of Holocaust book. *New York Times.* January 10, 1998. Section 2, B, 7.

Bohlen, Celestine. Pope ties "unjust teachings" to anti–Semitism. *New York Times.* November 1, 1997. Foreign Desk. Section A, 6.

_____. Catholic-Jewish panel meets on Holocaust document and agrees to dig deeper. *New York Times.* March 27, 1998. Foreign Desk. Section A, 6.

Bomb destroys gravestone of German Jews' ex-leader. *New York Times.* December 21, 1998. Section A, 6.

Braune Suppe im Boden. *Der Spiegel* 8:28–29, 1998.

Brentzel, Marianne. *Nesthäkchen kommt ins KZ: Eine Annäherung an Else Ury 1877–1943.* Frankfurt am Main: Fischer Taschenbuch Verlag, 1992.

Browning, Christopher R. *Ordinary Men: Police Battalion 101 and the Final Solution in Poland.* New York: Harper Collins, 1992.

_____. *The Final Solution and the German Foreign Office.* New York: Holmes & Meier, 1978.

Chernow, Ron. *The Warburgs.* New York: Random House, 1993.

Chronik Berlin. 3rd updated edition. Munich: Chronik Verlag, 1997.

Cowell, Alan. The past erupts in Munich as war guilt is put on display. *New York Times,* Late Edition (East Coast). March 3, 1997. Foreign Desk. Section A, 3.

_____. Hitler's genocide order: 5 days after Pearl Harbor? *New York Times.* January 21, 1998. Foreign Desk. Section A, 4.

_____. Bonn journal: Germans, Jews and blame: new book, new pain. *New York Times,* Late Edition — Final. April 25, 1996. Foreign Desk. Section A, 4.

Craig, Gordon A. *The Germans.* New York: New American Library, 1983.

Daten zur Geschichte des Musikverlages Peters. Leipzig: Ministerium für Kultur der DDR und der Hauptverwaltung Verlage und Buchhandel, Erschienen anläßlich des 175jährigen Bestehens des Musikverlages Peters am 1. Dezember 1975.

Dawidowicz, Lucy S. *The War against the Jews: 1933–1945.* New York: Bantam Books, 1975.

Documents of Destruction: Germany and Jewry 1933–45. Edited with a commentary by Raul Hilberg. Chicago: Quadrangle Books, 1971.

Eichmann Interrogated. Transcripts from the Archives of the Israeli Police. Edited by Jochen von Lang in collaboration with Claus Sibyll. Translated from the German by Ralph Mannheim. New York: Farrar, Straus, & Giroux, 1983.

Elbogen, Ismar, and Eleonore Sterling. *Die Geschichte der Juden in Deutschland.* Frankfurt and Main: Europäische Verlagsanstalt, 1966.

Elon, Amos. The antagonist as liberator. *New York Times Magazine.* January 26, 1997. Section 6, 40.

Encyclopædia Britannica. 15th edition. Chicago, 1986.

Engelmann, Bernt. *Germany Without Jews.* Translated by D. J. Beer. New York: Bantam Books, 1984.

Evers, Marco. Analen des Todes. *Der Spiegel* 13:268, 1999.

Faure, Michel. Argentine: Sur le piste des derniers Nazis. *L'Express.* April 9, 1998, 44–51.

Feldman, Gerald D. *Hugo Stinnes. Biographie eines Industriellen. 1870–1924.* Munich: C. H. Beck, 1998.

Finkelstein, Norman G., and Ruth Bettina Birn. *A Nation on Trial: The Goldhagen Thesis and Historical Truth.* New York: Metropolitan Books/Henry Holt & Company, 1998.

Frankel, Max. Willing executioners? Essays by two scholars dissect the work of Daniel Jonah Goldhagen. *The New York Times Book Review.* June 28, 1998, 7.

Friedlander, Henry. Die Vernichtung der Behinderten, der Juden und der Sinti und Roma. in Kinder und Jugendliche als Opfer des Holocaust. Dokumentations- und Kulturzentrum Deutscher Sinti und Roma. Edgar Bamberger/Annegret Ehmann (Hrsg.). Berlin: Gedenkstätte Haus der Wannsee Konferenz, 1995

Friedländer, Saul. *Nazi Germany and the Jews.* Vol. I, The years of persecution, 1933–1939. New York: Harper Collins, 1997.

_____. *Pius XII and the Third Reich: A Documentation.* Translated by Charles Fullman. New York: Alfred A. Knopf, 1966.

Friedrich, Otto. *Before the Deluge.* New York: Harper & Row, 1972.

Gay, Peter. *Freud: A Life for Our Time.* New York: W. W. Norton, 1988.

_____. *Freud, Jews, and Other Germans.* New York: Oxford University Press, 1978.

Gerlach, Christian. Die Wannsee-Konferenz, das Schicksal der deutschen Juden und Hitlers politische Grundsatzentscheidung, alle Juden Europas zu ermorden. *Werkstatt Geschichte.* 18:7–44, 1998.

Getuschel im Treppenhaus. *Der Spiegel* 41:148–49, 1997.

Gies, Miep (with Alison Leslie Gold). *Anne Frank Remembered.* New York: Simon & Schuster, 1987.

Goldhagen, Daniel Jonah. *Hitler's Willing Executioners: Ordinary Germans and the Holocaust.* New York: Alfred A. Knopf, 1996.

Goldhagen — ein Quellentrickser? *Der Spiegel* 33:156–58, 1997.

Goodman, Walter. Crime and punishment: the trial of Eichmann. *New York Times,* Late Edition (East Coast). April 30, 1997. Section C, 14.

Grimes, William. Capturing the man who caught Eichmann. *New York Times.* November 10, 1996. Section 2, 18.

Headen, Susan, Dana Hawkins, and Jason Vest. A vow of silence. Did gold stolen by Croatian fascists reach the Vatican? *U.S. News and World Report.* March 30, 1998, 34–37.

Heydrich, Lina. *Leben mit einem Kriegsverbrecher.* Pfaffenhofen, Germany: Verlag W. Ludwig, 1976.

Hilberg, Raul. *The Destruction of the European Jews.* Chicago: Quadrangle Books, 1961.

Hitler, Adolf. *Mein Kampf.* Translated by Ralph Mannheim. Boston: Houghton Mifflin, 1943.

Hochhuth, Rolf. *The Deputy.* Translated by Richard and Clara Winston. New York: Grove Press, 1964. (At the end of the book, Hochhuth has written an essay, "Sidelights on History," describing the factual background material on Pius XII and references he used in his play.)

Hoge, Warren. Rare look uncovers wartime anguish of many part-Jewish Germans. *New York Times,* Late Edition (East Coast). Foreign Desk. April 6, 1997. Section 1, 16.

House of the Wannsee Conference Guide and Reader. Permanent Exhibit. Edition Hentrich. Berlin.

Hughes, Rupert. *Biographical Dictionary of Music.* Revised by Deems Taylor & Russel Kerr. Garden City, New York: Blue Ribbon Books, 1940.

Joachimsthaler, A. *Korrektur einer Biographie. Adolf Hitler 1908–1920.* Munich: F. A. Herbig, 1989.

Johnson, Jeffrey Allan. *The Kaiser's Chemists.* Chapel Hill: University of North Carolina Press, 1990.

Jones, Ernest. *The Life and Work of Sigmund Freud.* Edited and abridged in one volume by Lionel Trilling and Steven Marcus. New York: Basic Books, 1961.

Kalthoff Jürgen and Martin Werner. *Die Händler des Zyklon B.* Hamburg: VSA-Verlag, 1999. (A 254-page history of Zyklon B, from its invention to its use today.)

Kempner, Robert M. W. *Ankläger einer Epoche. (Prosecutor for an Epoch.) Lebenserinnerungen.* Frankfurt am Main: Verlag Ullstein, 1983.

_____. *Eichmann and His Accomplices.*

Kinzer, Stephen. Germany marks place where horror began. *New York Times.* January 20, 1992. Section A, 1.

_____. Old demons are roused on a street in Berlin. *New York Times.* April 28, 1996. Section 1, 4.

Klahn, Karl Wilhelm. *Fehmarn. Ein Insel in Wandel der Zeiten. Von der Badekarre zum Ostseeheilbad Burg auf Fehmarn.* Neumünster: Wachholtz Verlag, 1996.

Klein, Peter. *Die Wannsee Konferenz vom 20. Januar 1942: Analyse und Dokumentation.* Berlin: Edition Hentrich. Gedenkstätte Haus der Wannsee-Konferenz, 1997.

Kohl, Christiane. *Der Jude und das Mädchen: Eine verbotene Freundschaft in Nazi Deutschland.* Hamburg: Spiegel Buchverlag Hoffmann und Campe, Hamburg 1997.

Krumm, Reinhard. Luftdicht in blechdosen. *Der Spiegel* 11:63, 1999.

Leonard Maltin's Movie and Video Guide. New York: Dutton Signet, 1995.

Lewy, Günther. *The Catholic Church and Nazi Germany.* New York: McGraw-Hill, 1964.

Lifton, Robert Jay. *Medical Killing and the Psychology of Genocide.* New York: Basic Books, 1986.

Longerich, Peter. *Die Wannsee-Konferenz vom 20. Januar 1942: Planung und Beginn des Genozids an den europäischen Juden.* Edition Hentrich. Berlin: Gedenkstätte Haus der Wannsee-Konferenz, 1998.

Lyman, Rick. Martha Gellhorn, daring writer, dies at 89. *New York Times.* February 17, 1998. Section B, 11.

MacDonald, Callum. *The Killing of Reinhard Heydrich.* New York: Da Capo Press, 1998.

Malkin, Peter Z., and Harry Stein. *Eichmann in My Hands.* New York: Warner Books, 1990.

Maser, Werner. *Adolf Hitler.* Munich: Bechtle Verlag, 1971.

Owen, Wilfred. *The Poems of Wilfred Owen.* Edited and introduced by Jon Stallworthy. New York: W.W. Norton, 1985, 117.

Pätzold, Kurt, and Erika Schwarz. *Tagesordnung: Judenmord. Die Wannsee-Konferenz am 20. Januar 1942.* Berlin: Metropol Verlag, 1992.

Perutz, Max. The cabinet of Dr. Haber. *New York Review of Books,* June 20, 1996. 43:31–36.

_____. Le cabinet du Docteur Fritz Haber. Comment un égal acharnement produit des engrais, des gaz de combat et le Zyklon B. *La Recherche* 297:78–84, 1997.

Picker, Henry. *Hitler's Tischgespräche.* Bibliothek der Zeitgeschichte. Frankfurt: Verlag Ullstein, 1989.

Piekalkiewicz, Janusz. *Der Erste Weltkrieg.* Düsseldorf: ECON Verlag, 1988.

Read, Anthony, and David Fisher. *Berlin Rising.* New York: W. W. Norton, 1994.

Rosenbaum, Ron. *Explaining Hitler.* New York: Random House, 1998.

Sachor Nicht Vergessen. *Erinnerung an Joseph Wulf.* Berlin: Aktion Sühnezeichen/Friedensdienste, 1989.

Schnäppchen aus Judenkisten. *Der Spiegel* 5:66–68, 1998.

Schoenberner, Gerhard. *Der gelbe Stern. Die Judenverfolgung in Europa 1933–1945.* Durchgesehene, erweiterte Neuausgabe. Frankfurt am Main: Fischer Taschenbuchverlag, 1991.

Selten Gnade. *Der Spiegel.* 20:20, 1998. (This article summarizes the article in the *Vierteljahresheft für Zeitgeschichte* dealing with Hitler's personal Aryanization of part-Jews.)

Sereny, Gitta. *Albert Speer: His Battle with Truth.* New York: Alfred A. Knopf, 1995.

Sievers, Leo. *Juden in Deutschland: Die Geschichte einer 2000 jährigen Tragödie.* Munich: Wilhelm Goldmann Verlag, 1983.

Sims, Calvin. Film stirs Argentines' memories of a Nazi. *New York Times.* March 5, 1996. Section C, 11.

Snyder, Louis L. *Encyclopedia of the Third Reich.* New York: McGraw Hill, 1978.

Speer, Albert. *Inside the Third Reich.* Translated by Richard and Clara Winston. New York: Avon Books, 1971.

Steinmetz, Greg. A German historian probes Nazi-era deeds of his father's bank. *Wall Street Journal,* October 16, 1997. Section A, 1.

Stern, Fritz. *Gold and Iron: Bismarck, Bleichröder, and the Building of the German Empire.* New York: Random House, 1977.

Stolzenberg, Dietrich. *Fritz Haber, Chemiker, Nobelpreisträger, Deutscher Jude: Eine Biografie.* Weinheim and New York: VCH Publishers, 1994.

Tekeli, S. "Fritz Haber" in *Dictionary of Scientific Biography.* C. C. Gillespie, ed. in chief. New York: Charles Scribner's Sons, 1972.

Thyssen, Fritz. I Paid Hitler. New York: Farrar & Rinehart, 1941.

Toland, John. *Adolf Hitler.* New York: Random House, 1976.

Tuchel, Johannes. *Am Großen Wannsee 56–58. Von der Villa Minoux zum Haus der Wannsee-Konferenz.* Edition Hentrich. Berlin: Gedenkstätte Haus der Wannsee-Konferenz, 1992.

Tuchman, Barbara. *The Guns of August.* New York: Macmillan, 1962.

Turner, Henry A. *German Big Business and the Rise of Hitler.* New York: Oxford University Press, 1985.

The Vatican's Holocaust report. Editorial. *New York Times.* March 18, 1998. Section A, 20.

von Leitner, Gerit. *Der Fall Clara Immerwahr: Leben für eine humane Wissenschaft.* Munich: C. H. Beck, 1996.

von Werner, Anton. *Geschichte in Bildern. Herausgegeben von Dominik Bartmann.* Munich: Hirmer Verlag, 1997.

Wistrich, Robert S. *Who's Who in Nazi Germany.* London: Routledge, London 1982.

Zentner, Christian and Friedemann Bedürftig, eds. *The Encyclopedia of the Third Reich.* English translation edited by Amy Hackett. New York: Macmillan, 1991.

Ziegel, Vic. Taste of 45 yrs. at Zabar's. *Daily News.* February 14, 1998, 22.

Index

Abd el-Krim revolt 13
Abraham, Max 45, 46, 47
Adlon Hotel 103
Aktion Reinhard 88
Albert, Wilhelm 60
Albertz, Heinrich 134
Albrecht, Duke of Wurtemberg 10
Alsen 3, 4, 5
Alte Kämpfer 158
Arendt, Hannah 96, 109, 110, 181
Aryanization 36, 39, 40, 41, 62, 186
Augstein, Rudolf 123, 126, 181
August Bebel Institute 132
Auschwitz 16, 39, 90, 91, 92, 96, 98, 99, 100, 104, 106, 129, 132, 135, 168

Bach, Johann Sebastian 43, 46
Badische Anilin und Soda Fabriken 8
Badoglio, Pietro 130
Baeck, Leo 133
Bajohr, Frank 40, 41
Baum, Vicki 101
Baumgarten, Paul O.A. 4, 5
Beckhaus, Friedrich 180
Beethoven, Ludwig van 43, 44, 46
Below, Nikolaus von 159
Belzec 67, 71, 98, 100, 157
Bergen-Belsen 101
Berger, Gottlob 167

Bergmann, Rudolf 61
Berlin Gas Company 30, 32, 42, 48, 51
Berlin Morgue 107
Besold, Heinrich 116
Best, Werner 60
Birn, Ruth Bettina 111, 112, 183
Bismarck, Otto von 20, 187
Bloch, Ernest 75
Blumenthal, David 123
Bockmann, Gerd 180
Bohlen, Celestine 122, 181
Böhme, Carl 44
Bonhoeffer, Dietrich 75
Bormann, Martin 133, 162
Born, Max 11
Bosch, Carl 8, 9
Böß, Gustav 32
Bradbury, John 21
Brahms, Johannes 45
Brandt, Karl 85
Brecht, Bertolt 101
Breitman, Richard 64, 65
Breuhaus, J.A. 51
Brockdorff-Rantzau, Count Ulrich von 20, 28
Browning, Christopher 111, 155, 182
Brüning, Heinrich 33
Bücher, Hermann 23
Bühler, Josef 72, 77, 78, 97, 146, 152, 153, 155, 156, 157, 176, 178, 179
Bülow, Hans von 45

Canaris, Wilhelm 61
C. F. Peters 36, 43–47

Charité Hospital 107
Chelmno 67, 71
Chopin, Frederic 44
Churchill, Winston 20
Clemenceau, Georges 20
Cohen, Sam 105
Concerning the Jews and Their Lies (Luther) 37
Conrad, Wilhelm 4
Craig, Gordon A. 36
Cuno, Wilhelm 21, 26
Cunow, Max 33
Czerny, Carl 44

Dachau concentration camp 53
Darré, Walther 162
Degesch 16
Deimling, Berthold von 10
Deputy, The (Hochhuth) 123
Deutsche Allgemeine Zeitung 19, 22, 24, 33
Diepgen, Eberhard 135
Divini Redemptoris 125
Dohnanyi, Hans von 75
Dollman, Eugen 53
Domarus, Max 112
Dörffel, Alfred 45, 46
Dorotheenstadt Cemetery 107
Duisberg, Carl 13, 157
Dulce et Decorum Est (Owen) 11

Ebert, Friedrich 21, 27, 29
Eichmann in Jerusalem (Arendt) 96, 109, 110

Eichmann, Adolf 69, 71, 73, 76, 80, 81, 82, 89, 90, 91, 92, 93, 94, 95, 96, 109, 141, 142, 145, 146, 154, 163, 167, 174, 181, 182, 184; assigned to drive Jews out of Poland 90; assigned to oust Jews from Bohemia 90; atrocious German of 94; early years 89; interrogated in Israeli prison 93; Israeli precautions to prevent suicide of 94; joins Austrian Nazi party and SS 90; kidnapped by Israeli agents 92; leaves Germany in 1950 92; organizes deportation of Jews 91; sends Heydrich's invitation to Wannsee conference 69; witnesses shootings and gassings 91
Einsatz-groups 66, 163, 164, 170; attack Rumanian Jews 66; destroy Ukrainian Jews 66
Einstein, Albert 9, 15
Elon, Amos 111
Elsas, Fritz 49
Emerson, Ralph Waldo 25
Exner, Helene Maria von 75

Fabro, Wilhelm 114, 116
Falkenhayn, Erich von 10
Faulhaber, Michael 125
Ferber, Karl 120, 121
Feuchtwanger, Lion 101
Field, John 44
Finkelstein, Norman G. 111, 112, 183
First World War 1, 5, 19, 20, 26, 38, 55, 65, 68, 73, 164; *see also* World War I
Fischer, Emil 9, 13, 52, 182, 186
Fraenckel, Paul 107
Franck, James 11
Frank, Anne 101
Frank, Hans 77, 144, 155, 170
Frank, Otto 101

Franke, Wilhelm 39
Frankel, Max 112
Frankfurter Zeitung 22
Frederick the Great 120
Frei, Norbert 111
Freiburg, Gröber von 127
Freimann, Käthe 115
Freisler, Roland 120, 146, 157, 158, 159
Friedländer, Julius 45
Friedrich Wilhelm (former crown prince of Germany) 34
Friedrich, Otto 33
Fritz, Peter 180

Gabcik, Josef 84, 85, 86
Galen, Clemens August Graf von 127
Galinski, Heinz 135
Gebhardt, Karl 85
Gellhorn, Martha 101
Gerlach, Christian 64
German hyperinflation 19
Geßler, Otto 26, 27
Gestapo 40, 57, 60, 62, 68, 73, 74, 75, 86, 90, 91, 96, 98, 104, 110, 112, 132, 157, 162, 163, 167, 170
Gilger, Babette 116
Globke, Hans 172
Globocnik, Odilo 98, 179
Goebbels, Joseph 76, 127
Goethe, Johann Wolfgang von 44
Goldhagen, Daniel J. 64, 109, 110, 111, 112, 113, 183, 184
Goodman, Walter 95
Göring, Hermann 47, 77, 88, 143, 145, 147, 168, 169; bans Jewish business activity 39; cross-examined at Nuremberg 77; declares Jews would pay for their sins 117; letter to Heydrich regarding Final Solution 70
Gospel of St. John 36
Gospel of St. Matthew 36
Greiser, Arthur 67
Grieg, Edvard 45, 46
Grynszpan, Herschel 39

Gürtner, Franz 75
Gute Hoffnungshütte 31
Gutterer, Leopold 82, 144

Haber, Clara Immerwahr 7
Haber, Fritz 3, 6, 7, 8, 9, 10, 11, 12, 13, 14, 15, 186, 187; at the front 11; character of 7; consults for industry 7; death of 15; early years 6; finds posts for Jewish colleagues 15; flees to Switzerland 13; frustrated at lack of victory after first gas attack 12; gas warfare and 9; marries Clara Immerwahr 7; organizes chlorine production for warfare 10; rejected for military duty 9; resigns from Kaiser Wilhelm Institute 15; suicide of first wife 13; synthesizes ammonia 8; tries to extract gold from sea water 14; wins Nobel Prize 9; work ethic of 7
Haber, Ludwig 10, 11, 12
Haber Process 6, 8
Hagen, Herbert 90
Hague Conventions 10
Hahn, Otto 10, 11
Hallgarten, George W. 30
Händel, Georg Friedrich 46
Härtel, Gottfried Christian 44
Hawthorne, Nathaniel 2
Haydn, Franz Josef 43
Heiden, Konrad 28
Heilmann, Johann 114, 115, 119
Heilmann, Peter 134
Helfferich, Karl 20, 22
Helmholtz, Hermann von 52
Hente, Karoline 18
Hertz, Gustave 11
Herz, Richard 120
Hess, Rudolf 139, 162
Heydrich, Bruno 53, 84
Heydrich, Lina 55, 57, 58, 59, 79, 84
Heydrich, Reinhard 1, 2, 52, 53, 54, 55, 58, 59,

60, 62, 67, 68, 69, 70, 71, 72, 73, 76, 77, 78, 81, 82, 83, 84, 85, 86, 90, 96, 131, 140, 143, 147, 150, 152, 154, 157, 164, 166, 167, 169, 174, 175, 176, 177, 178, 179, 185; access to money stolen from German Jews 60; attacked by assassins 84; buys Wannsee Villa 61; calls Wannsee Conference 65; character of 53; death of 86; describes Wannsee Conference to his wife 79; early years 53; expelled from navy 53; inaugurates Prague music festival 84; joins Nazi Party 53; Kristallnacht and 39; marital infidelity of 54; marriage of 56; named governor of Czechoslovakia 84; names Peter Wiepert to control SS property on Fehmarn 60; only speaker for most of Wannsee Conference 70; organizes Nordhav Foundation 55; renovates Wannsee Villa 62; Wannsee Protocol and 76

Heydrich, Thomas 88
Heymann, Klaus 104
Himmler, Heinrich 53, 57, 58, 59, 60, 64, 66, 67, 68, 71, 77, 83, 85, 88, 98, 100, 110, 133, 148, 150, 154, 161, 167, 168, 172; becomes head of Munich police 57; character of 57; designates Auschwitz principal extermination site 99; early years 57; Fehmarn and 58; funds archeological excavations 59; impressed by Vitzbyer Steenkiest 58; interest in early German history 58; orders that Berlin Jews not be liquidated 68; orders use of poison gas

for execution 58; organizes extermination camps 57; urges Wiepert to continue archeological research 58; visits mortally wounded Reinhard Heydrich 86

Hindenburg, Paul von 86
Hinrichsen, Henry 46, 47
Hitler, Adolf 1, 6, 14, 15, 22, 26, 27, 28, 29, 30, 35, 40, 47, 50, 53, 57, 58, 64, 66, 67, 73, 74, 75, 84, 88, 90, 91, 97, 100, 106, 109, 110, 112, 120, 121, 123, 126, 127, 128, 130, 131, 139, 154, 156, 158, 159, 161, 162, 164, 170, 171, 172, 184, 185, 186, 187; anti-Semitism of 39; beerhall putsch and 26; blinded in gas attack 14; concordat with the Vatican 124; contempt for Himmler's interest in early German culture 59; declarations of German blood and 74; disparages Hugo Stinnes 30; expounds on fate of the Jews 97; Friedrich Minoux and 1; goals of 124; Hamburg citizens and 40; harangues Max Planck 14; ideas about sex 121; intervenes in sentencing of Irene Scheffler 121; Katzenberger case and 121; murder of institutionalized children and 66; 1924 trial of 28; no written order for Holocaust 64; paternal grandfather of 74; predicts disappearance of Jews 65; rejects Jewish finance minister 28; religious affiliation 123; takes and holds Rome 129

Hitler, Alois 74
Hitler's Willing Executioners (Goldhagen) 110
Hochhuth, Rolf 123, 184
Hoettl, Wilhelm 54

Hoffmann, Heinz Hugo 120, 121
Hoffmann, Max 86
Hoffmeister, Franz Anton 43
Hofmann, Otto 97, 144, 146, 150, 152, 160, 161
Höppner, Rolf Heinz 141
House of the Seven Gables (Hawthorne) 2
Hudal, Alois 92, 129
Humani Generis Unitas 126
Hummel, Johann Nepomuk 44
Huss, Pierre 54

I Paid Hitler (Thyssen) 30
Imhausen, Artur 75
Irving, David 64

Jackson, Robert 77
Jacquier & Securius 31, 32, 41, 49
Jaenicke, Johannes 14
Jesus 36, 122, 123, 130
Joachimsthaler, Anton 75
John Paul II 122, 130
Joseph Wulf *Mediothek* 135

Kahr, Alfred Ritter von 27
Kaiser Wilhelm Institute 9, 13, 14, 15
Kaltenbrunner, Ernst 101, 171
Katharinenhof 55, 58, 59, 60, 61
Katzenberger, Claire 121
Katzenberger, Lehmann 113, 114, 115, 116, 117, 118, 119, 120, 121, 122; arrested for racial desecration 119; beheaded by guillotine 121; convicted and imprisoned 121; decides to emigrate 117; declares innocence in court 120; flattered by Irene Scheffler's attentions 114; forced to sell possessions 117; meets Irene Scheffler 114; no interest in emigration 116; police interrogate 117; sentenced to death

120; suspected of supporting Irene Scheffler 115; writes letters from prison 121
Katzenberger, Max 121
Kausch, Hans Joachim 33
Kempner, Robert M. W. 78, 79, 80, 162, 163, 169
Kerl, Hans 158
Kerrl, Hans 127
Kessler, Max 48, 50, 51
Kissinger, Henry 105
Kissinger, Paula 105
Klein, Georg 131
Klein, Peter 77, 80
Kleist, Heinrich von 3
Kleylein, Betty 116, 119
Kleylein, Paul 116, 118, 119, 121
Klopfer, Gerhard 144, 146, 161, 162
Kohl, Christiane 113, 122, 185
Koppel, Leopold 9, 13
Kristallnacht 39, 40, 42, 47, 88, 117, 118, 119
Kritzinger, Friedrich Wilhelm 144, 146, 162, 163
Kroll Opera House 97
Kube, Wilhelm 68
Kubis, Jan 84, 85, 86
Kuhlau, Friedrich 44
Kühnel, Ambrosius 43, 44
Kuhnke, Hans Helmut 51

Lammers, Hans Heinrich 78, 121, 163
Lange, Rudolf Erwin 69, 146, 163, 164
Laue, Max von 15
Law, Bonar 21
Ledóchowski, Wladimir 126
Leibbrandt, Georg 144, 146, 165, 166
Less, Avner 93, 95
Liebermann, Martha 98
Liebermann, Max 4, 5, 98
Liebknecht, Karl 34
Lipchitz, Jacques 106
Liszt, Franz 45
Litolff, Theodor 45
Lodz ghetto 68, 91
Loret, Jean 74

Lösener, Bernhard 173
Lossow, Otto von 27, 28
Louis XIV 20
Lubavitcher movement 75
Ludendorff, Erich 25, 26, 27, 28, 29, 30, 103
Lüer, Carl 41
Luther, Hans 23
Luther, Martin 13, 37, 38, 72, 76, 77, 83, 96, 143, 144, 145, 146, 150, 154, 155, 168
Luttge, Martin 180
Luxemburg, Rosa 34

MacDonald, Callum 84
Madagascar Plan 76
Mahler, Gustav 46
Malkin, Peter Z. 92
Maltin, Leonard 180, 185
Mann, Heinrich 101
Mann, Thomas 101
Marlier, Ernst 1, 4, 5
Mäsel, Hans 114, 115, 119
Maser, Warner 74
Mathwin & Son 49
Mattausch, Dietrich 180
Mehlhorn, Herbert 60
Meidinger, Kurt 103
Mein Kampf (Hitler) 30
Melchior, Carl Joseph 28
Mengele, Josef 92, 99
Messel, Alfred 4, 5
Meyer, Alfred 4, 72, 144, 146, 153, 164, 165, 166
Meyer, Gustav 4
Meyerbeer, Giacomo 43
Milch, Erhard 74
Minoux, Friedrich 1, 5, 17, 18, 19, 22, 23, 24, 25, 26, 27, 28, 29, 30, 31, 32, 34, 35, 36, 41, 42, 48, 49, 50, 51, 52, 131, 187; break with Hugo Stinnes 25; business interests 31; buys Aryanized business 42; buys Wannsee Villa 5; coal price fixing 49; collapse of political plans 30; condemns socialism 34; death 52; early years 17; education 17; enthusiasm for fascism 34; German

hyperinflation and 22; ideas for overcoming unemployment 33; imprisoned for fraud 50; joins with Hugo Stinnes 18; meets with Hitler 29; military service of 18; plans for authoritarian regime 25
Minoux, Katherina Reffert 17
Minoux, Margaretha 17
Minoux, Michael 17
Mit brennender Sorge 125
Mittasch, Alwin 8, 9
Mommsen, Hans 38, 64
Mommsen, Theodor 38
Moravec, Ata 86
Moravec, Marie 86
Morell, Theodor 85
Mossad 93
Mozart, Wolfgang Amadeus 43, 46
Müller, Arthur 51
Müller, Heinrich 73, 76, 91, 96, 167, 168
Müller, Herman 33

Nathan, Charlotte 14
Nernst, Walther 9, 13
Nesthäkchen books 101, 102, 103, 104
Neumann, Erich 73, 141, 144, 146, 152, 168, 169
Neurath, Konstantin von 84
Nobel Prize 9, 10
Nockermann, Hans 61
Norddeutsche Grundstücks-Aktiengesellschaft-AG 5
Nordhav Foundation see Stiftung Nordhav

Offenheimer, Lucie 42
Offenheimer, Philipp 41
Okriftel 41, 42, 43, 52
Oppenheim, Franz 62
Oppenheim, Kurt 62
Oppenheim, Margarete 62
Ordinary Men (Browning) 111
L'Osservatore Romano 126
Ossietzky, Carl von 133
Owen, Wilfred 11

Pabst, Waldemar 34
Pacelli, Eugenio (Pius XII) 123, 124, 125
Paderborn, Lorenz Jaeger von 127
Papen, Franz von 124
Paul VI 123
Peters, Carl Friedrich 43
Pilot, Friedrich (pseudonym of Friedrich Minoux) 22, 23, 24, 29
Pius XI 124, 125, 126
Pius XII 92, 109, 122, 123, 125, 126, 128, 129, 183; aversion to becoming a martyr 128; character of 125; expresses regret over Hitler's invasion of neutral countries 126; forbids Bishop Preysing's anti-Nazi activity 127; helps hide Jews from Nazis 129; indignant at Nazi arrest of Roman Jews 129; learns of mass murder of European Jews 128; silent about murder of European Jews 128; silent about SS atrocities in Poland 126; stays in Rome during war 130; urged to recall Berlin nuncio Orsenigo 130
Planck, Max 14, 15
Plötzensee Prison 159
Pomme, Kurt 60
Pope, William 15
Potsdam 3, 4, 50, 144
Preysing, Konrad Graf von 127

Rademacher, Franz 76, 77, 82, 83
Rall, Gustav 57
Rascher, Sigmund 100
Rath, Ernst von 39
Rathenau, Walther 21
Rauter, Hanns Albin 171
Reemtsma, Jan Philip 67
Reger, Max 46
Reich Citizenship Law 39, 137, 138
Reich Security Main Office 55, 59, 66, 68, 78, 97,

101, 141, 142, 146, 154, 166, 167, 171
Reichsbank 22, 24, 99
Remarque, Erich Maria 101
Ribbentrop, Joachim von 154, 155
Rigg, Mark 73, 74, 75
Robert Blum Gymnasium 104
Röder, C.G. 45
Roosevelt, Franklin D. 34
Rosenbaum, Ron 75
Rosenberg, Alfred 166
Rosenzweig, Ludwig 118
Rossignol, Robert Le 8
Rota Boiler and Engineering Company 31
Rothaug, Oswald 119, 120, 121
Rothschild, Louis 42
Rothschild, Salomon 40
Rowolt Verlag 133

Sachs, Willy 57
Sachsenhausen (concentration camp) 107
Sackur, Otto 9
St. John Chrysostom 36
Sauerbruch, Ferdinand 52
Sawicki, Jerzy 157
Schacht, Hjalmar 23, 24, 34
Scheffler, Irene 113, 114, 115, 116, 118, 119, 120, 122; reduced contact with Lehmann Katzenberger 118
Scheffler, Oskar 114, 119
Schellenberg, Walter 53, 54, 55, 60; arranges for purchase of Katharininhof 60
Schinkel, Karl Friedrich 3
Schirk, Heinz 180
Schleicher, Kurt von 27
Schmidt, Helmut 74
Schneersohn, Joseph 75
Schöngarth, Eberhard 97, 146, 169, 170, 171
Schubert, Franz 46
Schulenberg, Fritz Detlof Count von der 131
Schumann, Clara 45, 46
Schumann, Robert 44

Schütz, Klaus 134
Schwerin, Lutz Graf 59
Seeckt, Hans von 24, 25, 26, 27, 28, 29, 30
Seiler, Hans 116, 119
Seißer, Hans Ritter von 27, 28, 29
Sereny, Gitta 88, 159, 186
Servatius, Robert 94, 174, 175
Seydelmann, Gertrude 39, 41
Siemens family 52
Sievers, Albert 59, 186
Simson, Ernest and Martha von 62
Snajdr, Vladimir 85
Social Democratic Party 132
Society for the Study of Fascism 34, 35
Speer, Albert 59, 159, 186, 187
Der Spiegel 113, 122, 123, 181, 182, 183, 184, 186
Spielberg, Steven 105
Spoerrie, Günter 180
Spohr, Louis 43, 44, 45
Springer, Ferdinand 4
Stadelheim Prison 121
Stahlecker, Franz Walter 90
Stalin, Josef 127
Stauffenberg, Claus von 131
Steeg, Ludwig 50
Steinruck Company 107
Stiftung Ahnenerbe (Ancestral Heritage Foundation) 58
Stiftung Nordhav 1, 2, 55, 60, 61
Stinnes, Hugo 18, 19, 22, 23, 24, 25, 26, 29, 30, 31, 35
Stolzenberg, Dietrich 10, 11, 187
Stolzenberg, Dr. Hugo 13
Strauss, Richard 46
Streicher, Julius 113
Stresemann, Gustav 22, 23, 27, 29, 30
Stroop, Jürgen 100
Stuckart, Wilhelm 60, 82, 97, 141, 144, 146, 152, 171, 172, 173, 176, 177
Der Stürmer 38, 120

Suhard, Emmanuel 128
Süssmuth, Rita 135

Tannenberg, Battle of 86
Tchaikovsky, Peter Ilyich
46
Tesch and Stabonow 16
Thyssen, Fritz 30, 34, 187
Tiemessen, Johannes 48,
50, 51
Tisserant, Eugène 128
Toland, John 159
Treitschke, Heinrich von 38
Tuchel, Johannes 59
Turner, Henry A. 30

Ullstein Verlag 42, 133
Ullstein, Hermann 22, 186
Ury, Else 101, 102, 103, 104,
182
Ury, Emil 102

Versailles Peace Treaty 19;
see also Versailles Treaty
Versailles Treaty 1, 13, 21
Victor Emmanuel III 130
Vitzbyer Steenkiest 58

Wallenberg, Raul 133
Wannsee Conference 1, 3,
6, 16, 52, 60, 63, 64, 67,
69, 76, 77, 78, 79, 81,
82, 89, 96, 97, 98, 101,
131, 135, 144, 154, 156,
157, 159, 162, 165, 166,
168, 169, 172, 173, 174,
176, 178, 179, 186; as
motion picture (1984)
180
Wannsee Protocol 70, 71,
76, 77, 78, 79, 80, 81,
82, 135, 145, 146, 157,
169
Wannsee Villa 1, 2, 3, 4, 5,
17, 19, 25, 29, 51, 52, 59,
60, 61, 62, 70, 79, 80,
104, 131, 132, 134, 135
Warburg, Max M. 28
Warsaw ghetto 100
Wawel Castle 156
We Remember: A Reflection
on the Shoah 123
Weber, Carl Maria von 44
Weglein, Leo 116
Weglein, Walter 116
Weimar Republic 27, 111
Weismann, Wilhelm 47
Weizmann, Chaim 7
Weizmann Institute of Sci-
ence 15
Weizsäcker, Ernst von 129
Weizsäcker, Richard von
129
Werfel, Franz 101
Werner, Anton von 4
Whistling, A. Th. 44
Wiepert, Peter 58, 59, 60;
gives Himmler archeo-
logical tour of Fehmarn
58; visits Himmler in
Berlin 58
Wilhelm II 9, 13
Wirth, Josef 21
Witkowitz Steel Works 42
Witzleben, Erwin von 131,
159
Woermann, Ernst 77
Wolf, Hugo 46
World War I 6, 18, 24, 25,
48, 57, 74, 160, 162, 167;
see also First World War
World War II 16, 53, 57,
64, 106, 126
Wulf, Joseph 24, 132, 133,
134, 186; early years 132;
joins resistance 132;
leaves Poland for Paris
132; publishes first book
132; sent to Auschwitz
132; spurned by German
politicians 134; suicide of
135; urges creation of
Holocaust document
center 134
Wulf, Peter 24

Ypres 10, 11, 12

Ziegel, Vic 105, 106, 187
Zipfel, Friedrich 134
Zuroff, Efraim 112
Zyklon B 6, 16, 98, 186